The Unusual Suspect

The Unusual Suspect

Paul Flynn MP

Edited by Ruth Winstone

First published in Great Britain in 2010 by
Biteback Publishing Ltd
Heal House
375 Kennington Lane
London
SE11 5QY

ISBN 978-1-84954-017-9

10 9 8 7 6 5 4 3 2 1

A CIP catalogue record for this book is available from the British Library.

Set in Kepler and Franklin Gothic
Printed and bound in Great Britain by
TJ International Ltd, Padstow, Cornwall

A stranger asked my wife Sam whether I took her advice. 'If he did,' she said, 'he would be Prime Minister now.' Had I not taken her advice in 1985 I would never have been a candidate for Newport West. She has been my best friend, my lover, my guru and my ever-present companion whose advice has never been wrong. Her loyalty has been frequently tested but has never wavered. Through difficult and demanding years she has unselfishly worked for the causes of the family and the party. I owe her immense gratitude.

Contents

Foreword

Paul Flynn comes from the essentially freethinking and courageous tradition of Welsh politics. The loyalty of the electors of Newport West to Paul can best be understood by reading this book, in which this most talented of MPs describes his commitment to the world peace movement, to radical reform of the Commons and the voting system, and his opposition to the insidious corruption of politicians and civil servants, to the chimera of nuclear power and to despotic regimes. He argues for more power to independent-minded backbenchers, of whom he is one of the foremost. There are millions of people in Britain who are uneasy with the choice offered between two parties who agree on so much and argue so poorly on the alternatives. Paul is their natural candidate and in this book he reveals his strength, through his entertaining and thought-provoking style, and why he is such a brilliant representative.

Tony Benn
January 2010

Preface

If I had known what fun it was I would have written my first book when I was twenty-two not sixty-two. The apparent permanence of books stirs strong emotions. An article in a tabloid newspaper might be read by millions. Its impact is slight and ephemeral. The praise or blame in a book has a prolonged potency even with sales of a few thousand. After the modest success of *Commons Knowledge*, published in 1997, I was hungry for more excitement. Sadly there were more failures than successes ahead.

For thirty years I have written newspaper columns. They were sprints. I was daunted about a marathon of writing. After all I did have a day job. Out of the blue I was asked to write an autobiography in Welsh. Gwasg Gwynedd published one autobiography a year, in a series grandly named Cyfres y Cewri (Series of the Giants). Vanity made the offer irresistible. Who could turn down the accolade of being a giant of the Welsh nation? I used the August recess of 1998 to splurge my megalomania. It was a strange experience recalling the joys and sorrows of sixty-four years. I was as honest as I dared be while avoiding providing too much ammunition to political opponents.

My preferred title was 'Staggering Towards Innocence', to illustrate both my uncertain gait and my lifetime's wayward progress to idealistic causes. It sounded awkward in Welsh. The title was simplified to 'Staggering Forward', *Baglu 'Mlaen*. A few weeks before publication the publishers asked me to cut the book down from 70,000 to 60,000 words.

Inadvertently, I cut a vital story but left in the hook, which said 'No one could foresee the terrible tragedy that would befall this family'. There was reassuring proof that the book was being well read because many letters demanded to know what the excised tragedy was. The book was well received. The RNIB produced a very pleasing audio version. All the reviews were friendly. They mentioned the humour and the honesty. It had to be that way: the Welsh-reading audience is an intimate one where false or pretentious claims are severely punished.

Two books done, how many to go? Writing novels was an appealing possibility. Political writing is cramped by the tedious need to check facts, quotations and dates. The world created by the novelist is infinitely malleable to the will of the writer. Freedom to create characters of substance who behave oddly would be liberating. I wrote a few chapters. It was to be a futuristic tale after the death of Tony Blair, killed by a falling support of the Millennium Dome at the closing ceremony. He was then at the height of his popularity. Blairism became a religion, as a sub-churchlet of the Anglican communion. The year 2000 became year zero and subsequent years were named after Blair, starting with AB1. The title of my novel was 'AB20'. In an effort to grab the reader's attention the story began:

> Slowly he woke up after his binge on heroin beer. The world was swimming out of focus. He felt a line of warmth alongside his body. He had slept with someone. He prayed that it was a man.
>
> Panic rippled down his spine. It was the same tingling fear and sickly excitement that preceded all his worst moments. Had he junked his chance of becoming Britain's first gay Prime Minister? The rough skin and the musty smell of his compassion was reassuring. His braying snore was rudely male. It was the barman of the previous night. Unwelcome memories of the coarse chat-up and the drunken fumble were coming back.
>
> Another stupid act of disloyalty but not the one Jason feared. He cursed himself. Thirty years ago, in 1990, the political career of a would-be Prime Minister would be finished by a homosexual one-night stand. The new morality prized fidelity above any sexual orientation.

My next book was written in haste and anger. It was an uninhibited howl of outrage against the wiles of New Labour. *Dragons Led by Poodles* exposed the stitch-up of the election of the leader of the Welsh Assembly. The book was published in a new and, then, unique way. Tentatively, I called it guest writing. The key chapters were posted on my website on 15 September 1999. I invited surfers to help write the final version. My writing was influenced by my own subjective views as a Rhodri Morgan supporter. I asked if it was a fair account.

On the first day, 15,000 hits on the site were recorded. Within three days the total passed 33,000. The media gave it wall-to-wall coverage and a shoal of emails and letters flooded in. Newsrooms I visited were littered with downloaded pages and pictures from the web version. All Welsh newspapers gave the embryo book generous and provocative attention.

I sent Alun Michael and Ron Davies hard copies of the text. Ron came back denying a few details but confirming the truth of the main narrative. I amended the text on the lines Ron requested. Alun never got back. Readers outside of Wales may ask if one side *really* committed all the sins while the other was blameless. Although unlikely, that is still my view on what happened.

Perhaps it was inevitable that the central message of the web book was eclipsed by my colourful depiction of fellow politicians. I salted and peppered the serious text with mischievous and malign word cartoons of my Welsh colleagues. They were awarded up to five flames for dragon courage or five pompoms for poodle servility. The images of flaming dragons and pompomed poodles were seductive. They roused strong emotions.

A few weeks after the web edition, the printed version was published. Testing the patience of my publisher Iain Dale I bombarded him with fresh text variations by email. Inevitably, the book was printed from an early file that had not been properly proofread. Few people noticed, apart from the red-faced author.

The compelling message from Wales and Scotland was that voters were going to reward those that New Labour had cheated. Downing

Street should have studied the election triumphs of the expelled Dennis Canavan in Scotland and the ill-used Rhodri Morgan.

I hoped that sense would prevail and the selection of the candidates for Mayor of London would be fair and democratic. The shared fury of the Labour Party in Wales was bottled up during the Assembly and Euro elections. But silence was still demanded. There must be no whisper of dissent after an election, or in an election, or before an election, or before a conference, during a conference and especially after a conference. Must our mouths be permanently bandaged? The autumn of 1999 was two years distant from any election. It was a good time to put the party in order. Not to tell the truth about the stitch-up would have been to collaborate with it.

'Caught in the Rigging' was a planned exposé of the New Labour stitch-up of the Ken Livingstone/Frank Dobson selection. I looked forward to telling in print the story of when Frank's failing campaign really troughed. A cunning New Labour wheeze had been planned. Tony Blair was to be photographed flanked by Frank Dobson and Trevor Phillips in front of a statue called *London Pride* – the work of a sculptor also named Frank Dobson. Tony Blair panicked, sensing the potential gaffe. He refused to allow the salivating photographers to take any pictures with the statue in the background. The photographers protested. They had their stepladders in place. Tony moved the photo shoot to the nearby tube station. *London Pride* is a bronze nude with full breasts at head height to the trio. Blair feared that the tabloids would caption the picture 'Blair and his pair of tits'.

Frank Dobson amassed 13 per cent of the votes. Ken was elected Mayor. Blair confessed that he had been wrong. There was no longer any point in publishing 'Caught in the Rigging'.

I sketched out another book, 'How to Succeed in Coarse Politics'. The theme was the belief that most political successes are the results of deceptions, misdemeanours, error or luck. What was the advice? That it's dangerous to over-estimate the intelligence of voters. That no lie can be so preposterous that the majority of voters will not swallow it.

The book also planned to expose legislative incontinence. Dogs bark. Babies cry. Politicians legislate. Each year provides more examples of coarse politics and futile legislation. Parliament is not always a rational entity. The Regulatory Reform Act 2001 was designed to facilitate reforming legislation. It was so incomprehensible that another Act, called the Legislative and Regulatory Reform Act, had to be passed in 2006 to explain what the previous Act had meant. A contagion of group pre-election hysteria lubricated the passage of the demented Drugs Act 2005 through Parliament. It classified magic mushrooms in the same category as heroin.

And so to *The Unusual Suspect*. Parliament must be nurtured through a metamorphosis that will restore our reputation. Speaker Bercow will lead. Backbench scribblers will stimulate and chronicle the re-creation. I'll be one of them. Chronicled here is my daily experience of being delighted, astonished and humbled by this infinitely diverse organism called Parliament.

Part I

Baptism of treachery

1

Machine Gunner Flynn

My father died when I was five, but it was not until I was seventy-four that I found out the full story of his life and death. I realise now that almost all of my present passions are rooted in incidents from my childhood.

I can recall only one visit to Dad's grave in Cardiff's Ely cemetery with my weeping mother. Their marriage was not perfect. Only later did I learn of the despair of a man whose self-respect was destroyed by the First World War. His humour and good looks were celebrated and frequently recalled with pride by his three brothers, two sisters and by his many friends. We were shielded from the occasional excesses of the drink to which he turned. My few memories are of a rumbustious, lovely man who brought fun and laughter to any company he joined.

My information on my father's record in the First World War was sketchy. He had added a few months to his fifteen years to become a soldier. He was made a machine gunner. Both sides in the First World War regarded machine gunners as pariahs because of the number of lives that they took. The canard was that neither the Germans nor British would spare a machine gunner. He would be killed, not taken prisoner.

The family knew that during the war he had been shot in the leg, that he was marooned in no man's land and could not escape from his machine-gun placement. He heard a German-speaking group approaching, took his rosary beads and said his Hail Marys with his eyes shut. He waited for the bullet. It never came. The officer leading the Germans was a Catholic. They carried him three miles on their backs to a field hospital. He would have bled to death in the foxhole. My father believed that the rosary beads saved his life. The officer ensured that he was well treated at the hospital where he had surgery for his wound. The officer was from Cologne. His name was Paul.

My father's injuries cast a shadow over the rest of his life. Never again could he do a man's job. But any occupation not calling for physical strength he judged demeaning. Work was infrequent and unsatisfying, including heartbreaking spells trying to sell the *Golden Knowledge* encyclopaedia. It was impossible during the 1930s to persuade enough people to invest in the full twelve volumes. Mother remembered with bitterness watching the daily humiliation of a man who could not make a living wage for his family.

A set of the encyclopaedia found its way to our home, and it was a rare treasure-trove of information for my three siblings and me, full of gorgeous coloured photographs and wonderful pictures of bisected toads and fish. In the mid-1930s my father suffered another blow. The tiny family income had been supplemented by a pension for his war wound. The government needed to cut spending. His war pension was reassessed and cut. The justification was that his health problems were considered not to be 'attributed' to his war wounds, but to have been 'aggravated' by them. He went to war as a healthy sixteen-year-old and he was shot. Aggravated? The family slumped from poverty to dirt poverty.

The injustice of this decision was grievous. It happened in the week of Armistice Day. With tears in their eyes, the great and the good stood in eternal tribute to our war heroes, many of whom passed up unnoticed, unemployed, wounded, cheated and robbed of hope. My father's brother Miah shared his First World War years in the trenches. He recalled how he and his comrades-in-arms lived in a shed on the edge of no man's land. 'Every night there was heavy shelling. We were terrified. All we had in abundance was cigarettes and booze. So we drank too much and chain smoked,' he told us. Miah left the army broken and shell-shocked. My father died of lung cancer in 1940.

In April 2009 I gave a great yelp of joy when I received a letter from the Red Cross in Geneva. The Red Cross has an archive of prisoners of war in Germany in the First World War. A simple request to their HQ had been answered with precise details of the four prisoner of war camps where my father spent most of 1918. I thought this information had been lost forever. The family anecdotes had indicated that my dad was captured on the Somme in 1914. The Red Cross proved that he actually endured three and half years in the front line. He was shot and captured on 10 April 1918. That day was very significant. For the first time the Germans broke through the front line in Flanders at Ploegsteert Wood. Thousands of British and Australian soldiers were killed. The Germans held the area until September.

My father had always been grateful for the surgery that saved his leg. The Red Cross document proved the truth of other parts of family folklore. There was a military hospital in his first prison camp at Limburg where he was listed in May 1918. He spent time in a second PoW camp at Giessen near Frankfurt, and two others at Parchim and Gustrow in the far north of Germany. My brother Michael has a stock of old postcards that he inherited when my father's brothers and sisters died. The cards are of First World War vintage. One is captioned 'Ready for transport prison camp Gustrow' and shows a group of British and French prisoners arriving at the camp. My father had collected these images of one of the places where he was held as a prisoner of war. The Red Cross had solved another puzzle.

There is a wealth of information on the web about the German advance on 10 April and even photographs of the camps and the hospital where my father was treated. The Flemish town of Ploegsteert (known as Plug Street to our troops) has honoured the war dead with a fine memorial. The last post is played on the first Friday of every month. Many of the names on the memorial are of soldiers who were killed on the day my father was captured.

I visited the Ploegsteert memorial on a beautiful spring day in 2009. It was a moving experience to follow the paths trodden by Machine Gunner James Flynn. He and his comrades suffered danger, cold and squalor for four years from 1914 to 1918. The names of thousands of Welsh soldiers are remembered. But for a stroke of good fortune and the intervention of a compassionate German officer, my father's name would also have been carved in stone in Ploegsteert and my family and I would not have existed. The shame of his suffering in war, the legacy of his wounds and his premature death are a spur of anger that drives my parliamentary work now.

2

Triumph of shame

My first day as an MP was filled with June sunshine, media interviews and a visit to my mother in Cardiff. Alas, there was no national Labour victory in 1987. But I had a whirl in Newport's John Frost Square for the television cameras, milking the euphoria of a local triumph. The victorious campaign team gathered at the HQ to wallow in self-congratulation.

The campaign had been a decade ahead of its time. It was two years of shameless publicity seeking. Our posters were vast, stylish and very visible. They outnumbered all others by twenty to one. Tens of thousands of personalised target letters were delivered to individuals, all ostensibly signed by the candidate. Thanks to my agent David Mayer the literature and battle bus had been tastefully and strikingly designed. Platoons of workers from the party and the public were daily marshalled by my wife Sam in the headquarters. A reporter from a Dutch television crew described our work as 'very American'. He was trying to flatter us.

There had been no chance of debating with my Conservative rival, Mark Robinson. He adhered to the prevailing view, shared by almost all sitting MPs, that a challenger's status would only be elevated by a shared platform. There were, however, debates in the neighbouring constituency of Newport East, in which the Tory candidate, Graham Webster-Gardiner, was challenging Roy Hughes. A Christian fundamentalist, Webster-Gardiner's technique for winning over an audience of CND supporters was to explain to them that the CND symbol was the cloven foot of the goat, the sign of the devil. He seemed surprised at the resulting hostility.

There were many moments when my defeat had seemed likely. A body blow in the final week before polling day came in an article in the local paper, the *Argus*. It devoted one night's editorial to each of the Gwent seats. They advised voting Labour in all six – except Newport West, where they recommended a vote for Mark Robinson. In a contest which could have been decided by a handful of votes this was extremely bad news. The *Argus*'s message was to 'vote Labour in every seat where your vote does not matter, but in Newport West where it can count, vote Tory'.

Years later I found out that the English proprietor of the newspaper (Lord Stevens) had contacted the editor after reading the early editorials. He demanded balance. There was only one way to give him what he wanted. The writer had to put the boot into me, the last candidate to feature.

My mother's home in Grangetown, Cardiff was where I first fell in love with politics. There was no moment when I became a supporter of the Labour Party. We *were* Labour. Just as we were Catholic and Welsh. I can still recall the names of the members of Attlee's cabinet of 1945–50 with more certainty that I can the last cabinet of Gordon Brown.

The 1945 election was the first in the lives of my brother Mike and me. We were very impressionable ten- and eleven-year-olds. Labour opened its committee room in an empty shop opposite our home in Penarth Road. We threw ourselves into the campaign with excitement and gusto. Our offers of help were welcomed and we spent endless hours stuffing envelopes. The local *Echo* newspaper reported that one election dirty trick was to slash the tyres of opponents' cars. Mike and I were given the sacred duty of guarding the tyres of the only car in Labour's campaign in Cardiff South. My mother encouraged our interest but warned us that disappointment was a certainty. 'The Labour candidate here cannot win,' she said. 'Like us he's got an Irish name. They won't vote for anyone in Wales who is Irish. There's no future in politics for anyone called James Callaghan.'

Our interest survived the election. Mike and I were allowed to attend

Grangetown Labour ward meetings, held in a loft over a stable in Franklin Street. I treasure the memory of Jim Callaghan thanking us at one meeting with the forecast that we were 'two fine socialists in the making'. Our greatest hero was the beguiling political giant, Aneurin Bevan. Not only Labour, but also Welsh, witty and passionate. My idol-worship included pasting cuttings from the *Sunday Pictorial* and other papers of all he said and did. Especially prized were his hilarious put-downs of Winston Churchill. His death in 1960 robbed a whole generation of young socialists of a leader who might have fulfilled our supreme aspirations.

I dreamed of becoming an MP. There was no active role in the Labour Party for fourteen-year-olds so I wrote large numbers of letters to the *South Wales Echo* under the pseudonym Dafydd Llewelyn. At that time the *Echo* had an infuriatingly provocative letter-writer with the *nom de plume* Malfew Seklew. Dafydd Llewelyn was the next best, to such an extent that the then Tory MP for Cardiff North – David Llewellin – issued a denial that he was definitely not 'Dafydd' and they were not his letters. Writing to the papers was not a respectable activity and anonymity gave me the delicious freedom to say anything I liked without arousing parental wrath or the ridicule of friends. Subjects were not limited to political issues. They included a defence of the daffodil as the symbol of Wales, the need for Wales to have Cardiff as its capital, and an impassioned plea demanding rights for atheists.

Many venerable Labour Party members look back on the 1945–51 government as a golden age. We forget the popular disillusionment at the mid-term of the Attlee government. In 1948 in Cardiff's Sophia Gardens I heard Aneurin Bevan dominate and captivate his May Day audience. His vivid presence is a clear memory. In a litany of the achievements of the health service while he was secretary of state, he mentioned the improved birth rate and added, 'Not that I am taking personal credit for that.' On the same platform was my MP for Cardiff South, George Thomas. The whispered excuse for his faltering nervous speech was his health was 'shot to pieces'. The vigorous, robust Bevan died at sixty-three. George lived on to be Speaker and died as Lord Tonypandy at the age of eighty-eight.

The lowest point in Grangetown political life was the emetic sentimentality of George's meetings. His omnipresent mother sat alongside him on every platform, poised for George's ghastly grovel to the virtues of mother love. A writer of abysmal doggerel who hailed from Cromwell Road sent him sycophantic drivelling verse about the messianic qualities of 'Our George'. Unembarrassed he read them aloud at public meetings. As the son of a teacher, George's approval of this literary dung proved that there was room for improvement in Welsh education. Even as a twelve-year-old, I squirmed in embarrassment at the MP I was supporting. This was an experience I was doomed to repeat later.

Many MPs were dim-witted to the point of embarrassment. It was a party tradition. I accepted that even dismal MPs are the solid essential workforce for building our socialist Jerusalem. It was a great reassurance in my own lowest moments as a councillor and MP. However hard the press harried me for some foolish or untimely remark I had made, there was consolation. Labour supporters forgive all in the name of the cause.

Forty years later, on Election Day 1987, my mother, already worried about the prospects of defeat, watched the declaration of the Newport West result live on television with my sister Mary and her family. My mother had endured a hard life. She suffered in the 1930s and blamed the Tories. For her, an MP in a working-class family was deeply satisfying. There were a few tears because my daughter and one of my brothers could not share our joy. We had a celebratory cup of tea and laughed a lot. Practical as always, my mother fretted because I planned to replace my corned-beef-tin car with a second-hand Rover priced at a frightening £8,000. How could I possibly afford that?

There was other great election news. Margaret Thatcher was still in power but Labour had won back more Welsh seats. Before the election, hopeful Welsh candidates met on Sundays in the Channel View Leisure Centre, Cardiff. This 'M4 group', named after the motorway which linked south Wales and London, was convened and led by Rhodri Morgan who was standing in Cardiff West. All other new local Labour candidates attended: Jon Owen Jones (Cardiff Central), Alun Michael (Cardiff South & Penarth) and Win Griffiths (Bridgend). It was a useful gathering for exchanging gossip and ideas. Rhodri produced a number of position papers that were treated seriously, identifying a new Labour approach. All of us except Jon Owen Jones were elected. Jon's success came later. But the 1987 result was a Welsh Labour triumph that reversed the hideous Welsh losses of 1983. None of us could have guessed at the bitter divisions and extraordinary careers that lay ahead for the M4 group of MPs.

To milk the good publicity, Welsh Labour boss Anita Gale insisted on a photo call at Cardiff railway station. Rhodri's unique personality was having difficulty fitting into the expected persona of an MP. He was genuinely baffled when, on Cardiff station as we lined up for the cameras, I removed the Tesco bag in which he was carrying his smalls. I hid it behind a pillar on the platform. The rest of us had smart cases. For his first TV appearance as an MP he defied the media gurus and wore jeans and an open-necked lumberjack shirt. Looking smart was a baffling concept to Rhodri. He was eventually bullied and forced into a suit thirteen years later when he became the Welsh Assembly's First Minister. The nation smiled.

Fifteen years later I mentioned this incident in a *South Wales Echo* column as an example of Rhodri's wayward personality. I was emailed by a member of his staff. 'You've solved the great unanswered question. How the hell did Rhodri lose his new shirts and Tesco bags on Cardiff railway station? I know he had them when I left him at the station. Rhodri phoned me at home at 11.30 p.m. and I had to go to the station to find his luggage. I found them in lost property labelled "I think these belong to an MP".'

Another newly elected Welsh MP, Paul Murphy, considered the departure from Newport station as one of the most painfully embarrassing moments of his life. The train was held up until members of the Newport West party and the new MPs sang 'The Red Flag'. Paul Murphy was by then already New Labour, convinced that singing, and left-wing politics, should be confined to consenting adults in private.

Ron Davies, the Labour whip, welcomed us to Westminster. He was the sheepdog who guided the new lambs around their magnificent but daunting new habitat. My first three days as an MP were packed with surprises. In the cloakroom, it was comforting to see that a ribbon was in place to support my sword. Medieval technology sat cheek by jowl with sophisticated databases; desks equipped with nibbed pens and fully charged ink wells nestled comfortably with computer terminals on the splendid Library desks. Described as a vital life-support system for members, the Library provided a welcome telephone-free calm for the new members battling to control the deluge of paper that threatened us.

The abiding impression of that first morning was of a beautiful confusing labyrinth of a building whose main function was to feed paper to Members: a formidable pile of correspondence, masses of information from the Serjeant at Arms, the whips, the Fees Office and (surprise! surprise!) a handful of letters of congratulations from Tory MPs offering to pair with me. As an eager newcomer this was not what I expected. 'Pairing' is the gentleman's agreement between two MPs of opposing parties to abstain from voting in divisions. It reduces the No and Aye vote by one and has no effect on the ultimate result.

Standing in the Members' Lobby I suddenly became aware of a shambling tottering figure bee-lining towards me. His first words sounded like an order: 'You must pair with me.' His voice was a posh, breathless, gasping staccato. I was perplexed. 'You come from Newport. So we must PAIR.' Close inspection revealed a figure of apparently great age freely shedding dandruff and cobwebs from his shoulders. 'You see, my wife's father used to come from Penarth. We must PAIR!' He turned on his heels and staggered off unsteadily across the Lobby. That was it. There was no need or advantage for me in pairing or wasting time in organised truancy from a job I had longed to do for forty years. But senior MP Alan Glyn had decided. It was weeks later that the tenuous nature of the link on which the pairing was forged was explained. His wife's father did not just come from Penarth. He owned Penarth, Grangetown, Ely and other large tracts of south Wales. He was the Earl of Plymouth, who had lived in St Fagan's Castle until, as Alan later explained, 'all that dirty socialist legislation left him with just one castle to live in'. *Just one castle.* All poverty is relative.

There were other puzzles. The chamber itself presented ticklish problems. Where to sit? A policeman told me kindly but firmly that

Honourable Members are entitled to sit anywhere they like, but Michael Foot usually sits where you're sitting. Clapping was frowned upon, and practice was needed to produce the Dalek-like braying noises that express joy or scorn.

There were more women members than ever before, four black members and the courageous David Blunkett. He was not the first blind member but he was the first to be accompanied by a guide dog. Ted was to become a star of the new parliament, and a superstar once television was introduced. Straddling the area between the two front benches he was the focal point in the chamber. He proved to be an astute critic. He turned his head and cocked his ears at the amusing speakers, yawned and scratched in response to the pompous and rolled over on his back at the boring. Ted became the Greek chorus to the continuing drama of the chamber. He barked once – at Norman Tebbit.

At first hand I witnessed one hallowed tradition of the Palace of Westminster being rudely violated. And not for the last time either! At 5.15 p.m. on Thursday 18 June 1987, accompanied by a policeman, Ted used the lawn in New Palace Yard for an essential purpose for which it was never intended. Would Parliament ever be the same again?

We were grateful for the welcome from Ron Davies, then an obscure Caerphilly MP. It was a rare act of kindness from the sullen and resentful whips. The patronage of another whip, Ray Powell, was crucial in allocating desks and an office to us. Being Welsh, we all had an offer of a room on our first day, and all seven of us were happy to share. The office measured 25 by 12 feet and was on the second floor of a building across the road from the House of Lords. Crammed in with me were Rhodri Morgan, Alun Michael, Paul Murphy, Elliott Morley, John McFall and Eric Illsley. A sign was pinned on the door: 'Little Wales beyond England'.

The cooperation between Rhodri, Alun, Paul and myself continued. Survival through the first months was greatly helped by the solidarity of other novice MPs. We were all learning on the job. I wrote the book *Commons Knowledge* ten years later because of the hostility of Parliament to new recruits. It was a baptism of indifference. Less like starting at a new school than starting a term in prison.

The space in the office shrank quickly. Researchers were expected to share a corner of the single desks we each had. Alun Michael was an inveterate territory-expander. He assembled his work in piles on the floor. They rapidly spread, filling all the empty spaces between the desks. Rhodri's heaps of unread reports grew in great pillars on his desk until he disappeared behind them. Three years later Rhodri's new researcher Jane Davidson dismantled the columns. By then they were 5 feet tall. They were like the rings of a tree: 3 inches down was December 1989, another foot lower September 1988.

Paul Murphy incited homicide. He is pathologically tidy. Not only was there never a piece of paper on his desk but also he regularly polished it. It gleamed mockingly at our chaos and untidiness. Ringing phones and the constant buzz of conversation made the place uncongenial for working. John McFall fled from the room and took to working in the Library.

Differences between Rhodri and Alun on the Cardiff Bay barrage scheme introduced tension into an already claustrophobic domain. They had combined to buy office equipment. Neither had experienced divorce. When they fell out there were serious difficulties on who was to take custody of the young socialists. Also, how do you cut a fax machine in half?

My first blunder was not to recognise good news. As an innocent in the ways of Westminster I was angered that I was to be appointed to the Treasury Select Committee. No one had asked me which committee I wanted. I would have had more interest in almost any of the other committees than that one. I did not know that new backbenchers in Parliament had a status lower than earthworms. To consult us would have been a degrading surrender of authority by the omnipotent whips. A fellow novice Keith Bradley told me, years later, that what he remembered about his first meeting of the Parliamentary Labour Party was this brave newcomer who had the temerity to speak at his first PLP. I had objected at the meeting to being put on the Treasury committee (I later discovered it to be a coveted and prestigious position). The whips have long memories. I was not to get another chance to sit on a select committee for seven years.

Equally surprising and unwelcome was being press-ganged onto a standing committee for the first bill of the new parliament, the United Kingdom Local Government Bill. I was already more than fully occupied trying to set up my offices and dealing with the tidal wave of post. How could I find time to be on a committee from 10.30 a.m. to 1.00 p.m., from 4.30 p.m. to 7.00 p.m. and from 9.00 p.m. to the early morning, twice a week? I was told that was the job of an MP. More abominable was the discovery of the tawdry role played by opposition MPs on these committees. There was none of the expected line-by-line intelligent examination of the weaknesses of the bill with the aim of improving it. Jack Cunningham was leading for Labour. He explained that the only weapon of opposition was to delay the bill by obstruction, filibuster and bloody-mindedness. It was not the quality of a speech that mattered but its length. 'We'll keep the Tory bastards up all night. If we all do our bit, we'll all be here when the sun come up over St Thomas',' Jack assured us.

Already fatigued by the demands of the first weeks I was horrified at the prospect of all-night sessions. We had to produce endless streams of verbal ectoplasm to fill the hours until dawn. Jack was right. We drove them into the ground as promised. But there were seventeen of them and just eleven of us. We drove ourselves even deeper into the ground. The bright excitement of the first days was soon replaced by exhausted resignation and disappointment. This was no way to run a legislature.

The maiden speech of an MP is a frightening hurdle. The longer the wait the higher the hurdle rises. But the pressure to speak in the chamber was on. My predecessor for Newport West had followed the usual advice to wait until there was a debate on a subject about which he had knowledge. He delayed for six months and then spoke about China. The people of Newport were perplexed. 'We didn't send you up there to say nothing about Newport for months, then talk about China.' The truth was that he was better acquainted with China that he was with Newport.

I put a note in every day after the Queen's Speech, saying that I hoped to catch Speaker Weatherill's eye. The message came back that he was intending to call me six days after the Queen's Speech on 1 July. I rang Sam in Newport. By the time I was called to speak at 7 o'clock on the appointed day, she was perched in the gallery.

She said afterwards that she knew I was nervous but that no one else would notice. Kindness always. There were only about twenty members in the House and the place felt intimate and non-threatening. In the belief that it is best not to change the speech but to change the audience, most of what I said were golden oldies from previous speeches. My theme was housing and the success of Newport Borough Council in its innovative policies, including selling 20 per cent of its houses for good socialist reasons. That had been decades before Thatcher had the same idea. Aneurin Bevan had dreamed of the rich tapestry of a mixed community. I concluded by saying that we did not have a housing tapestry but an ugly jigsaw broken by lines of division and injustice. On one side, estates of fear, crime and neglect that are shunned. On the other, privileged suburbs behind barricades and security guards. Kenneth Baker replied to the debate and reminded me that he was born in Newport and warned me to look after the town.

Sam and I had an idyllic celebration meal in the Commons dining room. We really had made it at last. I could not have done it without her and the Newport West party. It was the team that did it. We toasted our good luck. The future was sure to be brilliant.

3

The Sewing Circle

In 1987 two Tory MPs, Jill Knight and David Wilshire, introduced what was to become the hated homophobic Clause 28 into the Local Government Bill. The bill also introduced compulsory competitive tendering. This was the grimace-to-grimace snarling political match that I relished as a novice MP. I was summoned from the committee one morning with a command to ring Neil Kinnock's office.

'How you getting on, Butt?' Neil asked. 'I'd like you to go on the front bench with Alan Williams.' Alan was the shadow Secretary of State for Wales. I had had only a few months of parliamentary experience and I had already bungled the offer of a place on the prestigious Treasury Select Committee. I agreed, astonished and grateful. It was so simple. No summons to the leader's office, or handshake – only a half-minute phone call. Later that day, the announcement was made that the first of the 1987 intake to be made frontbenchers were Mo Mowlam, Sam Galbraith and me.

It was generous of Neil Kinnock to give me the Wales spokesman job because our relationship had been rocky and his explosive temper had been directed at me on several occasions. Alan Williams welcomed me warmly and told me that I was his second choice. He would not say who his first choice was, and I did not press the point. I believed it was Paul Murphy because of their shared prejudice against the Welsh language and devolution.

Fellow Newport MP Roy Hughes was the third member of the

frontbench Wales team. He seethed with resentment at my appointment. Storms were just ahead. Roy always had a low threshold of rage, especially when he thought his dignity was being undermined. In 1968 Harold Wilson was invited to a Chartist commemoration dinner in Newport's Westgate Hotel. Roy was placed in an inferior position down the table to Pontypool MP Leo Abse. There was already bad blood between the two, partly because of Roy's enthusiasm for the Arab cause. An alleged anti-Semitic remark of Roy's was passed on to Leo Abse's wife. There was a scene in front of the assembled guests across the main staircase. 'What did you call my husband?' shrieked Mrs Abse. 'You shit! You shit!' – the word had more force in those days. The story was endlessly retold in the ranks of the Labour movement in south Wales. There were no more commemoration dinners for twenty years.

Even more colourful language was exchanged at a Commons reception given by the National Farmers' Union for Welsh MPs. Ron Davies, as a knowledgeable spokesperson on agriculture, was given the most prominent place at the dinner. Roy thought he should have been so honoured. An almighty row ensued within earshot of the hosts.

Roy was unhappy with Alan Williams's Welsh frontbench team meetings. He was a broad-brush hard-working politician who served Newport well. But he was baffled by the fine detail of policy, especially when discussed by the bright researchers at the team meetings. One of his areas of responsibility was housing, on which his knowledge was woefully superficial. When Roy played truant, buttering up farmers at the Royal Welsh Show instead of being on the front bench for the monthly Welsh Questions, Alan Williams's anger exploded. Roy was now certain to go.

It was at my first frontbench question time that I raised the need for a Welsh Language Act to tackle Wales's most divisive issue. It was a new experience to be speaking from the Dispatch Box, opposite Peter Walker on the Tory front bench. It was hard to ignore his constant mutterings 'Legislation, legislation! . . . Why do we need legislation?' It was Wyn Roberts from the Tories' side who answered my question. As always kind and courteous, he generously said my question was 'a tour de force'. I think he meant it was too long.

Roy Hughes jumped before he was pushed and resigned with a poisonous unjustified kick at Alan Williams. Peter Walker sneered that he was going to miss Roy's 'jocular performances from the front bench'. Like many other members of his generation Roy measured his worth in seniority rather than the quality of his parliamentary activity. Never mind the quality, count the years. He once complained to the head of the BBC because I had been interviewed on a transport issue rather than him, with all his years of experience. The fact that I was on the Transport Committee had not registered with Roy. He was also excessively territorial about the sanctity of his constituency. No MP should enter it without his say-so. It was alleged that some MPs marked their territory, canine fashion, by urinating on their boundaries. Most MPs take a more relaxed attitude. Many issues span constituency boundaries. If a factory is to close, it is unlikely that all the workers live in a single constituency. Former Monmouth MP Donald Anderson told me he was scalded by Roy's venom for trespassing into half a street that Roy judged to be exclusively his own.

Roy was not replaced on the front bench. I greatly enjoyed supporting Alan Williams. But he was in a losing fight with Peter Walker. Alan was a valuable mentor to me. An ex-minister and ex-shadow leader of the House, he knew all the intricate by-ways of Parliament's rules. He had also worked as a reporter for BBC Wales. Sadly Alan was better at teaching than performing himself. He outdid all other Welsh MPs in combating Peter Walker's superficial stunts. But Alan had forgotten his media skills. He not only sounded like an apology, he looked like one. With eyes downcast, hostile body language and faltering arguments he was a model of defensive negativity.

Welsh MPs grumbled and plotted against him. The formidable and resourceful Elizabeth Bachelor had long been his researcher and secretary. She was a past aspirant parliamentary candidate whose hopes had been frustrated by male chauvinism. Her experience of Parliament was greater than that of most Welsh MPs, but in 1988 she was the Berlin Wall, protecting Alan from the hostility of the outside world. She had once worked for Labour deputy leader George Brown – who needed protection from the press because of his alcoholic excesses. Alan did not.

I have heard her tell reporters and MPs, with Alan standing by her side, 'Alan is not here at the moment, but I can tell you what he will say.'

A group of over-the-hill Welsh MPs, Donald Coleman, Roy Hughes, Ray Powell (and occasionally Brynmor John), were nicknamed the Sewing Circle. It was rumoured that they met together to gossip maliciously while knitting their anti-macassars. The Sewing Circle was plotting to replace Alan Williams with Barry Jones. In my innocence, I did not know that they were able to rig elections. That was to be a future shock. Meanwhile Alan and I were suffering the full Peter Walker bombardment. He was like a B-movie trailer. He used the words 'colossal', 'staggering', 'tremendous' and 'fabulous' in almost every one of his press releases, sometimes more than once. He fumed when I pointed that out. He then replaced them with a new set of adjectives: 'lively', 'vibrant' and 'vigorous'. It was a case of incurable hyperbolic incontinence.

The truth slowly dawned on me. I was doing the most miserable job in Parliament, that of a junior frontbench spokesperson in opposition. The responsibility was immense. Every word uttered was carefully crawled over by opponents. No extra resources or staff were provided to juniors like me. Yet we competed on even terms in debate with the pampered government ministers, who were shored up with a small army of advisers and civil servants. Speeches and answers were written for them. In debate notes would be passed to them providing in-flight fuelling when they ran short of facts or inspiration.

With terror I prepared for my first major speech. It was on education. Alan generously allowed me to make the opening speech. Much midnight oil was burnt as I prepared. On the day I had enough material to deliver a Castro-style five-hour oration. It did not work out that way. At least half of my allotted thirty minutes was spent disputing Wyn Roberts's speech. Wyn said Wales was in the fast lane; I said Wales was stuck on the hard shoulder with hazard lights flashing. Far from oratory, but it was genuine debate. This was easier than I expected.

But in my bliss of early promotion, I was innocently unaware that an elephant trap was being dug for Alan and me.

4

Election rigging

My 78-year-old mother was determined to get the most out of having a son in Parliament during the few years that were left for her. She managed a tour of Parliament in a wheelchair. She spent hours monitoring my performance on the television, as my most severe critic. She once proudly explained how she had squashed a stranger whom she had met casually. The woman, having noticed my mother's Dutch name of Rosien, asked her how long she had been in this country. Miffed, she zapped back, 'Long enough to have a son as an MP.'

My stepchildren enjoyed the exciting new life, especially visits to Parliament. Alex, ten, and Natalie, six, had their own way of grading the worth of politicians. None enjoyed any status unless they had been portrayed on *Spitting Image*. Bernie Grant was a revered hero; Tony Blair a boring nobody. They had kept their father's name of Morgan. Few of their friends or teachers realised that they were related to an MP, and any worries I'd had on their behalf proved unfounded. We searched for a suitable building to set up an office in the centre of Newport. As a stopgap we ran the constituency from a spare room in my house. Sam had previously worked for Social Security, and had all the skills to work as my secretary. Home was far more convenient than Rhodri and Alun's new habitat in a trade union building in Cardiff. I was more available. Faxes could be sent out at weekends. Emergency constituency cases could be dealt with immediately. Having a secretary who was always on hand,

and whom I could trust implicitly, was perfect. It is much safer to make your spouse your secretary than risking the disruption and heartache of making your secretary your spouse.

Immediately after the recess in October 1987 the annual Labour Party beauty contest – the shadow cabinet election – was held. The members of the Sewing Circle were silently plotting to oust Alan Williams in favour of Barry Jones. The whips had enormous power of patronage in allocating jaunts abroad, offices, days off and other favours. It was common for toadies to hand their blank ballot papers to the whips for them to fill in. Even though Ray Powell had an official role as a whip, he still unashamedly canvassed my vote for Barry Jones. I refused. The next move astonished me.

Barry, who had been a former Welsh minister in the 1970s, was known as an assiduous cultivator of popularity from his fellow MPs. A handwritten congratulatory note from him would follow the most banal of maiden speeches. New members were impressed. The notes were on the lines of 'I was not in the chamber to hear your speech but I read it in Hansard and it was great. You will go far.' In the shadow cabinet election his direct approach was, 'I am standing in the shadow cabinet election. I know I've got no chance. But you won't see me humiliated, will you?'

With me he tried a new tactic. He had kindly visited Newport in 1986 during my election campaign. At my home he picked up a discarded picture drawn by five-year-old Natalie. He asked if he could take it to Parliament with him. Natalie later received a note saying how much Neil Kinnock and Margaret Thatcher liked her picture every time they dropped into Barry's room. During the shadow cabinet election Natalie received another note: 'I have moved offices and lost your picture. Can you draw me another one please?' Partly due to this heavy duty wooing, Barry was elected in 1987 to the shadow cabinet. Alan Williams was not. Barry replaced Alan as shadow Secretary of State for Wales. Peter Walker was delighted. He had little respect for Barry and had a cruel nickname for him.

The result made no sense. Alan was popular and had done the donkey work against Peter Walker, the media darling. Many years later Alice

Mahon and Brian Sedgemore revealed that the elections were rigged in a way that no one guessed at the time. Brian described in his book *The Insider's Guide to Parliament* how

> Alice Mahon, elected to scrutinise the counting of votes in the shadow cabinet, discovered the scam. The ballot boxes were opened by a Whip the night before voting officially ended. A preliminary count was made, thus enabling one of the Whips, who had a fistful of empty ballot papers handed to him by sleazy MPs, to vote in such a way as to ruin the chances of some MPs who would otherwise have been elected and ensure that other MPs who should not have made it, did so.

I am sure the revelation of vote rigging was as big a shock to the genuinely honourable Barry Jones as it was to me. The process was changed after Alice spilt the beans.

The sacking of Alan Williams was too much for me. He had done a good job without loyalty or support from many of his fellow Welsh MPs. Now he had been ousted on the back of a rigged ballot. Against my interests as an ambitious MP, I let my heart rule my head. I believed that Neil Kinnock should disregard the ballot result – as Tony Blair did later. I put out a press release saying Alan's sacking was cruel and unfair politics. Personally loyal, politically suicidal.

Kinnock called me in. 'There is no choice really, mate. You've sacked yourself, haven't you?' I did not argue. Life working with Barry as my boss was not appealing. Neil shook my hand and told me he would keep me in mind for another job, if one came up. I appreciated that I was being let down lightly but accepted the sacking as final.

I prepared a press release for the announcement the next day. It said how glad I was that my friends Paul Murphy and Alun Michael were joining the Welsh Office. I hoped they would gain as much from the experience as I had. I gave David Cornock of the *Western Mail* a copy of the press release, embargoed until the following day. Later that evening I had a telephone call from Neil: 'How would you like to go on

Social Security, kid? Just up your street?' It was a wonderful way out and I agreed enthusiastically. Working with my hero Robin Cook was a dream job. How could I get that press release back from Cornock? David respected the embargo and there were no reports that I had been sacked. It was seen as a sideways move.

The *Argus* was impressed. They recanted their election attack. In words that were sweet to read, their editorial on 11 November 1987 said, 'Readers with long memories will remember that at the general election we advised Newport West voters to return Tory incumbent Mark Robinson. Readers will have seen how Paul Flynn has made us eat our words. We did not expect him to be such a good MP.'

The *Argus* continued to be fair and reasonable for a few years, which was exceptional for a regional paper. Many of my colleagues wilted under the unending barrage of sneers from their local rags. It affected their value as MPs. They became debilitated when everything they did was interpreted in the worst possible light for their voters. It was impossible to challenge popular opinion, prejudice and ignorance on any cause. Fear of ridicule and abuse confined some MPs to the shallow waters of politics. They backed only the obvious causes, the trite and the bland. I felt sorry for them in their desolate half-life of intelligence-free cages. Little did I realise that enforced silence and a thought-free holiday was a wonderful preparation for office. Many of them became ministers in 1997.

The *Argus* was the essential conduit to the voters of Newport. When I was first elected the editor was the fair-minded Steve Hoselitz. He was of German-Jewish stock. He had a past in extreme left-wing politics but had settled down to middle-of-the-road Gwent nationalist views with added journalistic integrity. He offered me the chance of writing a fortnightly column under the title of 'The Red Rose' which became 'Commons Knowledge', a title suggested by Sam. I became very fond of it and later used it for a book. The new column ranged over all the delicious gossip, the wicked anecdotes and the witty comments of Welsh MPs. It was still a thrill just to walk into the wonderful buildings of Westminster. To be a witness and participant to all that happened there was an endless turn-on. In 'Commons Knowledge' I tried to pass on to the *Argus* readers my enduring feelings of exhilaration, wonder and excitement. I had built up a fruitful relationship of trust with the *Argus* and its staff for eight years. It collapsed hopelessly later. But it was fun while it lasted.

The euphoria of my new job as a shadow social security minister was soon replaced by silent gnawing panic. There was a morsel of truth in Kinnock's comment that it was just up my street. I had been the secretary of the Child Poverty Action Group in Newport since the 1960s and I understood well a handful of social security issues. But comprehending the vast encyclopaedic tangle of social security rules was beyond my tiny brain.

Ron Davies came to my rescue. It's just number crunching, he explained. None of us thoroughly understand our briefs. We are all walking on egg shells. The trick was to do it convincingly. Speak with a cultivated air of authority that disguises the fact that your knowledge of the subject is exhausted when you come to the end of your prepared notes. That's fine for set-piece speeches until an opponent intervenes and asks 'What precisely do you mean by that?' or 'Would you explain that in words that would make sense if you were addressing a bus queue?' or 'What did Labour do about this in 1964?'

A guardian angel appeared one morning. Weaving his way between the desks in our over-crowded office, a strange figure approached me. He looked like an Old Testament prophet: thin, with a long black beard and a face shaped like a map of Israel. 'I'm Tony Lynes,' he said, 'I work for Margaret Beckett. I think I may be able to help you.' Tony was the best stroke of luck I have ever had in my chequered parliamentary life. He is one of the country's greatest experts on social security. An ex-civil servant, he left to form the Child Poverty Action Group, which he headed for years before Frank Field joined it. The author of several standard books on social security, he had never sought wealth or status. He was single-mindedly devoted to improving the efficiency and justice of social security.

He taught me the concept of excess earnings. He had been receiving at one time in his life more money than he needed to survive. He set up a trust to hold the 'excess' cash so he could later give it away to worthy causes. Tony is one of the very few saints that I have known. He was then working part-time for Margaret Beckett, one half of the Health and Social Security portfolio. Robin Cook headed the team. My hero worship would soon prove to be justified. Robin kindly welcomed me to the job, explaining that he had been offered several names. He picked me because he thought I was a hard worker who would do the research.

Gulp! Research? I was already doing a more than full-time job as a backbencher. I had other ideas. I employed Tony Lynes on the one day a week that he was not working for Margaret Beckett. I rapidly grew to admire the awesome powers of Margaret, especially on the committee stages of the bills that soon dominated our lives. She was a toweringly authoritative presence in a bill committee.

Social security frontbenchers are plagued with at least one bill every year. I was hopelessly out of my depth. Tony Lynes kept me afloat with briefings that were clear and infallible. As each clause was debated on bills, teams of different civil servants would troop in to advise the minister. Margaret and I relied on Tony alone. He never let us down. So confident did I become in him that I happily stood my ground when ministers told me I was wrong. When Tony was nodding his head at me at the end of the committee room I was never caught out.

Working on social security trapped us in parliamentary purdah. No one was interested. Decisions were being taken that would drastically affect millions of people on tiny disposable incomes. Try telling that to the world outside. Journalists knew and cared about mortgages. They had mortgages. None of them were on housing benefit or income support or a state pension.

There were millions more people on each of housing benefit, income support and state pensions than had mortgages. But it was close to impossible to capture the interest of hacks. Their interest would have encouraged radical change from the Tory government. Many times I briefed them on some cataclysmic government decisions that were robbing defenceless millions of substantial amounts of their tiny disposable incomes. Their eyes would glaze over. If the point was pressed, they would stare skywards, focusing on a spot in the firmament just to the left of Jupiter.

And, in the absence of good information from the press, the public did not know that the government was picking their pockets. In one of my first speeches in the chamber, on the report stage of a social security bill, I warned that in the future MPs would have dozens of constituents complaining about the unjust claw-back of compensation payments that we were about to enact. Four years later the sago hit the fan. A fellow MP began a campaign against the unjust grabbing of the payouts. What were he and everyone else doing when the law was going through? The whole process of social security legislation is inevitably so complex that an intimate private priesthood of gurus makes decisions. No MP foresaw with clarity the hideous consequences of the Child Support Agency when the bill was drifting through Parliament. There were many further horrors of useless, malign and damaging bills that became law. The legislative process is an ossified idiocy long overdue for reform.

It had been a pleasure working with Margaret Beckett and Robin Cook. In one swift shuffle of ministers I lost both. They were replaced by Michael Meacher and Clare Short. Relations with Michael were cordial but never warm. I believe I was his second choice to his preferred old pal Gavin Strang. Clare had twice the warmth and half the ability of Margaret. The quality of our work deteriorated. Clare was racked by emotional resentments. When aggrieved she appeared to be sneering and whining. It is a false picture that has done her reputation harm. Her knowledge of Social Security remained superficial. But she maintained her authority by invention and native ability. She was a loyal supportive colleague who kept the morale of her team high by liberally distributing Fishermen's Friends.

Margaret and Clare, in common with almost all woman politicians, shared an aversion to confrontational politics. Previous bosses of mine, Jack Cunningham and Alan Williams, delighted in the aggressive parliamentary warfare of insult and counter-insult. Clare and Margaret were reasonable, cunning and civilised. Although I was to disappoint her later, my admiration for Margaret Beckett knew no limits.

There was no futile bravado of 'we'll keep them up until dawn' tactics. Rather, the women negotiated with the government on bill timetables. A deal was struck on when the committee would conclude. That allowed the government to timetable their programme. The opposition in return won a deal to debate controversial items at times of our choice when the media might notice our arguments.

Practical women's power allowed us infantry on the committees to organise our diaries in sensible orderly ways. This was intelligent constructive opposition. Bliss.

Part II

Shame is the spur

5

The portmanteau carrier

It is impossible to say whether my first semi-focused images are true recollections or tricks of the mind. My first memory was of lying in a cot, hearing women's soft voices and seeing smiling faces looking down on me, against the background of the sloping ceiling of an attic room. We lived for a short stay above Tony Mahoney's cobbler's shop on the corner of Clive Street. We flitted from these rooms to a large terraced house on the Penarth Road, the main Grangetown artery from Cardiff to Penarth. I sensed the fear and the excitement of night-time departure, clothes and bedding tied together in bundles, the whispered instructions and shushes as the family and a friend or two clambered down the darkened three flights of stairs. It was many years later that I discovered the meaning of a moonlight flit.

I heard the word 'jubilee' repeated several times in a conversation my mother had on the doorstep. It was a day of sunshine, flags and excitement in May 1935 ... the jubilee of George V. All these events happened before I was six months old. They are indelibly etched on my memory. My brother Michael and I started infant school together, although he is fourteen months older than me. My mother wisely knew that we would settle in better if we remained inseparable, as we had always been. I believe I disgraced the family honour by bawling on my first day. I was consoled with a ride on the school rocking horse. That first time on the horse was also the last. The terror of that torment ended my crying.

Infant school was a haven of warmth and gentle kindness from the all-women staff. Religion was taught by rote, by chanting the answers in the catechism. To the question 'Where is God?' the response was recited by the class with a powerful rhythmic chant. We in the second-year class learned the music of that catechism answer from Mrs Clarke's class next door a year before we learned the words, and a lifetime before we learned their meaning. This was learning by rote. Understanding the message was not important.

> As God Je-sus Christ is ev-ree-where,
> As God made man
> He is in hea-ven
> And in the Bless-ed Sac-ra-ment of the al-tar.

The week climaxed with the Friday raffle of a bag of sherbet. After faithfully investing a halfpenny a week for the Holy Souls through my five years at infant school, not once did I win and taste the exotic concoction. It proved to be a lifelong inoculation against gambling.

Infant school life was electrified by preparations for war. German bombing targets – the docks, the main railway station and Currans munitions factory on the river Taff embankment – ringed Grangetown. Relatives on my father's side warned that, when the air raids began, poorly aimed bombs would scatter down over the terraced streets of Grangetown, and so my paternal grandparents and a clutch of uncles and aunts decamped from their Cardiff home to the safety of Caerphilly. The air raids were events of wonder for me aged five and my brothers Mike, six, and Terry, nine. They were nights of terror for my mother. My sister Mary was born on 29 December 1940. The first major air raid struck Cardiff four days later on 2 January 1941. We scampered the 100 yards to the communal shelter in Clive Street weighed down with blankets and overcoats, my mother clutching the tiny baby.

It was midnight but the sky was bright with golden flares that burned and crackled as they fell. In our naivety we mistook the dropping flares for bombs. We were running through a cauldron of noise: the German bombers braying a characteristic engine throb, augmented by the howling banshees of the air raid warnings and the shouts of ARP wardens to 'get to the shelter, quick now'.

The communal shelter was a line of simple buildings that stretched down the centre of the unusually broad Clive Street. It gave psychological protection only, constructed of fragile brick with a concrete roof. The 200 mortals jammed into a single shelter were more exposed to bomb strikes than they would have been in the houses they had deserted. The threadbare consolation was that there was more chance of being killed outright in the shelter and less of being buried alive under the collapsed debris of a house. That night a shelter at the rear of Hollyman's bakery in Stockland Street, a few streets away from Clive Street, was bombed. It was a direct hit and at least thirty-three people were killed. Most of them were parishioners from St Patrick's Church who had rushed to the shelter from the church. The bodies were never recovered and a hardware store now stands on their unmarked graves.

Many other wartime precautions were equally futile. My father's brother Ted Flynn was a special constable charged with guarding the Canton bridge over the river Taff during air raids. Dutifully he hurried from his home to the bridge at the bidding of the siren. No one ever told him how to guard the bridge. If the Germans parachuted out of the sky, he had no weapon to defend it. Ruefully he concluded that his job was to spot bombs that were about to hit the bridge, catch them and throw them in the Taff.

The scariest warden's job of all was forced on a team of steelworkers. They had to climb up the main gasometer at Guest Keen steelworks in Splott and operate a Lewis gun mounted on the top. In peacetime and in daylight I later found that climb a terrifying experience. Those who did it in the blackout to take pot shots at enemy planes were true heroes. The rain of small phosphorus incendiary bombs on the gasometer was constant. They burst into flames on landing. The wardens' task was to kick them off the edge of the gasometer before they burnt through the metal cladding. A direct hit with a large bomb would have launched the gasometer, the wardens and the Lewis gun into the night sky and eternity.

Our infant invulnerability to grief shielded us from the worst suffering. We accepted the empty desks at school the morning after a bomb destroyed four houses in Paget Street, killing two classmates. Worse horrors were ahead. Land mines wiped out entire neighbourhoods in Grangetown and Riverside. We had a dim understanding of the scale of the tragedies, but our grief and fear were stunted and superficial. There was the rich excitement of watching a dog fight as planes battled at midday against a summer sky. Roaring engines, the crackle of guns and cottonwool puffs of smoke was a wonderful drama above our heads.

We experienced the raids through the noises of guns and bombs and the vibration of explosions. When a bomb was heard, beginning with its screaming fall to earth, there was a ritual bowing of heads. Bodies braced themselves for a possible impact. The scream grew louder, sharper. Boom! Relief and mutual congratulations that we were in the right place, again. Alive. Untouched. Wise heads would then announce 'That one was close' as they guessed our distance from the sound and flash.

The war came very near in two instances. The first was when the Tresillian Hotel was wiped out by a bomb intended for Cardiff railway station. It was situated on the corner of Tresillian Terrace and Penarth Road where we lived. For more than ten years the ruins remained, broken and gaunt, the shattered lift shaft door permanently hanging open, 50 feet above the ground.

The second was worse. We deserted the Clive Street communal shelter when each home was supplied with an Anderson shelter. It was family sized, half buried in the back garden. For company two or three families shared one shelter. There was no heating during the winter raids. We huddled close, wearing a couple of overcoats each and a heap of blankets. Children wore balaclavas, and a neighbour, Granny Edwards, sported an unlikely flat Dai cap. The master plan was that families should remain in their Anderson shelters all night. But cold and discomfort drove us back to our beds as soon as the All Clear siren sounded. To ease possible escape we slept downstairs. Following the return to our beds after one raid, my mother woke us up. There was a strong smell of gas. She opened the windows to let it out. That did not help. A time bomb had severed the gas main in the road six houses distant from ours. A passing lorry set off the bomb. There was an almighty explosion as a sheet of flame roared high above our three-storey homes. Even at 30 yards' distance the heat was unbearable. We were moved out into Granny Edwards's house where we continued to pull her leg about the Dai cap.

The fuel-saving campaign to persuade people to have their 'Holidays at Home' was a bonus to working-class children who had never had a holiday anyway. Schools and libraries were press-ganged into organising 'Holiday at Home' events in the fields near Grangetown.

My father was to be spared the suffering of another war. A few fleeting memories of him remain. The precious recollection of his singing uproariously 'Oh! Oh! Antonio, he's gone away' and persuading us three boys to join in the chorus. I have a clear memory from the age of five of a pale, thin figure in a bed in the living room at Penarth Road with a dozen relatives crammed into that tiny space. He was dying from lung cancer, a disease that the family doctor claimed was rare for that time. My brother Mike remembers him waving at us through a window at Llandough Hospital.

We did not understand what was happening. One morning, our red-eyed mother told us he had been moved into our spacious front room. Tradition dictated that the dead were given more space than the living. We felt neither grief nor loss. There was an argument about whether we should see him laid out. Mother said no, but a relative took us in. I remember it now without emotion, that strange waxwork of a body that could have no connection with my lively, laughing father. But it was interesting and fun. The house was filled with exciting people. Many years later my mother urged me not to see the dead body of the one I loved more than anyone else in my life. I took her advice.

The memories of childhood are lifelong companions. We are what we experience as children. The context against which I judged my social security job in Parliament fifty years later was the painful, proud and honest poverty of working-class life in Grangetown. There were the surface wounds of stigma. They became deeper in retrospect. My abiding memory is of a happy home life and a loving family. My brother Michael was a constant stimulating companion and we were often mistaken for twins.

To her dying day my mother bore guilt for the poverty of the war years. There was the humiliation of having clothes made of a grey cloth that was supplied free. It was a coarse material available only through the welfare system. The poorest children wore this uniform of shame. My mother destroyed the grey suits when I told her of the painful stigma. The shame persisted. Its spur still wounds.

In all other respects poverty was near universal. We were fortunate to be shielded from the worst privations because of the absence of choice. We were not touched by the New Labour myth that choice is the path to contentment. The reverse is probably true. There was little envy of material goods because of the enforced uniformity of wartime Britain. No family we knew had a car. Food was rationed and there were no luxuries. There was a choice-free solidarity of shared shortages. After all, as we were constantly reminded, there was a war on.

Generally we did not consider ourselves to be very poor. We were not, compared with the families of up to fifteen children at St Patrick's School who dressed in rags and rarely looked clean. There were times when we thought ourselves to be privileged, surrounded by intelligent self-educated adults with wide cultural and political interests. But a lack of food concerned my mother. Visits to her home for the rest of her life were welcomed by lavish hospitality. It was constant overcompensation for a deficiency that was not her fault and which was not noticed by her four children.

Mike and I vividly recalled the kindness of our family doctor. The charge for a doctor's home visit was half a crown. That was five shillings when we were both ill. Although that is only 25p in today's money, it represented a sixth of a postman's weekly wage and half a widow's pension. One day Dr South of Clare Road had been called to examine us. My mother handed over the two large, precious half crown coins that she could not afford. The doctor paused at our front door as he was leaving the house and asked Mike and me to play a game. He rolled the half crowns down the linoleum of our hall. We scrambled around to catch the coins. Dr South quickly closed the door and walked away.

Mothers had dreadful decisions to make. There were no child benefits until after the war. In those years many children died from childhood diseases. The decision whether to call the doctor was often one of life or death. Call the doctor and food would be short. Not call the doctor and the children might die. This was a powerful unforgettable lesson for Mike and me. We needed no convincing of the value of the health service that the Labour government of 1945 created. The five shillings per child family allowance gave immediate relief from poverty to young families. The gratitude of the working class was profound and, in our cases, lifelong.

My ever-present mother, Kathleen, was the daughter of John Williams, who kept the Penarth Dock, a pub in Thomas Street, Grangetown. She was partly educated in a public school where she learned some French. That was a rare achievement of education in a working-class community. Her mother died when my mother was six. Lovingly she described her mother's long golden hair and the horror of hearing the death rattle as she lay dying in the room above the pub bar. She had watched her being placed in a hole in the ground. That night it rained heavily. She pleaded for her mother to be brought home out of the wet. Her grief never healed.

She became a strong loving mother determined to keep her children close. The dominant Catholic parish priest Canon Phelan visited her shortly after the death of my father. He meant well but he terrified her. He explained that she could keep my baby sister Mary and my eight-year-old brother Terry, but she could not possibly afford to keep Mike and me. We were then five and four. The canon had arranged places for us in the Nazareth House Catholic Orphanage in Swansea. In a show of defiance against the all-powerful priest, my mother refused to let us go. She gave us the love and safety of a family, and saved us from the bleak neglect, and worse, of an orphanage.

She also refused to allow us to be evacuated to the safe south Wales valleys away from the bombing targets in Grangetown. 'If we are going to go, we will go together' was her expressed view.

There is some truth in the romantic view of a warm, close, working-class community supported by mutual dependence. But life was often brutish, insensitive and harsh. Drunkenness was public and flagrant. So were the fist fights that inevitably accompanied the rare deliveries of beer that allowed the closed pubs to reopen for a few days. In Grangetown pubs the fights spilled over into the streets. Those who failed to scrape a living income were trapped into lives with all the foul indignities of raw poverty. Many women yoked to drunken husbands were friendless and defenceless, compelled to bear endless pregnancies with an early grave as their merciful release. Every street had at least one child with serious physical or mental health problems. They were left to wander exposed to the cruel mockery of other children.

My mother had once had expectations of inheriting money from a prosperous uncle on her mother's side. The expected benefactor was Phillip Fletcher, whose name still survives in Fletcher's Wharf in Cardiff. The first choice of name for me was Phillip, but there was competition with what was then the less common name of Paul. That, as I learned much later, was the name of my father's German saviour. I was baptised Paul Phillip. My mother was later assured that the large sum of money would have been hers if she had chosen Phillip Paul.

Grangetown was a melting pot of confused identity. Although the hysteria of wartime chauvinism was at its height, we never felt English. Thousands flocked to watch our friends, the Dimascio family, being hauled off from their Holmesdale Street ice-cream shop to be interned as enemy aliens for the duration of the war. Even the father of my best friend Basil Salvatore disappeared. His ice cream cart was not seen again at his pitch on the corner of Penarth Road and Havelock Street until the war was over.

My mother defined Welshness in three grades. We the Cardiff Irish–Spanish–Italian mongrels were Welsh, because we had all been born in Wales. Those from the valleys who had sing-song accents which bore the imprint of the cadences of the Welsh language were the 'Real Welsh'. The mysterious Welsh-speakers from the far north were the 'Proper Welsh' – deeply Protestant, and not only strangers but probably extra-terrestrial.

Being Catholic was to belong to a large but separate minority. We were bound together by a church, a school and immigrant status – even though the immigration in many cases, including ours, took place a century earlier as a consequence of the potato famine. Memories tumbled down the generations. We heard vivid tales of ancestors who had been stoned as they walked from the Cardiff docks where they had arrived down the length of Bute Street. They ran the gauntlet from the berth of the Cork boat to the Irish haven in the enclave of Newtown. Prejudice was respectable among the indigenous population. It was acceptable to sneer that St Patrick's Day was the only day when the Irish washed the backs of their necks.

Like all immigrant communities, there was a need to be identified as excelling within the host community. That was the way to become fully integrated. Although the Irish community was long established, religion had maintained the divide between Irish and Welsh. There was always much agonising on which side to cheer when Wales played rugby against Ireland. There was no problem when Wales played anyone else.

Even in sport, Grangetown and other working-class parts of Cardiff had their own distinctive personalities. Only areas of Newport and Liverpool share our devotion to Welsh baseball. Crowds of up to 10,000 would flock to important matches in parks in Roath and Grangetown. Not only was it the most popular summer sport in the war, it was the only one. Cricket was in hibernation. Few Cardiffians of my age saw a game of cricket before their tenth birthdays. Miss Lawson was in charge of baseball in the big school at St Patrick's. The only two male teachers were both away fighting the war. What a joy it was to meet her as Mrs Eileen Driscoll in 1996 and recall those days. Fit and active she lived in Whitchurch, Cardiff after a brilliantly successful career in teaching. She died in her nineties in 2007.

Throughout elementary school life, I was judged to be one of the least able scholars – until my final term. The first class in the big school was divided. The bright seven-year-olds were taught by Mrs Steel, the rest of us by Miss McCarthy. Even there I did not shine. I starred only in an often repeated cautionary tale of two boys. One worked hard at his lessons, the other joked and idled his time away. Years later the good scholar, successful and rich, arrived home at Cardiff railway station and summoned a porter to carry his portmanteau for him. The porter was his lazy school chum.

'When you all grow up,' the teacher asked, 'who will be the rich man?' 'Eugene McCarthy, Miss,' the class chanted. Fixing me with her accusing stare she asked, 'And who will be carrying his portmanteau?' I was the only silent dissenter in the unanimous prophecy of 'Paul Flynn, Miss.'

I dreamed and drifted through the years of junior school puzzled by the futility of most subjects and rebellious about the illogicality of spelling. The saintly and gifted teachers never managed to coax me into steady work until the scholarship year. That was serious stuff. Triumph in the scholarship of the 11-plus won a place at St Illtyd's College in Splott, then the Far East of Cardiff. There they wore white flannel trousers, played cricket and had never produced a portmanteau carrier. It was the dream ticket boast for Cardiffians: born in Grangetown, educated in Splott.

To the astonishment of the junior school teachers I was one of eight children from our year of thirty-five who gained a scholarship. I had consistently been in the bottom eight of the class in all other examinations. The only thing of any merit I did in the scholarship exam was an essay on 'My Favourite Animal'. I wrote about an Alpine deer based on an article I had recently read. The novelty of the subject may have aroused the examiner's interest after reading dozens of scripts about cats and dogs. I must have only just passed. On the basis of the scholarship result I was placed in the lowest of the three first forms in the grammar school.

Probably by a hairbreadth my life was changed profoundly. Failure could have determined my future as badly as it did for many others. At eleven they accepted the brand of failure, reduced their ambitions and never recovered from the insult to their self-esteem. The 11-plus was cruel and destructive. It still exists in England. In Wales, it will never be exhumed from its shameful grave.

There was a breath of scandal in 1943 when my widowed mother's boyfriend first lodged in the house. He was a Dutch sailor named Wilem (Bill) Rosien whose boat was in a British port when Holland was overrun by the Germans. He stayed to take his First Mate's ticket. Tongues wagged because such an arrangement was far from respectable. They were silenced after a few weeks when my widowed mother and Bill married. Bill was trained as an upholsterer before he joined the Dutch merchant navy.

He rapidly found work. Possibly for the first time in our lives a regular wage was coming into the home and we were off dependence. Before, the tiny widow's pension welfare payment had been the sole income.

That was a time of great optimism. The war was due to end. So many good things were about to happen. Peace. A Labour government. Bananas again. And we could afford to rent a radio. A brave new world.

6

Shame embedded

'What happened on your first day?' was the excited question of my family. I was the first Flynn to attend a grammar school, and I had a strange tale to tell. There was boy in class with the exotic name of Dilwyn Jones. St Illtyd's was a Catholic boys' grammar school. Everyone had an Irish name or one from southern Europe. 'Not only Jones, but Dilwyn as well,' Maurice Reynard explained in amazement to Julius Hermer. 'Never known anyone with a strange name like that,' Patrick Kelly told Bernard Dimascio.

Dilwyn was not a Catholic. His reason for being there was that he lived in Splott Road almost next door to the school. About 5 per cent of the school population were non-Catholics, mostly Jewish, including the future poet Dannie Abse. None escaped the endemic religious ethos of the place. Some converted to Catholicism. Others deepened their own convictions through constant defence of them. One of these was a Grangetown friend of mine, Graham Horwood. He became a Church of Wales priest.

Perversely the first year forms at St Illtyd's were known as 2A, 2B and 2C. Forms 1A, 1B and 1C were at the preparatory school of De La Salle in another part of Cardiff. That was a fee-paying crammer to get the sons of the rich over the scholarship hurdle. Even in the lowly 2C life was thrilling.

Science was a joyous discovery of unimagined wonders. It was the start of a life-long love affair. Shame and a sense of a lost cause forced me to abandon my fight for logic, so I surrendered and agreed to spell the English language in the irrational way the teachers did. Academic success was vital because my best friend Peter Sexton had achieved a better scholarship result than mine. He was placed in 2A. The only route to continuing our close friendship was for me to come first in the Christmas term exam. To the delight of parents, uncles and aunts, I did. It was first real sign of any academic distinction. My primary school teachers had written off my scholarship result as a fluke. I was promoted to 2B. In the next exam I came first in 2B and joined the intellectual crachach and my pal in 2A.

For the next four years I enjoyed a long sabbatical of delicious dreaming sloth. I never made it into the first twenty in form exam results, although I always came first in the subject of my other new love, the Welsh language. My teacher Glyn Ashton inspired my interest in the language. It has been a lifelong delight. Bad, incompetent, sadistic teachers, and the odd depraved one, smothered my curiosity in some subjects. Illtydians had the great good luck to be taught history by the polymath Martin Cleary. His brilliant wit and infinite imagination made his lessons fascinating. An unexpected bonus of this Catholic education was a refreshing mistrust of textbooks. Knowledge and truth had many facets. We had to know the history of the textbooks only because that was the junk we had to churn out to please the external examiners. Parallel to the books was the vividly persuasive Catholic view of history, which was the 'whole truth'. Martin Cleary's jokes remain with me long after the authorised view has been forgotten. To a senior class he once demolished a pompous textbook tribute to Queen Elizabeth I. 'Virgin Queen? . . .Virgin Queen? . . . she was as much a virgin as my wife is.' His wit and humour anchored new knowledge in the minds of fifteen-year-olds.

There was a deep suspicion that all outside examiners were hostile to Catholic schools and would discriminate against us. The example quoted in my day was the failure of three-brained Walter Marshall to win a state scholarship in his final school examination. His case was used to change the system under which schools were immediately identifiable by examiners. The Central Welsh Board agreed to replace the name of the school with a number, ensuring that examiners were marking the papers without prejudice. The brilliant career of Walter Marshall (later Sir Walter) as the head of the nuclear industry reinforced the belief that St Illtyd's candidates were being unfairly marked down.

Pupils with radical views were warned to disguise them in external examination answers. Particularly vulnerable were the Irish nationalists and supporters of Cardiff's thriving Anti-Partition League. A cautionary tale was told of an invigilator who peered over the shoulder of one St Illtyd's boy who was writing 'and once again the Irish People squirmed under the heel of cruel English oppression'. He presumably scored a record low mark from the Central Welsh Board examiners!

The Christian Brothers of De La Salle ran St Illtyd's. There were of French origin, their order made up of mostly Irish monks. Brother Augustine was a subtle teacher of English and I discovered the sumptuous joys of English poetry from him. Most of the Brothers were simple, honest men whose single-minded vocations made them at least adequate teachers.

A few were racked by what to them were the impossible demands of celibacy. There was a scandal of the mildest character by today's standards. One Christian Brother was accused of groping boys. The story was a familiar secret to many senior pupils. It was dragged into the hearing of a handful of senior pupils who were religious zealots. They contacted the headmaster and he called a meeting of senior prefects. I was one of them. What shocks me now, but did not surprise at the time, was the protective reaction of many senior boys. Action was demanded not because of the damage done to the Catholic victims; the great fear was that the Brother might have interfered with a non-Catholic boy. His parents would have been outside the closed protective circle of Catholic *omerta*. They might have created a public scandal. That was regarded as the worst possible outcome. There was no consideration of help for the Brother's victims. He was removed from the school within days and sent on retreat to rebuild his spiritual life. There was no scandal and all involved agreed on group amnesia.

Religion damaged my family's life. My mother's marriage to her second husband, Dutchman Bill Rosien, had been an early success. They were very fond of each other. In spite of prejudice against him as a foreigner he found regular work. But the Catholic Church had a merciless disruptive campaign against mixed marriages. Bonds between Catholics and non-Catholics were judged to be the greatest threat to the survival of the Church. The subject was rarely out of the weekly sermons, with no appreciation that marriage to non-Catholics could bring new people into the religious fold.

My mother was unhappy with her status. In the eyes of the Church she was living in sin, having been married in a registrar's office without the blessing of the Church. She was brutally reminded of this by the priests. Bill Rosien agreed to marry again in the Church and submitted to the compulsory weeks of instruction in the Catholic faith. He was fortunate in having a highly sympathetic and intelligent priest who tutored him and intellectually convinced him of the arguments of the Church. Not only were they remarried in the Catholic Church but Bill converted to Catholicism.

Things did not run smoothly for my eldest brother, Terry. He was engaged to pretty and intelligent Lilian. She was an ideal future daughter-in-law and proved to be a marvellous wife and mother. My mother should have welcomed her into the family with whoops of joy. She did not – because Lilian was a Protestant. Terry had passed his national service guarding immigrant Jews at camps in Cyprus. On demobilisation, he and Lilian decided to marry. My mother refused to attend the ceremony or the simple wedding breakfast. I insisted on attending on the grounds that I was unlikely to be corrupted for life by a Protestant event. Endless rows and hurt were inflicted on families because of the narrow bigotry of Catholicism. Those wounds did not heal for many years.

Catholicism shaped the lives of the Flynn family. My job as an altar boy, at the age of seven, provided perks – religious, educational and social. The Latin responses that we learnt by heart are a permanent resource to aid the understanding of Romance languages. We became skilled in the art of conversing out of one side of the mouth to avoid detection by the congregation, a skill we shared with the inmates of jails.

There was a financial booty of half a crown for serving at weddings and requiems. Best of all was the annual altar boys' outing to Porthcawl. We relished a rare day by the sea. It was always in September. The town was forlornly closing down at the end of the season. It always rained. But for fourteen-year-olds the journey and the fun fair made it a day of tingling excitement, rich in new thrills and warm fraternity. Even more exotic was Mike's and my first holiday away from home. With misgivings and an enormous financial sacrifice my mother found £22 to send the two of us to the Urdd Dysgwyr (Welsh learners) camp in faraway Llangranog on the coast of Cardigan Bay.

It was a cornucopia of thrilling new experiences. Clean sea and sand, communal living in tents, sun, a Welsh-speaking world, and the thrill of my first love. Myra Bowen from Llanelli was the object of my devotion. It was reciprocated – at least for that blissful week. We were liberated from iron parental control to enjoy the first taste of sensual pleasure. Not surprisingly Welshness became a lifelong turn-on.

I needed fresh impetus to study other subjects. Mine was the first generation of O- and A-level guinea pigs. Exams were the only thing that provoked me out of my habitual indolence. They generated a spurt of intense study. The O-level year was serious. I stuck to the three hours of homework every night demanded by our teachers. There was even an episode of rare praise for an essay I had written for my English teacher, Jack O'Connell. He compared it to one written by former pupil Dan O'Neil. Jack was unaware that Dan is a cousin of mine. He has had a lifetime as an inspired, witty feature writer on Cardiff's *South Wales Echo*. If Jack the teacher had lived to his nineties, he would have been amused at his far-sightedness. Ten years ago Dan and I were both writing columns for the *South Wales Echo*: his on Thursdays, mine on Saturdays. We share identical rebellious views on the issues of royalty, Grangetown nationalism and illegal drugs. Nature or nurture?

There were few chances to practise the Welsh language that I had opted to take as a subject in the sixth form at St Illtyd's. I found a Ceredigion Welsh-speaking farmer who agreed to let me to work for my keep during the summer holidays. The words '*Rhyddid i Gymru*' (Freedom for Wales) were painted on a rock on the side of the main road from Pont Erwyd to Capel Bangor. It marked the spot where an earth road ran down the side of the valley to the Blaen Dyffryn farm home of Llywelyn Bebb. The handwriting on the rock was almost certainly that of Llywelyn, who was an indefatigable nationalist.

The Bebbs had three delightful children: Bethan aged fourteen, Angharad, seven and Aled, two. They welcomed the stranger with kindness and curiosity. Bethan was a dark-eyed, red-cheeked beauty who captivated me from the first moment. My clumsy half-hearted advances were not welcomed. The four farm hands were contemptuous of the pasty-faced town weakling who had come to help them in their work. Although one of them was in his fifties they were still all known as *bechgyn* (boys).

Life was alien and exotic with some light humiliation. I was trapped against a wall by a leaning horse when I was removing his halter. A lamb went silly on me and refused to budge. I carried him down the hill until Llew Bebb told me to put him down. He scampered off unharmed. I wrestled with a ram to keep him in one place after I had misunderstood an unfamiliar Welsh shout to 'Let him go!' as an instruction to keep a tight hold of him. The spectacle of the ram and me in a whirling demented tango across the farmyard was hugely enjoyed by the farm hands. It was mortifying to hear the story constantly retold.

Holding the head of a cow from a neighbouring farm while it was being serviced by Bebb's massive Welsh Black bull was traumatic and grisly for an innocent city boy. One hand held one of the cow's horns, fingers of the other hand up her nostrils. The bull's head jerked a few inches from mine, wild eyed, snorting, gasping. He lavishly and widely sprayed yellow in a manner that was surprisingly defective for an evolved beast. What he lacked in a sense of direction he made up for in passion. The deed was eventually done to everyone's satisfaction. It was all experience – a treasured small investment in my memory banks.

To avoid the justified ridicule of the *bechgyn* I was determined to excel at the totally novel physical work. Especially harrowing was the task of being the one in the middle of three, all pitch-forking hay from a trailer to the top of a haystack. At harvest time, the slog of collecting the cut wheat from the ground and bundling it into sheaves pushed my body through successive barriers of pain. The respite of the midday break was bliss. There was no time to return to the farmhouse. We rested in the shade, lying on stooks in the fields, feasting on the jam sandwiches that Bethan had brought from the house. The sugar-free tea that she poured from a Thermos flask was as delicious and refreshing as champagne. Never since have I taken sugar with tea.

I enjoyed the hospitality of the Bebbs for two glorious summers. Blaen Dyffryn was a beautiful haven of warmth, laughter and learning. There was no inkling of the tragedies that were later to deal cruel blows to the Bebb family. Following the deaths of his mother and father in the mid-1970s, Aled lost his wife and mother of his children in a fall from a ladder.

Being the only sixth-former for fifteen years to choose to study Welsh at St Illtyd's I sought companions from other Cardiff grammar schools. There were a crop at Cathays High School who were destined to become giants of the Welsh nation, including the poet Bobi Jones, Ted Millward, Emrys Roberts and Alwyn Prosser. I saw them at the Ty'r Cymry Welsh centre and in the reading room at Cardiff Library. It was my refuge for the intense study that was difficult in my crowded home. The atmosphere induced quiet concentration and I became an habitué. This was the only place in the whole city where James Joyce's *Ulysses* could be read, but only after convincing the library staff that you were a bona fide student of English literature.

Several of us passed English and Economics A-levels in our first year of our two-year spell in the sixth form. It encouraged complacency. The incentive and pressure to learn were weakened and we wasted the second year. It was to be the last time that serious educational study captured my interest. At seventeen, I decided to devote myself to a religious life.

7

Dropout

I had been a semi-cynical critical Catholic with sporadic bouts of enthusiasm. At seventeen I had a profound religious experience. The event was sudden. My decision to go to the novitiate was made in consort with a fellow sixth-former, Gerald Moorcraft, who later became a monsignor, working in the top echelons of the Church at Westminster Cathedral. He is still a working parish priest in Princes Risborough at the age of seventy-four. I recall the evening I walked home from town with Gerald. Animatedly we discussed our adolescent excitement at our refreshed and new religious convictions. Through a process of osmosis, we decided together that we both had vocations. When I arrived home I went to my battered typewriter in my bedroom and typed '*Credaf*' (I believe) on a piece of paper. I stared at it and believed my life had changed for ever.

There was no enthusiasm from my family. My mother was enraged. She thought I had been emotionally blackmailed by the Christian Brothers at St Illtyd's. She said so to their faces. It was untrue but plausible. A Welsh-speaking Brother able to teach the language would be of great value to the Order of De la Salle. None of the Brothers were Welsh. They longed for novices who were deeply rooted in Wales. My closest male relative and confidant, Uncle Dan, warned about the difficulty of maintaining the celibate life. That was the obstacle that had dissuaded him from taking up his vocation. There was less evidence then of the corrupting burden that celibacy imposed. Many who perceived their vocations as God-given were doomed to live unhappy lives. The struggle between powerful passions and the strictures of celibacy induces self-loathing when passion rules.

My infatuation with religious life was deep and overwhelming. The future that I saw at the Kintbury novitiate was one of seductive certainty and security. The place is ancient, green and beautiful. The trees soar up into the sky, striving to reach the heavens. Life was mapped out precisely until death. A serene existence with no major decisions or crises. But my convictions and faith proved transitory. The experience was rich, unforgettable, turbulent and damaging. Ultimately the religious experience for me was one of emptiness and delusion.

The psyche of those who have lived through Catholic education is deeply affected for life. Catholic and Labour nostrums were two sides of the same coin for me. Both strain our ambitions beyond our abilities.

The turbulence of adolescence and the wounds of the broken promise of religion dwarfed my ambitions. Without fervour or hope I drifted into university life. Half-hearted efforts had failed to win me a place in Oxford or London and deepened the gloom. Health problems were intensifying. Life was a bewildering trial.

Attending university in a home town is always second best. The apron strings are only part loosened. Independence is limited. Bad habits of laziness, acquired when I coasted through my second year in the sixth form, continued at Cardiff University.

Being taught by the giants, Saunders Lewis and Gruffydd John Williams, was the equivalent of an English lesson delivered by Shakespeare or Tennyson. Saunders once set us to write a poem. Justifiably modest about my aptitude to write poetry, I did succeed in producing a few stanzas that the great man described as 'promising'. This should have animated me to a period of furious writing. Lesser words of encouragement later in life did propel me into serious work. But crumbling academic interests and the joys of Brains beer and girlfriends dulled my enthusiasm for study.

The back room at the Old Arcade pub in Cardiff was where we lamented the plight of the 'Good Ship Venus' and the cautionary tale of

'Four and Twenty Virgins'. Does anyone know who wrote these marvels? I remember explaining to a student from Italy, Gaspare di Mercurio, the finer literary merits of one neat verse that has historic and zoological value concerning 'The sexual life of a camel'. This was a textual analysis of the English language that was not central to his studies.

My contact with student politics was slight because I judged myself to be about fifty years older than my contemporaries. One incident in Rag Week stirred me into protest. A US Army band from a base in Gloucester had led the Rag Parade through the streets of Cardiff. Later, band members went to the regular Saturday night dance at the Victoria Ballroom on Cowbridge Road. The white American soldiers were allowed in but the blacks were turned away. The rule was that black males were admitted only if they were accompanied by female partners. The management explained that blacks asking white girls to dance would inevitably cause trouble. They insisted that they were not discriminating. Oh, no. They had the same policy for the many Cardiff young black men.

Here was conscious unashamed discrimination in my beloved multi-racial home town. I spoke over the public address system at the Students' Union Rag dance urging everybody to join a torchlight procession of protest to the Victoria Ballroom. Fortuitously, the union had a few hundred torches left over from a rained-off parade planned for earlier in the week. Almost everyone joined in. It was seen as fun as well as a politically worthwhile event. The Victoria Ballroom was shamed. Shortly afterwards they dropped their colour bar. I was back into politics.

College life ended unhappily in collapsing interest, illness and failure. Some of the memories of that time are still too painful to revisit. My world was shrinking. Horizons were narrow and domestic. Life could no longer capture my interest. Burdened with black cynicism I surrendered to a future course of drifting through life as unobtrusively as possible; without effort or excitement I had come to terms with the futility of life. Failure of my vocation and the empty promise of religious life had crushed ambition and hope. I applied to become a bus conductor. One of the key differences in my political odyssey and that of John Major was that I passed the interview for this taxing job.

My main intellectual and creative life was through the hobbies of cine photography and sound recording. I had one of the first reel-to-reel Grundig TK5 tape recorders sold in Cardiff. It was a great novelty and a cheap way of exploring what was, to me, the unknown treasure trove of classical music.

There was one moment of drama on the Western Welsh buses. My mate and I chalked up a record that I do not think was ever beaten. He was part of a Cardiff Chinese family called Wu, although he called himself Percy Wing. We worked happily together for a couple of years. There had been trouble on the last bus from Barry to Cardiff on Sunday nights. An unruly mob from the Ethel Street area of Canton made weekly binge trips to the Thompson Street red light area of Barry. Aggressively drunk they regularly caused trouble on the trip home.

Raucous, foul mouthed and insulting, they upset the other passengers. In a foolhardy act I ordered them all off the bus. They refused to go. I stopped the bus at the police station at Wenvoe and knocked up the local bobby. He ordered them off and they walked the five miles back to Cardiff. Subsequently they were fined. There were thirteen of them; it was the largest group ever thrown off a bus and punished in the history of the Western Welsh Bus Company.

One of them did try to attack me a few weeks later on the same route. He had got off the bus, but he jumped back on again as it was moving off. He tried to kick my bag of money. He missed. I pushed him. He fell off the bus and landed spread-eagled on the road. Wise heads at the bus depot warned me, 'Never mind what he did, you hit him, you're in the wrong and will take the blame for it.' In retrospect my dragon-slayer stand was foolhardy and dangerous. Taking unreasonable risks became a lifelong trait. What possessed me to act in this probably foolhardy way is a mystery. The memory of the risk alarms me now. But that happened in an age before confrontation avoidance was understood. There was deference to authority. Even to the uniform of a bus conductor. The *Cardiff Times* fulminated on the collapse of law and order in an editorial beginning: 'Meet Percy Wing and Paul Flynn, two ordinary men doing an ordinary job...'

After a couple of years on the buses, I went to work as a technician in the laboratory at the steelworks of Guest Keen in Cardiff. The work was undemanding, the people congenial and the pay good enough for me to buy a Mini in the first year they were manufactured, 1959. Drifting towards my late twenties, my Saturday night forays to local ballrooms took on a new search for a potential wife. In the vast auditorium of Sophia Gardens pavilion I asked a good-looking girl from Rhiwbina to take the floor. As a dancing couple we were a clumsy flop, moving in contrasting directions. Even though I had acquired some elementary competence in dancing, we were incompatible. I suggested a drink as an alternative to a second dance to avoid serious injury to one or both of us.

Her name was Ann Harvey. We fell in love and decided to marry. She was a Baptist. We married secretly to avoid the theatrics of more family warfare. We told no one. Only our two witnesses knew. It avoided a battle but the reasons were never fully understood, especially by Ann's family. In later life, I believe Ann, too, resented the loss of a proper wedding.

In the early years our marriage was happy and successful. We briefly lived in a flat in the Roath area of Cardiff. On an August night in 1962 Ann and I moved from our Cardiff flat to our Newport home. Because of disorganised arrangements we slept overnight in Cardiff on a settee in Penarth Road. We had not intended to start a family so early in our marriage. That night we conceived our daughter, Rachel.

I moved to Newport and, though I loved Cardiff, I developed an infatuation for my new home. I have never considered leaving.

Newport exists because it stands on an old ford across the river Usk that divides the city. At full tide the Usk is a vast expanse of attractive reflective water. At other times it's reduced to a modest stream flowing through a canyon of unsightly mudscape. The poet Gillian Clarke wrote of the beauty of the mud that was resculptured at every tide. A barrage across the Usk would have led to a welcome transformation, but it was a political issue. The Tories found elections difficult in Gwent. They preferred to exercise power by stuffing quangos with TWEMs – Tory Welsh Establishment Males. They were also known as Conservative and Unionist Nomenklatura Toadies. That has a more telling acronym. The Abergavenny triangle of Tory quangocracy on the salmon-fishing upper reaches of the river Usk was lobbying heavily to kill the barrage. The interests of the people of Newport were swamped by powerful up-stream voices shouting in the right places. The beautiful Usk tidal range similarly ravished a Welsh Office inspector. As a Friend of the Mud, he waxed lyrical in the report that turned down the barrage.

Newport urban areas have sprawled outwards like a doughnut, leaving a hole in the middle of land that is under-used or derelict. Much of it on the banks of the river would have been revitalised by the barrage. New housing and hi-tech development could be happily housed on the edges of a huge permanent freshwater lake. There is still fascination in observing the daily drama of the rise and fall of the second highest tide in the world.

One of the most beautiful areas of Newport West is the fenland area between Newport and Cardiff. Below the level of high tide, and sheltering behind the sea wall, the Gwent levels are divided by drainage furrows known as reans, and are lined by pollarded willows and rich in wildlife. A major cause throughout my political life was preventing Cardiff from spreading in Newport's direction. Had Newport and Gwent councils been as permissive as Cardiff's, the two cities would have merged into one megalopolis. It would have been possible to walk from Newport Civic Centre to the City Hall in Cardiff without seeing a field or a grove of trees. The battle to stop Cardiff doing a shimmy towards Newport continues.

Marriage was a great adventure. Number 52 Greenmeadow Road, Pont Faen was a tiny, year-old, semi-detached house. It had a large kitchen and one single room downstairs, three bedrooms and a bathroom upstairs. We were liberated from our grotty flat in Cardiff, but alarmed at the huge mortgage of £2,500. Ann and I delighted in furnishing our small house, preparing the nest for the family we wanted, while trade union work at the Llanwern steelworks dominated my working life. Although we were to be dealt a terrible blow, I prized the memory of those years. There may have been bad days, but all I can remember is the dawning love of two new lives, our wonder and delight as we explored the excitement and fulfilment of the loving world into which our children were born.

My Austin Mini was now unaffordable and had to go. Life was dominated by nest building on a tight budget. Endless hours of overtime were worked. That meant a double shift of sixteen hours of continuous work with only an eight-hour break before another shift. It seemed worthwhile at the time. Now I mourn the futile loss of precious time that could have been spent with my young family. I missed one complete August with them to buy a fridge.

Ann worked first at Llanwern, then in the social security office in Newport. I did my share of the domestic chores, including cooking and washing the nappies. Little in life can be as thrilling as the birth of a child. Rachel was born in Panteg Hospital on 20 May 1963. It was a time of soaring excitement and expectation. Etched permanently on my memory is the flood of paternal protectiveness and love that I felt when I first saw her. The image of that tiny red face and miniature hands sent a great surge of joy coursing through my body. James Patrick was born at home in Greenmeadow Road on 2 January 1965. He had a mop of black hair and a perceptible family resemblance. His birth was marred by worries of a potential abnormality with one of his feet. The worry passed.

Nothing could ever give me greater happiness than those early years of parenthood, years of discovery and hope. The family was my whole life. Work was a tormenting interference. I was fully absorbed in their growing up. From an early age I told Rachel and James bedtime stories which I had lovingly and painstakingly prepared. I used them to convey messages about road safety and to give them lessons in Welsh. But mostly it was to excite in them a joie de vivre for all the wonders of the universe that were opening up for them.

After a few years, a new second-hand Mini made trips and holidays possible. We had several idyllic weeks self-catering in an old farmhouse in Pembrokeshire, within a couple of miles of the sea. Acquiring new skills was a surprising part of fatherhood. Being a bloke and doing household blokey chores had previously not been for me. But I found myself dismantling the engine of the car, fitting electric circuits in the house and even building a brick Wendy house with a tiled roof for Rachel. For the first, and only, time in my life I had a practical use for trigonometry. Having built the four walls, I had to make deft calculations on the angle at which to build the sloping roof. Only trigonometry could answer that conundrum.

The years raced agreeably by. We had several Siamese cats and a Burmese one. A litter of Siamese kittens in the house was an intriguing diversion. Siamese kittens are creatures of wonderful grace and beauty. Much as I enjoyed the company and hero-worship that dogs give, I was captivated by the haughty splendid independence of these most sensuous of creatures.

Our family had outgrown our tiny first home and we moved in 1975 to a larger house, 22 Christchurch Road in Newport. It cost the then huge sum of £18,000. 'Will it ruin us?' we wondered.

It was a vast Victorian pile. The previous owner, a local businessman, had modernised the house while trying to retain many of its attractive Victorian features. There was a large garden with a couple of pear trees. Although it was detached it was on an unfashionable part of a main road. Huge trees and bushes towered in the neighbouring gardens providing valuable privacy. I loved that rambling house. But it was a nightmare to maintain and we were living above our joint incomes from the steelworks and the DSS. We got by through scrimping on cars and other non-essentials. I suffered a succession of wretched old vehicles, mostly Datsuns, held together with string and a prayer.

Some knowledge of car mechanics kept me mobile. For many weeks I drove a car without an accelerator around Newport. This is a conversation stopper even with the mechanical cognoscenti. The secret was to ram a few coins between the accelerator cable stop and the carburettor to keep the car running at about three times the tickover speed. The engine then ran at a fixed speed, slow enough to start in first and fast enough to move through the gears up to a speed of about 40 mph in fourth.

It required an approach to driving that had rarely been used since the early days of motoring in the nineteenth century. After three or four months I got around to asking a garage to fit a new cable. The mechanic in disbelief handed back the three coins worth 27p that had kept me moving. Bangers they were, but our family certainly got full value from them.

Newport is a wonderful place for parents and young children to visit and explore. There is the drama of the huge tidal range that reshaped the dramatic mudscape at Goldcliffe, and the splendid views across to Somerset. It is called the land of summer (*gwlad yr haf*) in Welsh because it is visible only on sunny days. At low tide the estuary is a vast expanse of rock, mud and treacherous sands. The beach is full of interest. It is strewn with fossilised trees, mollusc fossils in abundance, plus the detritus left by the retreating tide. There was even an ancient fishery where salmon were caught in cornet-shaped wicker cages called putchers, which are fixed on supports that face the incoming tide.

Newport has some of the best parks in Wales. Beyond them is a circle of woods and hills. A wonderland for Rachel and James throughout their childhood were Wentwood Forest, Coed y Caerau and Cwm Carn Forest trail. One of the boons of shift work was that a daily excursion was possible as soon as children returned home from school at 4.00 p.m.

Newport's historical radicalism derives among other sources from the Chartists. The memories of their sacrifices continue to inspire each new generation of Newportonians. Rain-sodden, hung-over and exhausted after their night sleeping rough, badly organised and poorly led, a group of Chartists charged trained soldiers lodged in the Westgate Hotel, Newport in 1839. At least twenty-two were killed. Every 4 November I recharge my political batteries by honouring the Chartist cause at the site of their unmarked graves at Newport Cathedral.

Five of the six reforms demanded in the original Charter were all won during the course of the nineteenth century (the call for annual parliaments being the only exception). The six points of 1839 were: annual elections, secret ballot, equal electoral districts, removal of property qualifications for parliamentary candidates, the payment of Members of Parliament and universal (manhood) suffrage. In 2009 the 170th anniversary of the Newport rising was celebrated, with glorious inspiring music and poetry in two weeks of glittering events. Wales's national poet Gillian Clarke wrote a special poem on the 'grudged gift of democracy'.

In my frequent visits to schools I retell the honoured tale of the noble sacrifice of the Chartists. Their memory is a constant inspiration. A core task of a Newport MP is to renew and rebuild the idealism and courage of the Chartists.

We need a new charter for the twenty-first century:

Point one: Make all votes of equal value. Our eccentric and irrational electoral system means that elections are decided by a small number of footloose votes of the weakly motivated and the least well informed. Voting in the second ballot at Assembly elections is a gamble that often perversely elects the party the voter dislikes the most.

Point two: Use national funding to liberate parties from any dependence on outside interests. Lobbyists still infest politics, promoting the causes of their rich privileged clients at the expense of the needy and deserving. We have the scandal of foreign millionaires spending vast amounts to buy victory in marginal seats.

Point three: Extend to all media the broadcasters' statutory duty of balance. A handful of newspaper moguls abuse their massive power. They proselytise irresponsibly without the discipline of balance imposed on broadcasters. Meanwhile, regional papers are dying and begging for state subsidies.

Point four: Extend the franchise to sixteen-year-olds. The election of a monkey in Hartlepool and more votes for *Pop Idol* than local elections proves that politicians are out of touch.

Point five: Make power the exclusive gift of the electorate, never to be inherited or bought. Only two countries in the world allow their hereditary chieftains to make laws: Britain and Lesotho. The hereditary principle must be finally buried.

Point six: Broaden political horizons to encompass all of humanity, one environment and one world. The narrow local focus of politics accelerates the global neglect and looting of our environment. All decisions should be on a worldwide scale.

Chartist history gives my convictions a historic legitimacy. I fear I would not have had their courage in facing the guns but I recognise the idealism in the letter of George Shell to his parents the night before he was shot dead. He wrote, 'I hope this will find you well, as I am myself at present. I shall this night be engaged in a struggle for freedom, and should it please God to spare my life, I shall see you soon; but if not, grieve not for me. I shall fall in a noble cause.'

Their story is a wonderful illustration to teach each new generation of Newport children to value their heritage of democracy. They warm to the heroism of their ancestors and empathise with the hope in the Chartist poems.

> For ages deep wrongs have been hopelessly borne;
> But despair shall no longer our spirits dismay,
> Nor wither the arm upraised for the fray;
> The conflict for freedom is gathering nigh.
> We live to secure it, or gloriously die!

8

A nation lives in her language

'I've learnt a Welsh song at school,' Rachel told me in 1969. Education in Newport then had no Welsh content in either language or culture. But as a gesture to Prince Charles's investiture celebrations one Welsh song was being taught. Proudly she sang me the words, 'The land of my fathers is dear to me . . .' This was 'Hen Wlad Fy Nhadau', the Welsh national anthem, *in English*. That was the final straw. Even in the cosmopolitan areas of Cardiff where I was brought up we sang the anthem in Welsh.

Furious, on the same day I wrote an article for the *Argus* calling for the establishment of a Welsh school. Unknown to me there was already an *ysgol meithrin*, a Welsh nursery school, in another part of the town. Dedicated parents in Risca had a school up and running in spite of fierce opposition from local councillors. A campaigning group was formed and I became its secretary. In September 1971 the first class of the Newport Welsh unit opened with eight pupils. It was a difficult task to convince parents to trust their children to what seemed an educational gamble. Dare they have faith in a tiny unit with an uncertain future?

Progress since then has been continuous, but against the solid bias and prejudice of local politicians. Shortly after the start of the Newport unit, I was invited to Merthyr to explain how it was done. The meeting of parents took place in the home of a young man employed at the local Hoover factory. His name was Dafydd Wigley. The future leader of Plaid

Cymru impressed with his organising ability. Happily, Welsh medium education had a few valuable friends in the education authorities of Gwent, including Hugh Loudon and Vaughan Williams. Without them, small-minded local councillors would have frustrated progress as it had been frustrated in other parts of Wales.

The pioneering parents made many sacrifices. Their tireless work resulted in the development of these units into the schools that spread throughout the county. Often it was two steps forward and one step back. Nothing ever came easily in the growth of Welsh language education in Gwent. There were many heroes of the campaigns to give the children of Gwent the chance to speak *yr hen iaith*. Members of the parents' groups at Risca acted, in the 1960s, as the Praetorian guard.

Many of the children have built on their hard-won knowledge of Welsh and developed fine careers in education and the media. Some are back teaching in Gwent passing on the baton to another generation at the first Welsh language school, Ysgol Gwynllyw. The Urdd Eisteddfod in Gwent in 1997 celebrated 4,000 children in Welsh medium education, an unbelievable increase. For the first time ever, Welsh was taught as a second language in almost all schools in the county. The progress has continued with new Welsh medium schools in what was once the Welsh Sudetenland of Monmouthshire, claimed by both England and Wales. Every single Welsh school established has prospered and grown.

It is now possible to greet the children with a '*Bore da*' in all Newport schools and get a strong confident reply back. It is no longer exotic to tell Gwent children tales of the Mabinogion and the reason why Bendigeidfran stretched his body across the river as a bridge for his army. My own involvement in those pioneering days lasted a few years only. Yet I am intensely proud of the results of the pioneering work of the parents of the 1960s. Gwent education has been transformed. Our children's connection to their linguistic inheritance was shamefully ruptured by a dullard Philistine generation.

It was a measure of the achievements of those pioneers that, twenty-five years later in 1988, Newport hosted its first Eisteddfod for more than a hundred years, having elected its first Welsh-speaking MP in the town in the twentieth century – or possibly ever. I was invited to be a *Llywydd y Dydd* (President of the Day). The President is expected to make a rousing speech to an audience of up to 8,000. I had vivid memories of a wonderful witty speech by the *Llywydd*, the actor and playwright Emlyn Williams, thirty-four years earlier.

That memory deepened my sense of inadequacy. I picked a striking image from Hungarian writer István Széchenyi, who, in answer to the question 'Where do you find the nation?', said, 'The nation lives in her language.' I decided to rejoice in the long history of Welsh in Gwent, its current miraculous revival and to give credit to our latter-day saviour of the language – the media.

I agonised over the style of the speech. Help came from broadcaster Huw Edwards, who was then the BBC's Welsh Language correspondent in Westminster. He was a patient tutor, although he never accepted the idea of living 'in the language', *yn yr iaith*. He urged me to say 'through the language', *drwy'r iaith*. I stuck with István's metaphor.

The celebrated writer Gwenlyn Parry said after my speech, 'You are more of a patriot than Dafydd Wigley.' Others were less happy. The Carmarthen Labour MP, Alan Wynne Williams, sent me a sulphuric letter expressing his astonishment and fury because 'you have given your blessing to all the illegal activities of Cymdeithas yr Iaith and the Welsh Nationalists'. He was especially incensed that I had praised Gwynfor Evans whose fast had persuaded Margaret Thatcher to surrender over the Welsh language fourth channel issue. This was simply a matter of recognising the truth of the events.

The Newport Eisteddfod will always be remembered with great pride and satisfaction by the city. Newport is still reaping the benefits. At Mold the next year I was received into the Gorsedd of Bards with a name I revel in: Paul y Siartwr (Paul the Chartist). It was a wonderful moment. The setting was dreamlike and magical. The Gorsedd of Bards met on a hill in a grove of tall trees with the dappled sun breaking through. It was the only honour I ever coveted.

There was no Welsh spoken in my family or anywhere in working-class

Cardiff when I was a child. It was an inspired teacher who kindled my love of the Welsh language. Glyn Ashton entranced his class of eleven-year-olds with a collection of ancient stories called the Mabinogion. I was a favoured pupil because for the first six months he was convinced my name was Flint – an interesting Welsh adaptation from the Irish nomenclature. Glyn was an oddity in Cardiff Catholic Grammar School. He was Protestant, lame, eccentric and a snuff user. His initials, GMA, were similar to the Welsh word *dyma* ('here it is') and inspired his nickname of 'Gyma Ashton'. He was a gifted teacher and a spellbinding storyteller.

To truly love a language, it's vital to know more than one. The monoglot usually accepts language as little more than a means of communication. Bilingual speakers constantly compare the endless delights in the unique personalities of languages they know. Those who live only in their mother tongue are often baffled by the passions that the possible loss of other languages arouses. Why bother nurturing a minority language such as Welsh when all Welsh-speakers are fluent in the great world language of English? Cannot everything be done in English? Now that the rest of the world is adopting English as the world's main language, why perversely cling to language spoken by half a million people?

A living language is created by the accretions of sounds, thoughts, imagery and wit that have echoed down the centuries. All languages are unique. Welsh has evolved over 2,000 years. From the ancient Celtic mother tongue and its Brythonic branch Cymraeg emerged. The language was passed down the generations, each one enriching it with new subtleties, strengths and poetic insights. Welsh has a continuous rich literary inheritance which began centuries before English existed. The greatest honour that Wales bestows is the annual Eisteddfod prize for writing a poem in a literary discipline that is unique to Welsh literature.

Love of the mother tongue is instinctive. The first words heard at the mother's breast, the language in which the world is discovered in childhood: the only adequate words to console, express tenderness or make love and to curse or express anger. The mother tongue is the medium of our most intense living until the final words on the lips of the dying. Insulting or disparaging the mother tongue is to wound at the deepest level of human nature. A haunting dread is a future in which no one could delight in Welsh literature and language. That has been the fate of other unique tongues.

The task of protecting and nurturing the Welsh *mamiaith* remains a national passion. Its survival and present vigour is remarkable. Wales has avoided the worst divisions of religion and race but language is a potential source of tension among the nation's majority of non-Welsh-speakers who fear exclusion. It was my great good luck to fall in love with the language and literature at an early age. It has been a companion that has allowed me to straddle both linguistic communities and heighten my sense of nationhood and appreciation of a precious culture.

Tolkien was attracted to Welsh as something ancient that had to be preserved and passed on. 'For many of us it rings a bell, or rather it stirs deep harp-strings in our linguistic nature. It is the native language to which in unexplored desire we would still go home.' He was determined to convey the beauty of Welsh to word-deaf and blind English monoglots. He recalled seeing the word *adeiladwyd* ('it was built') carved in stone. 'It pierced my linguistic heart,' he said. Then he discovered that Welsh was overflowing with words that are rich in sonorous beauty. The word *wybren* he found more pleasing than 'sky'. Boris Johnson learnt some Welsh when he was a candidate in Wales. He delighted in the prospect of a Roman centurion demanding his *cig moch* (pork) and *sglodion* (chips). Two of the Welsh words for 'butterfly' delight language learners – *pili pala* or *iar fach yr haf* (the little hen of summer).

The charm of Welsh was experienced by a world audience in the singing of the lullaby 'Suo Gan' in Steven Spielberg's *Empire of the Sun*.

> Huna blentyn yn fy mynwes
> Clyd a chynnes ydyw hon;
> Breichiau mam sy'n dyn am danat,
> Cariad mam sy dan fy mron.

(Sleep, my baby,

At my breast,

Comfortable and warm are Mother's arms that safely hold you,

Mother's love is under my bosom.)

To illustrate the quality of Welsh to schoolchildren, I ask them to close their eyes and listen intently to the soft dancing consonants of the poem 'Nant y Mynydd' ('Mountain Stream') or the muscular guttural strength of the 'll's and 'ch's in warrior poems. My hope is that one or two children may be stirred by the ancient sounds in the same way that Tolkien was.

My teacher Glyn Ashton told me that Welsh literature had no pornography. His generation had been shielded from the hidden treasures of the Middle Ages by language taboos. He knew nothing of the uproarious bombastic poem by Dafydd ap Gwilym in praise of the penis and the equally uninhibited work of the female poet Gwerful Mechain in praise of the vagina. Both poets celebrated unembarrassed relish and joie de vivre for all of life from the divine to the profane.

These heady delights are far removed from the mundane work of strengthening the place of language in legislation. It has been been my good luck to serve in parliaments that have created the framework for Welsh to survive and prosper. The Welsh Language Act 1993 put Welsh and English on an equal footing within the public sector in Wales. It has been welcomed by the people of Wales with renewed pride in our precious *hen iaith*.

The Act was the culmination of the work of a small group of enthusiasts. In 1962, national guru Saunders Lewis had warned that the Welsh language was destined to die before the year 2000. This galvanised lovers of the language. The campaigning Cymdeithas yr Iaith Gymraeg (The Welsh Language Society) was born. It brilliantly and successfully campaigned for bilingual road signs, mostly by breaking the law. Far more crucially, it called for a Welsh-language fourth television channel.

Luck gave me a small role in the politics of broadcasting in the 1970s. Although it ended in anger and frustration, it was a fulfilling task. Solicitor Gerard Purnell was the secretary of Newport Labour Party. He was on the unfashionable right of the party. His ambitions for a political career were never requited. He was New Labour twenty years too early. The party in Wales was seeking a policy document on the fourth channel. Gerard and I put months of work into collecting information that was published in 1973 calling for a Welsh-language fourth channel. The then journalist and future MP Ann Clwyd gave valuable support. The Labour Party in Wales adopted it as policy. We both spoke at the mass national meetings demanding a fourth channel. We also gave evidence to the Crawford Committee on broadcasting on behalf on the party. In 1974, Gerard was appointed a member the IBA advisory body for Wales and I became a member of the BBC ruling body, the Broadcasting Council for Wales.

It was rapturous for a shift worker in a steelworks to engage in erudite chat with the patrician scholar Glyn Tegai Hughes, the cerebral university teacher Alwyn Roberts and other luminaries of the nation. Our powers were limited but we did have a voice that penetrated through to the decision-makers in the BBC and the government. The Welsh fourth channel issue dominated my five years of membership from 1974 to 1979. The business was always strictly confidential. I assumed that it would always remain so. But historian John Davies's volume *Broadcasting and the BBC in Wales* reveals all. Davies generously notes that I was one of the most active members of the council who was particularly persistent about the fourth channel as the only answer to the broadcasting problems of Wales. He also records that I deprecated any attempt to seek palliative measures.

It was a bitter disappointment that my own Labour government had failed to honour a Welsh manifesto commitment to set up a channel in Wales, dedicated to serving the Welsh-speaking community, after our electoral successes in 1974. It was first of many times when my loyalty to the party was to be under strain. Our argument was simple and overpowering. The language would not survive without its own channel. The antagonism against the language in non-Welsh-speaking households would be placated only if an all-English service was also available to Wales. Aerials pointing from Wales to English transmitters were diluting the Welshness of life for monoglots. Non-Welsh-speaking communities were increasingly being anglicised.

The demand for the new channel united the people of Wales. In February 1977 Davies records that I welcomed the publicity for a Cymdeithas yr Iaith demonstration at the BBC World Service Centre. I said that it would draw attention to the absurdity of the BBC broadcasting more radio programmes in many obscure foreign languages than it broadcast for the indigenous Welsh-speaking population.

In June that year chairman Glyn Tegai Hughes, disappointed with government timidity, urged the council to consider a fall-back position. Future chairman Alwyn Roberts argued in favour of considering new approaches because a Welsh Channel Four seemed unlikely now. I remember my own anger at this apparent weakness and betrayal. My recollections are dim now but Davies reports that I argued that the Channel Four campaign was very much alive.

In September 1979, when I was acting chairman of the body, Home Secretary Willie Whitelaw announced that there would be no fourth channel for Wales. Could the long years of campaigning, the sacrifices and prison sentences endured by our brave young people be all in vain? All destroyed by a few sentences uttered by a man who knew little of Wales and nothing of Welsh broadcasting? I rang the BBC Wales controller, Owen Edwards, and told him that I would make the only possible effective protest.

My period as acting chairman is almost certainly a record that will never be beaten. It lasted fifteen minutes. I announced my resignation in protest at Whitelaw's decision. The council expressed their sympathy but understood. The protest was heartfelt but was quickly brushed aside by Secretary of State for Wales, Nicholas Edwards. My resignation had an ephemeral and slight influence. But Plaid Cymru's leader Gwynfor Evans's threat to fast to death terrified Thatcher. She was then studying Irish history. Her fear was that Wales would have a similar martyr to those of the Easter Rising in Dublin.

My part in the campaign was long but minor. Victory was sweet. At last, Wales had won a significant victory. The reality of S4C's spectacular later success was beyond the most extravagant dreams of those of us who planned it a decade earlier. S4C secured the future of Welsh as one of the world's most thriving minority languages. I feel modest pride in having played a small role as a Welshman in securing the future of Welsh as a living vibrant tongue.

9

Expelled to happiness

It was not part of my life plan.

I judged elected councillors to be a strange breed of self-important busybodies prepared to sacrifice their leisure time for small causes in exchange for one year of eminence as mayors. As with all the other major events of my life, becoming a councillor was an accident. I drifted into it. Campaigning for Welsh language education in Newport brought me into close contact with councillors on the Education Committee. Their general lack of understanding was a shock. I was a lifelong Labour Party loyalist but my energies were devoted to trade union work. Standing as a candidate would ingratiate me with Labour councillors and benefit the Welsh language campaign. But as the besotted father of two children, I shrank from the prospect of giving up hours of precious leisure time dealing with other people's trivial problems.

The answer to this dilemma was to seek nomination for an unwinnable ward. Allt-yr-yn is the most prosperous part of Newport. In 1972 Labour had never won it. The mainly professional membership of the local ward had suspicions that I was a Plaid Cymru plant. They selected me as their candidate even though one member objected to my using the word 'efficacious' in my speech. This was too posh even for Allt-yr-yn. 'Effi. . . fucking. . . cacious?!'

It was a novel experience. An attempt at humour in the election leaflet I sent out badly backfired. I denounced in acerbic language the brutalism of the architecture of a new car park in Newport, damning it as a suitable venue only for those contemplating suicide. During the campaign a young woman took her life by jumping from the car park roof. Few mistakes are more regrettable than the boomerang of macabre humour. I punished myself for my self-indulgent extravagance. Few others noticed. Nobody reads political leaflets. Many other similar indiscretions occurred later in my political life. Where practical, I now try to seek the second opinion of my wife or someone else I can trust before committing any risky original thoughts to print.

Those who delight in words are often destroyed by their own extravagance. Our wildest flights of fancy must be grounded. It is inhibiting and diminishing to cut poetic ideas to fit the Procrustean bed of public prejudice. Fresh soaring thoughts must often be suffocated at conception. I took a week's holiday to campaign. Most of it I spent alone banging on a seemingly endless succession of Tory doors. My record was twenty house calls without finding a single 'don't know'. The result was the usual massive Tory victory with a Liberal second. I was third with a slightly increased share of the vote. Of the thirteen wards in Newport, Allt-yr-yn was the only one that Labour lost in 1972.

I was hooked. Contact with voters was pleasurable and provocative. The sting of failure spurred me to stand as a candidate a few months later at a council by-election. The result in the safe Labour ward of Malpas was a formality. It was a unique occasion noted by the *Argus*. All thirteen wards had elected Labour candidates for the first time ever. My work as Councillor Flynn dominated life for the next twelve years. I reached the dizzy heights of deputy leader of Newport Council, chair of the Public Works Committee and chair of Gwent County Council's Transport and Special Schools committees. The work was stimulating and satisfying. The best of my Newport colleagues were admirable idealists of ability and integrity. A dozen of them would have been brilliant MPs.

In 1972 the children were growing into considerate bright young people. Rachel was nine and James seven. But cracks began to appear in my marriage. It was becoming increasingly apparent that Ann and I had little in common. Our paths were dividing. New social contacts for both of us, beyond the cocoon of early marriage, exposed the differences in our characters and left us open to the attractions of other partners.

There was a series of upsets and painful rows. Disloyalty happened on both sides. It is of no interest or of any significance who carried the greater share of blame. I don't really know. There were one or two periods of brief separation. Our deep shared love of the children kept us together in an increasingly empty relationship. Trust between us was dead. But life was still full and tolerable. We had two beautiful, bright, healthy children. We were relatively prosperous and material life was improving. The children had a full clutch of doting grandparents. Why destroy that?

Rachel was a constant delight. Clever and popular, she was growing into a beautiful young woman. James was highly intelligent and kind but life was troubling him. Always a thoughtful child, I recall his bringing a happy meal to a halt by announcing when he was five that we will all die soon. Rachel comforted him. Such thoughts had never bothered her. The challenges of parenthood were perplexing. Good intentions were far from adequate. Adoration changed to baffled unhappiness at the impenetrable problems of communication and helping adolescent children. The divisions grew deeper. We were four individuals sharing a house, rather than a family.

All my early speeches for Newport Council were made in the afternoon sessions of the council meetings. My fragile confidence needed to be bolstered. A glass of wine or two with the midday meal helped me. Happily that drug has never become addictive for me, but it was a useful prop. Unwillingly, nervous and ill prepared, I was plunged into making long speeches in my first weeks as a councillor. I was terrified but I had to halt the Education Committee's damaging policy on the vulnerable embryo Welsh school that I had worked hard to establish.

A lesson in the treachery of political life came with my de-selection from the Malpas ward after a year of bustling work. It was a deal settled without my consent. Two councillors who lived in Malpas, but represented other wards, were chosen as candidates. I was orphaned, left to seek selection elsewhere. Luckily the council estate of Alway, close to my home in Lliswerry, selected me. I had restrained my fury at the de-selection and said little. Aneurin Bevan had advised politicians to hide their wounds. They sadden your friends and please your enemies. Local politics dealt me future wounds and some good moments. The low points were expulsion from the Labour group on Newport Council and, later, resignation from Gwent Council.

Some councillors were very able. Others were dolts. Most were benign and ambitious to fulfil worthy ideals. I provoked their anger and sometimes their jealousies with my impatience, intolerant of their conservatism. I judged them to be imprisoned in a dead world of paralysed thinking. Unwisely I allowed my irritation to show. Inevitably, my excitement at fresh ideas and unorthodox policies was too much for them. I console myself that many of the outrageous causes I championed forty years ago are now accepted wisdom. It was a tactical error to extend myself beyond what was acceptable then as the lowest common denominator of public and councillor opinion.

Among the causes that gave me initial notoriety was opposition to a ban on the film *Last Tango in Paris*, support for homosexual equality, criticism of contemporary architecture and high rise flats, advocating the use of speed humps and the championing of poetry as a performing art. I campaigned for an end to animal dissection in schools, supported CND and opposed new road building. This was too powerful a brew for my fellow councillors.

A leader of Newport Council, Harry Jones, told me of his surprise thirty years ago when he heard me urge a solution to the building of a multi-storey block of flats. It was his first council meeting and I helpfully suggested that the half-built shell of the block should be filled with concrete. The edifice would stand as a giant tombstone, a statement of the architectural error of multi-storey living.

However, my support for more conventional causes diluted my off-the-planet image. New Labour may be surprised that I battled for the sale of council houses and for weakening the links between the Labour Party and trade unions. These were daring innovations then. For good socialist reasons, I argued, council houses should be sold to their tenants because 'rent is theft'. It was a battle that I and others won. Newport sold council houses to the tenants a decade before Thatcher did.

My expulsion from the Labour group at Newport came not from any exotic proposal. It was opposition to the unnecessary demolition of a street of council houses. This was politics at its worst. Ignore the evidence, just take action that is politically gratifying. I was later to discover that this trait infected politics at all levels. The houses in Maple Avenue, Somerton were in good condition but the area had fallen into a vortex of dereliction. The pattern is a familiar one. A few difficult families move into an area. They accept as normal discarded mattresses in the front garden and graffitied walls. Families with high standards move out. Families with conventional standards refuse to move into the street. Only other problem families find the street acceptable. The decline accelerates. What could be done? Demolish the houses, said the council. This was as sensible as cutting off a leg because of a pain in the toe. I was a councillor for Somerton and I condemned this crass decision. I said, 'Demolishing sound solid homes that cost £200 to build in 1920 and replacing them with £14,000 plastic and cardboard modern houses would be an act of criminal stupidity.' The council leader objected. The Labour group expelled me because I was destroying its coherence. Morally I took the right course but politically it was suicidal. Not for the last time in my life, I allowed my heart and reason to overrule political guile and caution. It is the lesson of my political life that I have found difficult to learn.

The expulsion hurt. I felt crushed, bullied and upset. It was hard to explain to Rachel, by then thirteen years old, and James, eleven, that I had done nothing wrong. Having scented blood several top councillors moved to expel me from the Labour Party. They failed. There was already a gulf between party and councillors that was to serve me well in the future. Nor could they expel me from the council. I remained as a councillor, but outside the Labour group. At the council elections, the Alway ward adopted me as their candidate and the group had no choice but to readmit me. Two years later all was forgiven. I was elected by Labour councillors as deputy leader of the council.

The fusion of Newport and Monmouthshire councils in 1974 was an amalgam of two political worlds. Apart from shared membership of the Labour Party, we councillors had little in common. It was a great thrill for me to join the same council that Aneurin Bevan served. Bevan had never been allowed to speak in council. He lacked seniority. Little had changed. Several members of the old Monmouthshire Council had been there since 1935. There was no opposition to Labour in the valleys. The senior councillors did not see themselves as accountable to electors. A county councillor was the local boss, the dispenser of patronage, the one to intervene when a job of head teacher was up for grabs. Or more importantly, that of a school teacher or caretaker.

Many had been denied a decent education. The story of one chairman of the library committee who spent his lunch hours reading children's comics was unfortunately not apocryphal. Most elderly Monmouthshire county councillors were arrogant, shallow and malicious. One of the glorious exceptions was Phil Abrahams. He had been imprisoned in the Blaina riots. To young councillors, he was the conduit to the past glorious history of the bitter struggles of the miners. He was an intelligent, dedicated idealist and a deep political thinker.

The council was biased against intelligence, innovation and debate. The all-powerful committees were the fiefdoms of their chairpersons. It was a matter of pride and congratulation to rubber stamp all decisions speedily and without debate. Opposition councillors such as the flamboyant liberal Angus Donaldson and the Communist Goff Miles were routinely abused because they dared to speak. Goff once made a speech of impenetrable labyrinthine complexity in which he complained that he tried 'nilly willy' to find out what was happening. Had he just broken wind for ten minutes he would have made a better impression.

I found a way of ventilating my irritation of the group on Gwent and Newport councils. I wrote an anonymous column in a local paper, first under the pseudonym Penderyn, then Orion. No confidential information was ever used but I did have the occasional dig at fellow councillors. To protect my identity I occasionally attacked myself and some of my causes. The column kept my brain ticking over in the long, empty hours while I toiled away at Llanwern steelworks. It was a wonderful release for the ideas in my teeming brain that were searching for an outlet. It was also a rallying call for the young councillors on Gwent County Council.

Former Newport councillors, who had themselves experienced opposition, would not stomach years of crude political thuggery and bullying. In 1975 the new combined authority moved to a splendid chamber that cried out for use as a debating chamber. Surprisingly I was elected as a whip of the Labour group. It was my job to write a report on the future procedure and conduct of the council. It was densely written, long and deliberately incomprehensible. Only the younger county councillors would read it. Buried deep in the document were recommendations for fundamental change to the council procedures that had existed since 1884. Councillors would in future sit alphabetically, not in party groups. All matters would be open for debate and decision in the chamber. The number of full council meetings was to be quadrupled. The leader of the Labour group would no longer chair group meetings.

Incredibly, the reforms were passed in seconds as one of the final items of a meeting that had spent hours discussing nothing. If the document had been fully debated few of the reforms would have been approved. The chamber was liberated. The council had several first-class debaters including Labour's Jon Vaughan Jones and future Tory quangocrat Geoffrey Inkin. Debates were often thoughtful and fierce. For the first time ever, decisions were taken on the basis of the force of the arguments, not personal and political imperatives.

My joy was in chairing the Special Schools and Transport committees. Their names belied a rich fulfilling experience. The old patronage on school appointments of the previous Monmouthshire Council ended. No longer was anyone appointed because they were 'one of us'. Chairing Special Schools with the help of splendid officers Hugh Loudon and Brian Mawby gave me real influence in helping to provide education of prime quality.

I regret the failure of good ideas I pursued. A realistic runner was a scheme to adapt one of the council's redundant farms into a halfway house for young people leaving care. I was appalled that young people were pitch-forked from the council's full-time care into the full-time neglect of harsh society. Many drifted into lives of crime or prostitution, leading to prison or mental institutions.

An organic labour-intensive farm could be a halfway home, a bridge from care to independent life. It would have been self-financing, selling its own produce. Although everyone thought it was a good idea, it was frustrated by inter-departmental jealousy, inertia and conservatism. Novelty challenged councillors' comfortable settled life. Twenty years later I raised the same crisis of care leavers in a parliamentary debate. The intervening period was Thatcher's epoch. The fate of care leavers had not improved.

Another proposal was to provide hostel accommodation at one of our county schools for boarders. The council were obliged to provide education for children whose families worked abroad. It would have avoided subsidising public schools and it would have widened the span of social classes in state schools. No one ever disagreed with the idea. Nothing happened. I was pulling on the rubber levers of power.

There were some cherished victories. The late Jon Vaughan Jones and I were the only members of the 78-strong council to oppose the 2,000 new jobs that a new nuclear power station at Portskewett in Gwent promised. It was not our oratory that changed opinions three months later. It was the shock of the 1979 Three Mile Island nuclear accident that persuaded the council to reject the planning application.

Always a reluctant celebrator of New Year, I do not recall whether I was especially gloomy about the prospects for 1979. I should have been. Now, I would love to erase the memories of those twelve months as the worst time of my life. It was the year of the defeat of the devolution that I had dreamed of all my adult life. The bleak age of Thatcherism began. And it was the year Ann and I suffered every parent's worst possible nightmare. Life dealt us a terrible bereavement. Rachel's death dwarfs everything else into nothing.

10

Cursed year

The year 1979 began with a political dirty trick. Even in the shark-infested waters of south Wales Labour, I did not expect such low political chicanery. The selections for the first European elections were held in 1979. Knowing some French and being an enthusiastic Europhile, I thought I had a chance. I won some nominations in three of the four Welsh seats for the European Parliament.

Many weary days spent canvassing in north Wales secured me a place on the final shortlist there. I lost the final vote, along with luminaries like former MP Wil Edwards and future MP John Marek. I have forgotten the name of the person from Wrexham who mysteriously won the selection and then lost the election. The choice was wholly unexpected.

My main campaigning push was in the European constituency where I lived, South East Wales. The Vale of Glamorgan party was kind enough to nominate me for the seat. Win Griffiths was finally selected. Hawking your wares around to dozens of wards and trade union branches invites bruising rejections. This time there was a novel, possibly unique, twist. The shortlisting process was abused to eliminate the strongest candidates. Nine candidates in all had nominations. Some were single nominations. Gwyn Morgan was a former deputy general secretary of the Labour Party. He had recently lost the general secretaryship because the party chairman had used his casting vote in favour of the left-wing and ineffectual Ron Hayward. In my view,

Gwyn Morgan's rejection cost the Labour Party dearly. It postponed Gwyn's reforming plans for Labour that could have made the party more elector-friendly in 1979.

Gwyn was the favourite to secure the nomination for the South East Wales seat. He and I had four nominations each – more than any other candidates. The short-listing meeting at Pontllanfraith adopted a bizarre manoeuvre. Instead of voting for the strongest candidates to be on the shortlist, a motion was accepted that Gwyn and I should be removed from the shortlist. It was passed because the supporters of the seven weaker candidates with few nominations had conspired to vote off the opposition. We had been cheated out of our chance to become MEPs by an unorthodox procedure.

Gwyn Morgan protested loudly and publicly. He denounced the fix. I remained silent. No rules had been broken even though it was transparently unfair. Like Gwyn, I bitterly resented a conspiracy that robbed us of the chance to present our case to the final selection meeting. The plotters justified it on the grounds that Gwyn and I were regarded as right wing. Even worse was the fear that speaking other languages marked us out as Europhiliacs. For most of my political life, 'left wing' was the equally inaccurate label pinned on me. Far easier to attach labels than intelligently appraise the worth of candidates. There were more dirty tricks. A surviving candidate was told that he would be given a new job if he stood down. He refused and stayed on the shortlist. He was not selected and he did not get the job. The final selection was won by Allan Rogers, who went on to become an MEP and an MP.

The Welsh nation disgraced itself on the international stage in 1979. It is a rare event in world history for a nation to declare it does not want to have a larger say in its own affairs. The battle lines on the devolution referendum were mainly between the Welsh people on one hand and the Welsh establishments of left and right on the other. But we the people were also divided. The establishment ruled. Gwent was typical. The 'Gwent Against the Assembly' movement was funded by a grant of £1,000 from the Labour-controlled county council. It was jointly chaired by Lloyd

Turnbull, the Labour leader of the county council from the left, and Richard Hanbury-Tenison, the Lord Lieutenant in waiting, from the right.

National divisions were cleverly exploited. The bilingual speakers were against monoglots. A politician in Pembrokeshire feared urban socialists from Cardiff and Newport would dominate a Welsh Assembly. The ultimate calumny was a half-page advertisement in the *Pontypool Free Press* paid for by Leo Abse. He warned that devolution would mean that 'Welsh-speakers from Cardiff would steal Pontypool jobs'. North Wales fretted that English-speakers from south Wales would steal their daughters and their diamonds.

With a few precious allies I fought the battle on several fronts. Plaid Cymru faded into the background. They knew that Labour votes would decide the outcome. We hoped to make it a Labour-versus-Tory fight. The Tories did the same, pushing the Neil Kinnock-led gang of six Labour MPs into the foreground. It was a vicious internecine Labour-versus-Labour fight.

The battle between comrade and comrade grew increasingly bitter. It troughed for me during a debate for sixth-formers in Cardiff. I was making an innocent point about the difference between public transport in Wales and in London. 'The valley trains are still the main form of transport, but those who live in London, in, say, Richmond, they use their cars to get—'

Neil Kinnock leapt to his feet and angrily interrupted me. 'It's nothing to do with you, Paul Flynn, or to this audience or to anyone else, where I live or where I send my children to school.' The audience was visibly taken aback by the force and venom of this outburst. There was no conscious reason why I had chosen Richmond as an example. But I had unwittingly hit a sensitive spot because Neil's home was in Richmond. There had been some criticism of his choice of school that I had missed. Possibly it was because he did not have his main home in his valley constituency. He thought I was about to repeat some criticism that had scorched him. When I finished my speech, Neil leant backwards in his chair and said to me behind the chairman's back, 'You had better watch your tyres don't get slashed.' I tried to persuade the chairman to relay to the audience Neil's comment. He refused. It was a dangerous trait:

the future leader of the party had lost his case with his temper. In future Neil treated me with great kindness and generosity. He saved our party from a descent into suicidal factionalism and has earned his honoured place in our history.

The count of the referendum votes in Gwent was an expected rout. The Gwynedd result had already been declared as a 'No' victory. There was the death of hope for Gwent. We were smothered by nine votes to one. I was one of the few surviving 'Yes' campaigners at the end of count. Contemplating embarrassment and humiliation, I did my best to be positive and breezy in a radio interview. Remembering my media training, I dredged up a few scraps of optimism. Memory has kindly buried the mock euphoric nonsense that I talked. The memories of March are gone. Those of the following month are indelible.

The fourth of April 1979 was a day like any other. Humdrum. Ordinary. I had worked a night shift. There was a council meeting in the afternoon. There was also a local authority election campaign in progress and I was candidate for my Newport ward seat of Alway. The election was a week away. Labour was not popular and defeat was possible. A full and exhausting day was likely. A few hours' sleep in the morning, council meeting in the afternoon and then an evening's canvassing.

Rachel had grown up to be a beautiful young woman. She had had a couple of boyfriends. One was a school pal. She had dumped him for her current one, an older boy who was a motorbike enthusiast. 'She left me for a motorbike,' her previous boyfriend complained. I feared motorbikes with their high accident record. I warned the new boyfriend about the precious person who was riding pillion with him. It was another nagging doubt to add to the ceaseless anxiety that all parents suffer throughout the lives of their children.

For understandable reasons, Ann was Rachel's best friend guiding her through the difficult years of dawning womanhood. Ann told me they had no secrets from each other until the final fortnight. But Rachel was also always close to me. Everything seemed to be going well. She was a gifted artist and had a close circle of school friends that she had known since infants' school. Her room in Christchurch Road was the biggest and sunniest one in the house. It overlooked the garden and she had painted the walls with pictures of her hero, the racing driver James Hunt. She had passed one O-level a year early and was set to do well. That day, she was unwell and was off school. I kissed her goodbye and went to my council meeting. All I remembered of it was a bad-tempered exchange with a Tory. I snapped at him and did not feel very proud of what I had said.

I returned home at about 3.30. Ann had been watching a film on the television. After a short period, she made a cup of tea. She took one upstairs to Rachel who, she said, was working in her bedroom. I heard Ann scream and give whimpering cries. 'God, God, God.'

'She can't be dead,' Ann sobbed as I ran into the room. Rachel was lying on her bed. Her face was red, mottled with blue marks. She was warm but did not seem to be breathing. I begged her not to die. I pounded her chest in order to try to get her heart beating. Distraught and cursing my own ignorance of what to do, I rang 999 for an ambulance and shouted at the operator, 'I think she's dead.' Probably minutes later, I rang again and demanded to know why they had not arrived. Never had I felt so helpless and inadequate. The one I loved more than life itself was dying and I did not know how to stop it.

The paramedics moved her now cold body to the floor and tried oxygen. They would know what to do. Ann and I held each other in a brief moment of false hope. A paramedic stared at us and shook his head. Ann lay on the floor and hugged Rachel's body. The paramedic tried to pull her away. I stopped him. The warmth of life was leaving her. Ann who had brought Rachel into the world was holding her as she left it.

The phone rang. It was the familiar voice of her previous boyfriend asking if he could speak to Rachel. 'I really wish you could,' I said. 'Dear God. I really do, but she's dead.' I could give him no explanation. 'She just died.'

The house was full of people. A doctor, the police and the men from the mortuary with a body bag. I protested that her body should be left at home. To no avail. As her body was being taken out of the house, James came in. He had taken the dogs out for a walk. He asked what the body bag was. 'It's Rachel,' I said, 'she's dead.' The words were alien, without meaning. Our Rachel. Dead? How could that be? James stared back at me, blank. Without understanding.

As ever, phone calls were coming in. A chirpy fellow councillor with a joke about that evening's canvassing. A constituent angry about a minor housing matter. A neighbour called at the door to complain that a hedge had not been cut. There was a great gulf between us and everyone else. They were still in the world. We were in hell.

A policeman wanted a statement. A statement? What was I tell him? Life that had been full and sweet an hour ago was now an agony that will go on forever. That the loveliest person I have ever known is no more. How could he write down my howl of torment in his notebook?

Ann, James and I stayed close. Hugging, touching each other for reassurance. As a family we had been ravaged. If we held on to each other, we could not lose anyone else.

The policeman kept asking me stupid questions. I imagined his face to be blue and blotched as Rachel's was. I suddenly laughed. Irrationally, I felt a thrill of relief. Nothing worse than this could ever happen to me, I thought. I am afraid of nothing. Life can never hurt me so painfully again as I am hurt now. I was suddenly strong, untouchable. I smiled. The policeman asked if I was all right. No explanation was possible.

Kind friends and relatives came to the house and tried to help. There was a note from Rachel saying sorry and goodbye. She had taken her life. Why? There was no reason. Ann said there had been a mild row earlier in the day. She was having her second period. The first was when she was away on an exchange visit in France and that upset her greatly. Was that the explanation? Ann said that she was angry and had stormed off upstairs. But there had been no warning. No threat. Never had she hinted that the possibility of suicide had ever occurred to her. Normally, before she took any tablets, she first asked Ann's permission. This day she had stuffed a handful of painkillers down her throat.

In our large house, we all had our own bedrooms. The three of us spurned the doctor's offer of oblivion through sedatives. Without a word being said we all moved to one bedroom and spent the night together. 'Don't either of you do anything stupid,' said James. We needed to be close. Only sleep stopped the pain until we woke next morning to be bereaved once more.

The death of Rachel brought Ann and me together in grief. Our marriage of seventeen years was long dead and beyond revival. Both of us had had other partners, although there were no permanent attachments to anyone else. We tried to look after each other as best we could to lessen the pain.

Together we took Rachel's ashes to be buried in the village of Malestroit in Morbihan, Brittany. There she had found happiness with her exchange friend from the Guegan family in their beautiful old water mill. There was a funeral ceremony in the village church attended by many children from the local St Julien School. It was twinned with Rachel's Lliswerry High School. We were touched to see friends from Newport attending, including her art teacher who admired her work. The French village authorities dispensed with all formalities and donated a plot in the cemetery for the burial. Her gravestone is inscribed with the words 'Rachel Flynn 1963–79 – Une Galloise qui aime cette ville.'

Ann, James and I found different ways to live through our grief. I found help by becoming a counsellor for the bereavement group Compassionate Friends. All the members had lost children. The belief was that loss was best understood by those who have suffered the same bereavement. A fellow member of the Broadcasting Council for Wales, Beryl Williams, sent me a touching note – 'The pain does get less.' Beryl had lost her son at Aberfan. Before that disaster Beryl's life was that of an unassuming housewife. The tragedy was the trigger to her transformation. With simple unaffected eloquence she spoke of her loss on television in a manner that others found penetrating and consoling. Beryl shared the experience of many. Bereavement had sensitised her. She was a different person. Almost certainly a better person. She gave the rest of her life to community work in Aberfan. She was a welcome breath of fresh air on the Broadcasting Council. After Rachel's death, I spent many hours in Beryl's company. We both had changed. Profoundly. A few months later I attended her funeral at Llwydcoed.

Beyond sense or reason, I was bereft.

11

Tribes at war

I had been lured to Newport in 1963 from my beloved home city of Cardiff by the new steelworks at Llanwern. By 1980 I had been working there for nearly twenty years, during which an inequality had developed among factory workers between works grade and staff. The shopfloor workers rightly enjoyed good conditions, pay and power. The previous advantages of 'staff' had withered. Pay was comparatively poor, overtime unpaid, bargaining power nil and status in decline.

I had been one of the movers in starting the first trade union branch of the steel union in Cardiff. When I moved from Cardiff the job of secretary of the staff union was thrust on me. The union was grandly titled BISAKTA, the British Iron Steel and Kindred Trades Association. Laboratory staff were kith and kindred. Our pay was £12 a week plus a few staff perks that were swiftly diminishing in value. Compared with the works grade we were badly off. I set up a new staff branch and continued with my job of branch secretary. Membership extended beyond laboratories throughout the plant to all technical staff including nurses.

We did have the snob value of being staff plus a pension and the choice of coming to work in our best suits. The novelty of a union among staff created hurdles for my fellow technician shop steward, Owen Rees, and me to overcome. There was hostility and suspicion from some staff who refused to join. Coaxing monthly unions fees out of our fellow workers was a dispiriting chore.

Our first awkward, nervous negotiation for a pay increase succeeded beyond our fevered imaginations. We gained a rise of nearly 25 per cent. We had asked for 40 per cent. My role placed me, psychologically, in conflict with the managerial tribe. There was no chance of any promotion. Shop stewards were cast as agents of antagonism and confrontation. One dispute about the safety of a new procedure for identifying nitrogen in steel resulted in a bitter altercation with management. My promotion goose was cooked. For the rest of my time at Llanwern I became resigned to my fate working under bosses for whom I had decreasing respect.

Work became a meaningless chore, which I performed with my mind and imagination detached. So what? I had the joy of witnessing the daily miracle of my two young children discovering their joie de vivre. I was content to prostitute my time in exchange for money to build the comfortable home that was the centre of my life.

The steelworks were a great national enterprise. A political fudge by Prime Minister Macmillan divided the giant plant between Ravenscraig in Scotland and Llanwern in Wales. Decades later, both plants suffered from that act of cowardice. The Llanwern steelworks had attracted an army of 6,000 incomers from steel centres throughout the United Kingdom. The accents of Glasgow, Llanelli and Birmingham were heard more frequently than those of Gwent. In the early 1960s Llanwern enjoyed great publicity as a model, newly minted works with staff that were the elite of British steelworkers.

The dream faded fast. In the bleak, self-destructive spirit of the early 1960s the simple-minded union bigots ruled. Management was weak. The huge site encouraged the creation of small protective self-contained units. The management was remote in their hutted village on the edge of the site, at Lliswerry. The union empire built around the Cold Mill was 4 miles away, skirting the village of Bishton.

The works Balkanised itself into nineteen separate conspiracies, all at war with each other and with management. Loyalty ended at the boundaries of each department. Success could only come from a united team, one that worked together from the point where raw materials entered in the west to the place where finished steel was dispatched in the east.

New equipment saw production records broken. But the works were plagued by disputes, strikes and an endemic atmosphere of bloody-minded lethargy. At a Labour Party conference in the late 1960s Michael Foot, MP for Ebbw Vale, answered a debate in which there had been a routine demand for more investment for industry. Michael pointed to Llanwern. 'They are up to their necks with investment there but they are not delivering the goods.'

The works were out of management's control. It became a deeply unhappy place. Pride, excitement and hoped faded. Stories spread about the indolence and inefficiency of the workers. Demand for steel was falling and international competition was threatening Llanwern's products in the marketplace. As a socialist and trade unionist, I was upset to see my convictions challenged. Justice for working people achieved through combined strength against greedy employers was a prime tenet of socialism. It was our answer to the bitter inequalities of wealth and power that created the cruelties of Crawshay Bailey's work slaves and the victims of the potato famine.

Equality of power between union and management had been the aim of early socialists: the dream was that it would evolve into shared responsibility between self and community interests. At Llanwern I witnessed a cherished ideal metamorphosing into waste and abuse. Ill-disciplined union power was a bloated brainless monster. Cowed management retreated behind the barricades of their departments' defences. The worst union leaders surfaced, ignorant, self-indulgent, naive and brutal. The arteries of that great works became clogged with futile contrived conflicts. Gloomy forecasts of doom were heard. The possibility of allowing the whole place to sink back into the marsh on which it was insecurely built was feared. Shock therapy was a long time coming.

In retrospect, I mourn for those wasted twenty-two years. All were on shift-work, the pattern consisting of shifts from 6.00 a.m. to 2.00 p.m., from 2.00 p.m. to 10.00 p.m. and from 10.00 p.m. to 6.00 am. The one upside was that there were substantial numbers of shiftworkers in the local communities. That made our status as a sub-stratum of society bearable. The pattern of our lives was abnormal. The shifts undermined the routines of family and social life.

Nights out were marred because of afternoon working. The need for an early start the following day or having to leave events early to start a night shift imposed an untidy routine. Young children could not understand why father was sleeping in the middle of the day. I resented the tyranny of a life that was out of kilter with the rest of society. The shared misery brought shiftworkers together in a freemasonry of mutual interest. My work was undemanding and the long hours were made bearable only by the stimulus of intelligent companions. Overtime was regular and essential to build a decent wage. Half of my waking hours were spent in the company of the same ten men who shared my shift.

Life was monastic in its intimacy. Relationships were close, intense and potent. The spasmodic nature of the work allowed for hours of chat. We were part of a production process which had peaks of intense activity separated by periods of idleness. Friendships were forged and broken. Faults and irritating habits were magnified.

To avoid boredom plots were hatched. Victims were found and persecuted. The boastful and the false were exposed. Hypochondria was a prime neurosis. One shift leader had bored and annoyed us with his symptoms of deadly diseases. A mild headache was a terminal brain tumour. A sudden pain the next week was liver/bowel/skin cancer. Any new fashionable disease that was in the news was certain to hit our boss within days. His visit to the steelworks nurse was a daily irritant to her and disruptive to our work. She was a willing ally when we struck back.

The night shift began with David looking and feeling good. This was the night when we had arranged to teach him a lesson. It started subtly with a concerned enquiry in the first ten minutes of the night shift. 'Are you feeling well, David?' 'Champion!' he answered. A quizzical look and a doubting shake of the head were enough to start David's queasy feelings. Subsequent questions were more direct, from 'Are you sure you're alright?' to 'What the hell's wrong with you?' The induced illnesses forced David to lie down in a corner of the laboratory. Then he complained of severe pains. Inevitable really.

The nurse was called. After a great deal of muttering and worried frowns she summoned the works ambulance to pack him off to the local hospital. He managed a few waves of farewell to his fellow workers and he was stretchered out, convinced that he might never see us again in this life. The nurse had previously worked in the intensive care unit at the Royal Gwent. She had warned the doctor there that a case of chronic hypochondria was on the way.

David survived and turned up for his shift the following night. A little cowed and resentful he told us that the hard-hearted doctor at the hospital had given him a terrible rollicking for wasting NHS time. David said, 'It may be hypochondria but it still hurts.' His personality was transformed. Months, possibly years, followed without his contracting a single fatal disease. The medicine was severe but effective.

The tedium of routine was relieved in 1980 with the national steel strike. Three months of sacrifice, treachery, heroism, cowardice and humour. The burden of debts from fourteen weeks without pay left a trail that stretched over many years. To some strikers it was the most vivid and worthwhile experience of their lives. Ordinary men doing humdrum jobs were catapulted into the spotlight. They were the standard bearers of the war against Thatcherism. The hopes of most of the nation were with them. Life was exciting, combative and with an agreeable touch of danger and flattering media attention.

There was polarisation between police and strikers. But there were also strange alliances. The familiarity of the daily contact between police and pickets at one site in Monmouth created friendships. Empty hours were filled with gossip about rugby and sex, interrupted by an occasional organised push that developed into a ritual. Twenty lorries were allowed out of the plant troubled only with the standard shouts of 'Blackleg!' and 'Bastard!' To break the monotony or to provide some pictures when the TV cameras arrived the strikers would occasionally block the road.

The game developed its own rules. Pushing and shoving was allowed. Punching was not. The police always won but they were expected to allow a decent period of struggle to introduce a little drama into the fight. No one was ever seriously hurt. A few on both sides were wrestled to the ground. An occasional policeman's button was torn off.

The only serious incident occurred one day when trouble was expected. Police reinforcements arrived from Cardiff. They did not know the rules of the game. When they overstepped them and tried a bit of strong-arm tactics, they were firmly put in their place by the local police. They intervened to defend their pals, the strikers with whom they had struck up warm friendships. 'What are you doing to Fred?' a Gwent bobby yelled at the Cardiffian. It came close to being a police versus police battle with the strikers looking on as bemused spectators.

After a month there was a morale-boosting rally in Newport Civic Centre. I had little previous experience of feigning indignation. I had to fake it. The *Argus* records that 4,000 steelworkers heard me say, 'We have been pushed into this strike by madman Joseph and Mother Superior Thatcher. The industry has been volunteered for suicide. This is a struggle between the Iron Maiden and the men of steel. We know a thing or two about metal. Under strain, iron is brittle and breaks; steel bends and has greater strength.'

Yes, it was a rant. I had been arm-locked into performing. My justification then and now is that it was all in a good cause. Flagging morale had to be boosted. For the first time in my life I felt that I was a local leader. The speech was based on golden advice given to me by Leo Abse on speaking in the open air. Never talk for longer than three minutes. Always use picturesque ideas and simple sentences without sub-clauses.

It was a thrilling and seductive experience. The small gang of speakers was perched on high ground where the Newport law courts now stand. The crowd – eager, intense and passionate – was spread out below us. The echoes of our booming voices roared back at us fortified by the cheers of the crowd. Demagoguery is an intoxicating brew.

We were asking for a 20 per cent pay rise. Success was not impossible but extremely unlikely. It all ended with a face-saving deal. We had a 16 per cent rise but 7,000 of the 24,000 Welsh steelworkers were on short time a few months later. The emotional Bill Sirs and other national leaders of the steel union ISTC had cracked without a single union member crossing a picket line.

Among the strikers there was neither bitterness nor any sense of failure or defeat. That would have been the rational reaction. The first weeks back at work were a joyous reunion. We plunged into self-indulgent reminiscences about the most enjoyable moments of the great adventure. One haunting urban myth that still survives is that this first steel strike for fifty years was the consequence of a lovers' quarrel between a union man and a management man. I wonder. It was an extraordinary stand made by a traditionally docile trade union.

The strike's failure and the union's capitulation had profound consequences. The subsequent miners' strike was already doomed. Thatcher had won. Humiliation was certain two years before Arthur Scargill picked the day to lead his troops over the precipice.

12

Permissive

I was troubled. I did not realise that my life was about to be magically transformed. At forty-eight I found myself to be the oldest technician in my department, doing work that demanded increased physical effort and strength which I did not have. I had previously spurned all offers of redundancy. The place was ludicrously overmanned but there was weighty political resistance to selling our jobs. 'They are not ours to sell. They belong to future generations,' I had said many times. I was trapped by my own bullshit.

The cycle of arthritis was at its worst. It was dangerous for me to climb gantries and seek a path through dense steam clouds to collect samples from the hellish boiling froth in the waste bug plant. Dismissal was a real possibility because I had refused to carry out new tasks that I thought were unreasonable. I had a major row with management.

It was helpful that I knew my way around employment legislation and I argued that I was being constructively dismissed. A way out was suggested. If the doctors agreed, I could retire on health grounds and start receiving my pension. This avoided the political problem. My job would not be sold. Someone else would do it. It was ethical too. The job had changed and I was no longer fit to do it. Retirement on health grounds left me about £10,000 short of the deal I would have had if I had accepted redundancy. To get my due share I must live, and receive my pension, until I reach the age of 120. So hard won was that pension through the weary years of shiftwork that I intend to do just that.

Retirement was a thrilling change. For the first time in my life I was unemployed. I was forty-eight, separated from my wife with a grown-up son living at home, and had a mortgage and £8,000 advance pension money in my pocket.

I was free from the tyranny of shiftwork, liberated from the burdens of council work, and romantically unattached. I had no idea what I was going to do with the rest of my life. Brilliant. The freedom was a great relief but the ignominy of signing on and receiving dole was an affront to my pride. I applied for several jobs, most of which were on the government's community programmes that had been set up to deal with the worst unemployment for a generation.

I failed in my attempt to become the race relations officer for Gwent but I was employed to run a community unit to have input into the newly established BBC Radio Gwent. It had been created as a spoiler to the new commercial Gwent Broadcasting Company. It was a year of intense creative work, plus a great deal of frustration and disappointment. On out-of-date inadequate equipment, two bright, prolific workers, Lydia Townley and Kim Findlay, produced a creditable output of items on community issues. Perhaps stretching the extent of our talents and resources we had a Calamity Family slot to illustrate consumer problems.

The family included veteran broadcaster Sally Harvard as Granny and Trevor Jones as Granddad. The BBC were nervous of the involvement of a newly resigned politician. My voice was banned from the items we produced. I cheated and acted the part of the father. I was ludicrously over-ambitious, expecting miracles of ingenuity and versatility from a tiny number of workers. The three of us were doing the jobs of a dozen specialists. We were writing the scripts, recording the interviews, cutting and editing the tapes and introducing the completed programmes. There were some modest achievements and many flops. It was a frantic, intense, ambitious romp of a year. Lydia Townley went on to a very successful career as a producer in Radio Wales which continues to this day. She gained her foothold in BBC Wales by recycling many of our old stories from Gwent Community Radio. I was involved in an unsuccessful bid for the commercial franchise for Gwent. That was a lucky break. The successful bidder, Gwent Broadcasting, had but a brief existence.

One of the frustrations of my time later on the Broadcasting Council for Wales was my failure to convince BBC Wales of the merits of radio broadcasting on a mini scale. There are thousands of tiny communities in Wales with distinct identities. Broadcasters in Ireland were using a small van as a self-contained broadcasting unit. It was on loan to Wales. In Ireland the van would turn up at a village community centre. The driver would find a plug for the electrics, make himself a cup of tea, put out the cat, switch on, sit at the microphone and start broadcasting. Locals were invited to knock on the door if they wanted to broadcast. Radio Wales tried some very successful experiments at Pwllheli and Gorseinion under the name of Radio Bro. On a visit to one I was redirected from the van to the local pub. It had been taken over by BBC Wales who had gone there mob-handed. At least twenty-five people were having lunch. They had not quite got the point. It seemed to be impossible for a big broadcasting organisation to scale itself down to the mini size that would have served a future Radio Splott or Radio Capel Bangor.

Having lived through my years of dawning sexual maturity in a world of abysmal repression, the period between my marriages was an unexpected consolation prize. The years of the late 1970s and early 1980s were times of excess and licence. There were lots of girlfriends and late nights, and far too much beer and wine. Many of the relationships were brief, wild and gorgeously satisfying. I was free and unattached in an age of permissiveness. It is difficult to convince contemporary teenagers of the restraint and innocence of most relationships in the early 1950s, when I was a teenager. The spur to seize these new opportunities for sexual adventures in later life was the memory of opportunities lost and experiences missed decades earlier.

Happily, the brief relationships ended peacefully and on good terms. It was a time of genuine sexual equality. There were many acts of foolishness that I now wish had not happened. But none of the relationships were exploitative on either side and I and my partners emerged unscathed and unburdened. One intermittent serious relationship lasted three years. We discovered that we had a great deal in common. Both of us were in ruined marriages. We sought fulfilment and escape. It was a loving relationship of trysts, separated by weeks and sometimes months apart.

As mutual therapy – and preparation for political office – it was beneficial. We each had a close trusted friend. In different parts of the country we were hawking our own wares to local Labour parties and begging for their nominations. We gave each other good-humoured encouragement after repeated ego-crushing rejections.

My mind was set against a new marriage. The wounds of bereavement were still raw and I shrank from any emotional burdens that marriage and a new young family would bring. She is now happily remarried to someone she met a few years later. My life was on the threshold of undreamt happiness and fulfilment. There was sunshine ahead.

13

Resigned to success

Although I did not recognise it, 1983 was probably the year of my mid-life crisis. I was unemployed, having just retired from Llanwern. I did not want to become a full-time councillor reliant on the council allowances and my works pension as my only source of income.

A campaign to ban fox-hunting on council land had taught me a bitter lesson. The campaign was successful but it was painfully protracted. Far too much time and energy were spent in dragging a predictable decision from the council. After all, it was Labour Party policy. Reluctantly I concluded that it was my leadership of the campaign that was responsible for the slow and painful progress. My passion on another cause, the peace movement, had lost me many friends. Was I a liability to anything that I espoused? Why continue? I resigned.

By accident rather than design, being 'Mr' and not 'Councillor' Flynn perversely helped my next step. Why not Parliament? I had once been shortlisted in the Gloucester City seat in February 1974 where Ann Clwyd won the nomination. In the second general election of that year I was the candidate for the north Wales nursery seat of Denbigh.

There was no chance of winning Denbigh in October 1974. It was a relaxed campaign free of the tension of a marginal seat. The local party were kind and welcoming. They tolerated my feigned delusion of possible victory. One voter told me, 'Listen, son, I'm more Labour than you are. But the only way to get rid of the Tory here is to vote Liberal.'

'But we really have a chance to pass the Liberals this time,' I begged. No one was convinced – not even me. It was a simple one-typewriter campaign. I took to rewording the editorials in the five local papers and sending them to their editors as statements from the Labour candidate. The papers gratefully reprinted my mirror image of their views. Rereading my election message to the voters of Denbigh thirty-six years later I was surprised to see this sentence: 'New problems posed by the reducing economy, genetic engineering or the ecological time bomb need new solutions.' What did I then know about genetic engineering? What did anyone know?

Michael Foot joined the campaign in Colwyn Bay and a drunk threw a punch at him. I intervened. There was a scuffle. I hurt my wrist. It was a great excuse for me to abandon handshakes that were already painful because of my arthritis. Also it created a good headline: 'Candidate hurts hand helping Foot'. It was a happy campaign. On visits to north Wales now, I fondly linger at the bridge at Llangollen or the square in Ruthin where I once bawled on a loudspeaker at crowds of tourists about the subtleties of Labour's pensions policy.

The election result in October 1974 was very similar to the one six months earlier. At least the Labour vote had not defected to the Liberals. It was an honourable draw for me in third place. In fourth place was the future leader of Plaid Cymru, Ieuan Wyn Jones.

It was nearly ten years before I had another good chance of standing for Parliament. My union came close to ruining my hopes. It was the selection for the 1983 general election and I was strongly placed to succeed retiring Speaker George Thomas. I had nominations from nearly half the wards in Cardiff West.

The talented Welsh Labour research officer Jon Vaughan Jones had presented himself as a candidate of the left but he was doing badly. He had won no ward nominations and was hanging on with the lone support of the Fabian Society. The union NUPE were backing me as an alternative candidate to the left of Jon. There were rumours that my steel union favoured Jon and that they were about to withdraw my name from the selection. I strongly protested. They relented. There was a shortlist of seven. The first to be eliminated was future megastar Alun Michael. He was then too absorbed in local politics to make a decent case on national issues. I reached the last two and I was beaten by the right-wing candidate, local councillor David Seligman. He narrowly lost the seat at the general election to Stefan Terleski. As soon as possible afterwards I resigned from the union panel. They had never been of any help to me and they had the power to block any future nomination I might have.

When New Labour arrived, hopeful candidates were drafted into safe parliamentary seats without the bother of fighting hopeless nursery ones. Previously, it was not abnormal for aspirant MPs to spend twenty-five years, as I did, hawking our wares around constituency parties. One of the reasons why I did not win a selection was my vulnerable domestic life. Order, respectability and electability came into my life when I met a new friend.

Sam Morgan was a regular at Newport Labour Party events. A mother of two young children, she had returned to politics because she was alarmed at stories of extreme militants taking over the party that she had worked for as a child. Very beautiful, highly intelligent and articulate, I was immediately drawn to her. Although she was anchored in her marriage we became inseparable companions at the après-meeting get-togethers in pubs. She became my companion and confidante. She is the most delightful company. There was a delicious meeting of minds and spirits.

Some eyebrows were raised because of our close relationship. Sam's family had a strong chapel tradition. Her parents were worried about our intimacy but trusted Sam to do the right thing. There was a large gap in our ages. Sam came to dominate my life and thoughts. There seemed to be no opportunity for the situation to change. At that time I was seeking to end the burnt-out relationship with my lover which coincided with a period of difficulty in Sam's marriage.

We decided to live together. Only Sam and I knew that this was the beginning of a permanent relationship. Our friends were incredulous and pessimistic. Sam's best friend begged her to see a psychiatrist before she made any move. There were good reasons for cynicism. I had just retired from work on grounds of ill health. I had severe arthritis. My political hopes were in ruins, having just resigned from Gwent Council and falling short in my efforts to win nominations for the European and Westminster parliaments. I had an adult son, a mortgage and two dogs. I was on the dole with a total income of £27 a week. My love life had been colourful, volatile and often chaotic. My home was run-down and carried the scars of prolonged bachelor occupation. Not much of a catch for Sam.

How could she leave what was ostensibly a stable marriage for the gamble of shacking up with an unemployed near-crippled no-hoper who was heading for Skid Row? Sam and I did not see it that way. We were intoxicated with optimism and a faith in our relationship. My mother, sister and brothers welcomed the news that we had decided to live together. Times had indeed changed. My mother, who had sabotaged my elder brother's wedding reception because he was marrying a non-Catholic, now hailed the prospect of my living in sin with a married woman. Sam's parents were horrified by the news. But they knew their daughter's nature. Within a few weeks they relented and gave us marvellous support.

Sam's children were already acquainted with my two boisterous springer spaniels. One of them was adept at performing circus tricks that my son James had taught him. Sam's small dog, a Lhasa apso, surprisingly found her level and fought her corner. Sam and the children moved in on May Day 1984. The intimacy of this relationship, with its openness, respect and trust, was exhilarating and novel. We were closer than I ever believed to be possible. With absolute certainty I knew that this partnership was for life. Nothing has ever shaken that view. Years later, Sam told me she did not always share my optimism about our future.

Sadly, Sam and I have never had children of our own. Sam's young children Alex and Natalie settled in happily at number 22 Christchurch Road, pleased to be living with 'the man with the dogs'. They have always spent part of each week with their father, who they continued to call 'Dad'. I have always been known to them by the Welsh word for father: 'Tad'. I have happily taken on a one-step-removed relationship with them. Relations between Sam's former husband and me were cold but civil. This time-share parenthood can be successful when all concerned have the welfare of the children as their paramount concern.

At the first opportunity after Sam's divorce was through, we married on 31 January 1985. The service was in Sam's family chapel, St Mary's Street Baptist Church in Baneswell, Newport. It was a happy, simple ceremony enjoyed by the children and members of both families, all of whom had become reconciled to the situation. My own family was intact then and my mother, brothers, sister and their spouses were there.

In the evening we had a great party with a couple of hundred people in the Ringland Labour Club. Sam audaciously married in red and wore a stunning black dress at the reception. She was beautiful in both. I can think of few days in my life when I have been happier or more certain of future good fortune. It was irrational, a triumph of optimism over reality.

This was the winter of the year-long miners' strike. One of the main events at our reception was a collection for the strikers. Our honeymoon was spent driving about mid-Wales, not a tourist Mecca in the first week of February. A highlight was a demonstration and march in Aberystwyth in support of the miners. We joined in, even though it was snowing. Surreal bliss.

When we returned from our honeymoon there was a job on offer. It arose out of my failure to gain the nomination for the South East Wales Euro seat in 1984. Allan Rogers had stood down from the safest MEP seat in Europe and moved to the safest MP seat in Britain. The strong shortlist included future MEPs John Tomlinson and David Morris, plus three future MPs: Paul Murphy, Llew Smith and me. Llew was the only candidate with no previous experience of elected office. He had followed Neil Kinnock and Allan Rogers as the organiser for the Workers' Educational Association in south Wales. Like them he used his position to build up contacts with Labour Party activists. He was addicted to the telephone, which he used with great skill to convince hundreds of people that he was their personal friend. Llew's organising work secured support in the face of experienced operators with brilliant futures. The simplicity and sincerity of his old-time socialist message endeared him to Labour comrades. He won the nomination. Unsophisticated and raw, he jumped straight from street politics to European politics. The Euro election was to be held after the funding for my community radio job had run out. I was unemployed. Generously forgetting our rivalry for the nomination he made me his press officer in the ensuing campaign. Once elected as MEP, Llew offered to employ me as his researcher. I enjoyed the work. On the major issue of the time, the peace movement, we agreed.

We avoided Welsh issues. Like all his opinions, his anti-Welshness had been set in concrete aeons earlier. Turning Llew from a militant ranter into a first division politician was a major task. He was then an inexperienced public speaker. He had little understanding of the subtleties of serious politics but his heart was in the right place. His first interviews with the press were disasters. They usually ended with Llew masking his incomprehension at the meaning of the questions by mouthing Militant slogans or by insulting the interviewers. There is no proof that he was a member of the Revolutionary Socialist League, the secret name for the Militant Tendency, but Llew was recruited into street politics by Adrian Jones, who was the main south Wales guru of the RSL. During my time working in Llew's office he welcomed Militant activists. I rarely did.

Drastic action was needed. I rehearsed every interview with him. We tried to anticipate every possible question and work out the best replies. I agonised over how far I could go without sapping his confidence and his natural charm. The worst interview was on national television with Robert Key. Llew tried to defend remarks made by then miners' leader Kim Howells on the death of a taxi driver crushed by objects dropped by striking miners from a road bridge. Kim and other leaders refused to be interviewed. Llew jumped in and drowned, out of his depth, trying to defend the indefensible.

The fiercely anti-European South Wales Labour Party had sent Llew to Strasbourg to destroy the European Union. Disillusionment was swift and crushing. Llew was baffled by the complexities of Euro-babble. To his credit, he spurned the consolations of the luxury lifestyle that seduced many of his fellow MEPs. He reverted to the role that he knew and understood. He became a street campaigner in the Euro-corridors of power. One day he charged into the parliament chamber with a miners' banner, rupturing all the rules. Euro aristocrat Otto von Habsburg tried to wrench the banner from him. The tug of war continued with Habsburg screaming 'Communist!' at Llew, who yelled 'Fascist!' back.

Worse was to come. Llew had arranged a small exhibition to collect money for third-world famine victims, an event acceptable in street politics. There was no talking him out of it. Part of my job was to promote and defend his public image. My worst moment arrived with a phone call from Strasbourg. 'We've had a bit of trouble here, brother,' he said. 'The collection was alright, but I've been involved in a bit of fight with a Tory MEP.'

'Not in the chamber?' I asked horrified.

'No, no,' he reassured me, 'it was outside on the landing.'

Relieved, I asked him whether anyone had seen it.

'Well, there were these two camera crews there, but I don't know whether they filmed it.' The BBC evening news led with shots that were going out on television all over Europe. They showed Llew blocking the path of the Tory MEP, the Tory trying to push past Llew, the pair falling to the ground and rolling over, wrestling each other.

Llew's explanation was that he thought the Tory was trying to take the money that been collected. The editor of the *Merthyr Express* witnessed the incident. He was on a freebie visit to Strasbourg, sponsored by Llew. He wrote a detailed account of the day. He reported that there was more than a hint of provocation in Llew's attitude to the Tory MEP whom he hated. A greatly exaggerated version of the clash filled the front pages of the next day's papers. The tabloids described how there was spitting, punching and clawing. Llew was destroyed by the incident. Six months later, when Llew's wounds had begun to heal, the Liberal–SDP Alliance used film of the wrestling match as the introduction to a party political broadcast. 'Here are a Labour MEP and a Tory MEP discussing the political situation in the third world.' At a Christmas party for the staff in the offices which we occupied someone gave him a joke present of a karate mat. Everyone enjoyed the gag but Llew was stony faced and upset.

Other MEPs settled down to the political impotence of the Euro Tower of Babel and consoled themselves by energetically milking the sumptuous expenses. Llew failed to find for himself any satisfying role in the European Parliament. He puritanically denounced them – and members of the British Parliament – in an article in *Tribune*. That provoked the first use of the 'Holier than Llew' jibe. As with every other article that appeared under his name at that time, it was written by me. My most productive work in my two years working for Llew was a monthly Euro Diary that was printed in several of the weekly papers across the Euro constituency. It reached 200,000 readers. My intention was to make the articles quirky, irreverent, punchy and readable. There was no room for the Euro-stodge that was the daily diet of Strasbourg and Brussels. Llew gave me a free hand to write anything, complaining only when I occasionally overlaid his views with mine.

I told Sam that I had the best job in the world. I was continuing the campaigning work that had dominated my life and I was even getting paid a modest wage for it. There was complete freedom to promote my political passions to a huge media audience. There is very little constituency work in an MEP's office. We filled the vacuum by becoming a print shop. Llew had located his office in Newport West because it was the only marginal Tory-held Westminster seat within his larger Euro constituency. Our main political task was to use the office as a base to ensure that Labour wrested the seat from Tory MP Mark Robinson.

It was a mission that I fully backed even though I had no hope of becoming the candidate. I had resigned my Gwent County Council seat and, in the opinion of Llew and many others, that had doomed my political career. Printing leaflets and newsletters for community and political groups was a useful task that the Euro office could perform. Printing work was dirty, exhausting and painful because of my troublesome arthritis. The leaflets were written, typed, etched on to plates and printed on an antique offset litho printer in our two-roomed third-storey office in Newport's Pillgwenlly. Tens of thousands of high-quality leaflets were produced at almost nil cost for the peace movement and community groups. These were the solid achievements of the office and a new skill for me. Sadly, relations between Llew and me were set to take a turn for the worse.

Sam and I had been living in the home I had previously occupied for ten years with my first wife. Sam never settled. It was someone else's place. Sam wanted us to build our own nest. Alex and Natalie had a long way to travel to school. There was never any question of changing their schools where they were happily ensconced.

When the Newport party split in 1983 into East and West constituencies, I was the first president of Newport East. There is neighbouring antagonism in Newport between the two sides of the river. Newport West has the town centre, the Leisure Centre and the Civic Centre and they tended to look down on the East for having little except two legs of the Transporter Bridge. In our comradely way, Newport Labour Members pleaded for cooperation between Jews and Arabs in Palestine, and Catholics and Protestants in Ulster. But between Newport East and West? Never!

Without a thought of its political advantage we moved in 1985 to Newport West. It was a large semi-detached three-storey house in Fields Park Road 50 yards from Newport Civic Centre and nearer the children's schools. Unconsciously we had made a decision that changed our lives.

Who would be selected as the Labour candidate to challenge Mark Robinson? Speculation on the likely individual dominated political gossip. My name was never mentioned by the *South Wales Argus*'s 'man in the know', Martin Mason. Sam had convinced me that Newport West turned me down for the Euro nomination the year before only because I was a Europhiliac. Perhaps unforgivably I also had a working knowledge of French. But I was being realistically pessimistic. Newport West had not just rejected me, they had given me a tiny seven votes out of a possible 140.

Sam advised that I had a good chance of getting the parliamentary seat nomination – but only if I kept my intention to stand a secret until the last moment. There were two leading candidates. On the right was Judi James, a capable teacher who had previously stood in Cheltenham. On the left was NUPE union official Adrian Jones with a reputation as a Militant godfather. For two years they had damaged each other in pre-selection skirmishes. It was then fashionable to be left wing. Adrian and Judi schemed to out-left each other. The abolition of the mayoralty and cancellation of the town's militaristic Tattoo were hot issues.

I kept neutral. Sam's advice not to show my hand until the last possible moment persuaded me. One heart-stopping moment was an announcement by Martin Mason, talking in Llew's office in Pillgwenlly. He told Sam and me that he knew the identity of a strong surprise candidate 'who works in this office'. Sam and I were aghast. Was he about to blow our secret and ruin any chance I had of winning?

Martin's technique was to pretend to know a great deal more than he did in order to coax the innocent to part with confidential information. We implausibly ridiculed his claim that there was a 'secret' candidate. A few days later, in his column 'Mason on Monday', he announced his coup: 'Llew Smith is to throw his hat in the ring for the Newport West selection.' What a relief! Luck stayed with us. Mason also revealed at least a dozen other possible hopefuls for the seat. Never once did he mention me.

Llew, at this point my boss, believed that I was a no-hoper, yesterday's man. When I confided in him that I intended to stand, he advised me not to. He had already thrown his weight behind other candidates; first it was his old mentor Adrian Jones, then Judi James. Llew was an accomplished fixer. He had organised brilliantly his own selections with one-to-one phone contacts. His support and influence could have decided the choice in Newport West.

The Labour candidate who had lost the seat in 1983, Bryan Davies, put his name forward. Had he nurtured the constituency party, the nomination would have been his on a plate for a second chance. But he had been chasing nominations in many far safer seats including Cynon Valley (won by Ann Clwyd).

I announced my candidature five weeks before the final selection meeting. With the immense hard work of Sam I won more ward nominations than any other candidate. In the final stage, I believe Llew was backing both Judi and me and secured a few union nominations for both of us. It was a nerve-racking time. At the age of fifty this was my last chance. Labour parties usually select the candidate they dislike the least.

Most delegates vote against, rather than for, people. Winners are the ones with the fewest enemies.

Then a fixer from the past arrived. The Labour Party's former Welsh secretary Hubert Morgan descended on Newport West, waving the biographical details of a dream candidate. 'This man has been our ambassador to the United Nations, a distinguished MP and a European Commissioner.' Hubert rang local stalwarts with the 'good news'. The distinguished Ivor Richard was willing to become our candidate. At that time local parties were independent and wanted local people, not national megastars. The chances of Ivor Richard getting the nomination were nil.

He did manage to get shortlisted for the Malpas ward. I recall the indignity of his squeezing into a nursery school chair with us candidates who were waiting to give our ten-minute speeches. He offered us miniature bottles of whisky which he appeared to have hanging from his belt under his double-breasted suit. Was this a new Euro-treat?

Union power was still strong. I was not a little irked that delegates from the branch of the steel union that I had founded and served as secretary for twenty years were ordered to vote for Ivor Richard. Presumably because of the years he had spent slaving in front of blast furnaces. Sam's father was an official of the ASLEF branch and he was ordered to vote for Richard. He did. Old Labour had a few dirty tricks in their locker long before New Labour invented fresh ones. The only support Richard received was from trade unions arm-locked by the party machine. He continued to hawk his wares around many other constituencies. He came closest to success in Cardiff West. He was favourite there until he announced that he did not intend to be a full-time MP. Rhodri Morgan won the nomination mainly because his jokes were good. Ivor gave up on democracy and accepted a peerage.

My battle for the thirteen Newport West ward parties started promisingly when I won Shaftesbury ward with a decent majority. Then the bombshell. Adrian Jones withdrew from the contest. He asked his supporters to back me. Judi James understandably judged this to be a cunning Machiavellian plot. If it was, I was never in on it. Adrian's reason was that he believed that Judi would move to the right in Parliament and that I would remain steadfastly left.

I ploughed on, winning a majority of wards. Some unexpected objections arose. At the Allt-yr-yn selection meeting one member whispered to Sam that she would not vote for me because I had 'stolen another man's wife'. Sam was able to talk her around without explaining that she was the wife under discussion.

The perfidy of parliamentary selections in south Wales is legendary. On the night of the key shortlisting meeting by the Newport party's executive committee, Sam returned home. 'It was dreadful,' she announced in terms of mock horror.

I froze in fear. The committee had the power to eliminate me from the shortlist. It would have been 'Bye bye Parliament' for ever. 'How dreadful?' I whimpered.

'Awful', she moaned, 'Ottaleen Dally was wearing the same dress as me.'

The executive committee had shortlisted all seven serious candidates. But the final arbiter – the General Management Committee – were wounded and in a vengeful anarchic mood when they were asked to approve the list. They attacked the big beasts of Gwent Labour. One member moved that Lloyd Turnbull, the leader of the county council, be removed from the shortlist. Lloyd had failed to turn up at the Rogerstone ward selection meeting. There was a majority in favour.

Treachery was contagious. It was then moved that future council leader Bob Bright be removed for not attending enough party meetings. He was dumped. The meeting was heading for a shortlist of none. The rot stopped when four were left: Bryan Davies, Judi James, Newport Council leader Harry Jones . . . and me.

The final selection meeting remains a blur. I remember making one boob when I confused proportions and allocated three lots of 50 per cent to one cause. Many other questions were aggressive, especially about my peremptory resignation from the county council. Would I do the same thing again? Sam and I had classified all delegates into four groups: 'For', 'Doubtful', 'Against' and 'Over their dead bodies'. We had calculated a narrow win. In a run-off with Bryan Davies I won by five votes. Life was about to be wonderful.

Ahead of us was a two-year election campaign. The local party members gratifyingly reunited in my support, including the 'Over my dead body' ones. They recognised the strength of any team that included Sam. Without the stability and savvy that she had brought to our marriage, I would not have been selected. We were not prosperous. The only income coming into the house was my £8,000 salary as Llew's researcher. We had settled in happily in our Newport West home. My car was a ten-year-old Avenger affectionately known as the corn-beef tin. One of its many faults was that the driver's door had the habit of swinging open after it was slammed shut. I was called up by the police in the early hours of one morning. They explained that my car had been broken into and 'they made a hell of a mess of it'. In fact the door had opened itself and the mess inside the car was my filing system.

In my twenty-year-long political life I had blown so many chances. Now I had one last one. Sam and I put all our eggs in the election basket. Everything was single-mindedly dedicated to that end. Llew was astonished at my selection. There was a new hint of competitiveness that cooled our friendship. 'Who is more important,' he asked, 'an MEP or an MP?' But he generously allowed me time for campaigning. Instant availability to the press was a great boon in promoting myself and in undermining Mark Robinson, who was very vulnerable with a 500-vote majority.

Mark was young and popular. He was a novel and attractive change from the lugubrious Roy Hughes, the only MP Newport had known for twenty-five years. His daughter was baptised in the crypt of the Commons. The Robinsons moved into a mansion in Caerleon, one of the most pleasant parts of the constituency. His constituency work was thorough and he sold himself well to the local press. He organised acres of favourable newspaper publicity.

His appointment as minister at the Welsh Office earned him local kudos but also exposed his weaknesses. He was an indifferent Commons performer and never improved. The *Western Mail* forecast his sacking after one dire performance at the Dispatch Box. At one point he dried up altogether. In answer to a question from Ron Davies about a constituent's missed appointment for a cervical smear test, Mark suggested the constituent got in touch with the Welsh Office 'if *he* wanted to'.

The *South Wales Argus* was fair in its treatment of me until the final week of the campaign. My agent, David Mayer, was a tower of creative strength through two years of relentless campaigning. With skill he used every weapon in the politician's armoury. We had a blizzard of press releases, media interviews, social events and ward newsletters, plus imaginative stunts and demonstrations in Newport's John Frost Square. So conscientiously did I attend all social and public events at which Mark Robinson appeared that, under present law, I could have been charged with stalking him. The campaign had energy, colour and humour. A few bull's-eyes were scored, especially when exposing false employment figures issued by the government. Mark exuded confidence throughout. He was convinced that a small boundary change, and Labour's peace policies to leave Britain defenceless, would bring him victory in 1987. After all, I was well known for my CND work.

Two activities that were unique to Newport West Labour campaigning were our merchandise and our birthday card. Sam organised the sales of pens in the shape of six-inch nails (to nail the Tories), plus key rings and a Euro 'rose in a fist' car sticker. A card sent out to every eighteen-year-old on their birthday showed a photograph of Neil Kinnock shaking me warmly by the hand. His balloon had the words 'You're looking cheerful today, Paul.' My balloon said, 'That's because [Name] is old enough to vote today.'

What little national newspaper coverage I had was hostile. In December 1985, the *Mail on Sunday* denounced me as one of fourteen hard lefties to watch. We were described as 'the extreme left wing', out to embarrass Neil Kinnock as soon as we got to Westminster. The list hilariously included David Blunkett, Keith Vaz and Paul Boateng, all future models of New Labour rectitude.

In those fraught pre-election days a bad newspaper report was taken seriously. The opinion polls were our barometer, causing us to rise to

giddy heights of bliss or fall into the gloom of despair. Local and by-
election results were crawled over and analysed to discover what the
Newport West result would be on the same basis. The worst moment
was about a month before the election was called. The SDP opinion poll
ratings passed Labour's. If the anti-Tory vote was divided in Newport,
Labour would lose. Failure was a dismal prospect. Not only the end of any
hope of a full-time political job, but serious financial troubles. We had
spent our own money lavishly on our campaign in anticipation of victory.
We had an overdraft of about £2,000. Penury threatened.

Sam and I were in Llew Smith's office when we heard the announcement
of the election date live from Parliament – 11 June 1987. We hugged each
other in excitement. This was it.

14

Nervous triumph

Voices in the balcony were chanting my name. No one seemed to have noticed that my piles of counted votes were 2,000 behind the incumbent MP I had hoped to unseat.

Most of my supporters were drunk or unhinged by a delirium of optimism. But the wise and sober council leader, Aubrey Hames, had congratulated me as the MP for Newport West about half an hour after the count had started. It was an outbreak of premature congratulations. I smiled weakly. I was pessimistic.

It had been a hell of a day. A last-ditch Liberal dirty trick was attempted at dawn that day. It hit hard. They circulated a leaflet door-to-door. They were known locally as 'yellow perils'. Because of their timing, there was no chance to refute any claims made. The message was:

> We the Liberals in Newport West believe in campaigning on the issues not the personalities. That is why we have not published the information given to us anonymously by the Conservative Party, that if published, would prove that the Labour candidate, Mr Flynn, is not fit to be an MP.

It was poisonous and imprecise, allowing the voters to invent their own major crime that made me unfit to represent them. It was certainly actionable. The Liberal candidate, Winston Roddick, subsequently apologised in person for it. There never was any serious possibility of suing because of the cost. But I was curious about this terrible secret that they claimed to have.

A well-known local Tory had shown them a fourteen-year-old report from the *Argus* that I had been fined because my MOT certificate was out of date. I was stopped returning from Greenham Common at 3.00 a.m. The news had already been reported to the local voters. The Tories believed in franchising their dirty tricks out to the Liberals. It was a demoralising blow. I was already jittery with a chronic case of candidate's neurosis. At mid-morning, I told Sam that I thought we had lost. She had other ideas.

It was odd that the two dirty tricks in the campaign had come from a party who was certain to come in third place. The Tory campaign in Newport West was invisible. The Liberals were irritating. Nationally they issued a list of 'hard left' candidates, dubbed the '101 Damnations'. The reason they gave for including me was inaccurate. One of their accusations was that I had backed the demented Militant schisms that had divided the Labour Party in the early 1980s. Rather, I had strongly opposed them as corrosive interlopers. I offered to pay £1,000 to charity if they could prove their claims.

I did not have £1,000. But I knew that they could not justify their accusation. The cash offer won a headline story in the *Argus* and a great deal of public sympathy. After the election, in response to a letter from me and the threat of a writ, David Steel sent me an apology.

At the count my solitary anxiety continued. The trend of the accumulating votes at the count was 6,000 for the Tory MP, 4,000 for me. Then 10,000 to 8,000, 14,000 to 12,000. The Tory had won the previous election with 14,000. My rising panic was a rational response.

The Tories were buoyed up. When the wife of the Tory MP met Sam she said, 'I don't think we'll need a recount tonight.' She had also noticed the trend in the accumulating piles of votes. Later when the candidates and spouses posed for a newspaper photograph, she smiled and said to Sam, 'I hope that this marriage lasts longer than his first one.'

An old friend from my years as a councillor winked at me. He was organising the counting agents. 'Watch their faces,' he whispered. He dragged a plastic tray of 4,000 counted votes from under a stage and carried them triumphantly on his head. They were all mine. It was his idea of a joke. I was propelled from 2,000 votes behind to 2,000 ahead, 16,000 to 14,000.

Sam had wisely left my side as my pre-announcement angst reached its height. She believed that a nervous breakdown shared was a nervous breakdown doubled.

After an age, the sweet words were announced into the vast echoing space of the Newport Centre: Paul Flynn 20,887, Mark Robinson 18,179.

My life was transformed. This was no routine career move. The result meant hell or heaven. From steelworker to statesman, hard up to well off, street campaigner to Commons legislator, from Newport citizen to Newport MP. 1987 was the realisation of a dream I had cherished since 1945. Losing an election at the age of fifty-two would have been terminal. Emotions welled up. Joy that my wife Sam was at my side and my eighty-year-old mother was watching on the television. Sorrow for lost loved ones who could not share the moment. Happiness that two years' slog by hundreds of tireless Newport comrades had succeeded. Newport was Tory-free again.

Mark Robinson was dejected. He had expected victory and spoke to the press on election day about his planned champagne celebration. He was young and popular. There was no pleasure in his downfall. He was a decent compassionate man who was doomed to lose again in 1997 after another single-term tenure as MP for Somerton & Frome. Then he drifted into New Labour until they became too right wing for him.

The Liberals were crushed, demoralised and eventually invisible. They slunk out of the Newport Centre leaving a malodorous slick behind them. The Labour team lingered, reluctant to leave the field of victory. Sam was keen to get home. She had never slept with an MP before. Exhausted but happy, I drove my ten-year-old Avenger home. It was 3.00 a.m. I carefully parked outside our Victorian three-storey house in Fields Park Road and quietly shut the door. As I walked away from the car, I heard the door click open and creak mockingly at us.

The future would be better, with a car with doors that locked.

15

Cage breakout

My work as an MP led me into unexpected and unknown territory. The first three years of parliamentary life, as a committee member, then as a frontbench spokesman on Wales and on social security, were spent in a narrow world in the company of a small band of fully qualified enthusiasts. Almost all of the Labour members on the committee on social security bills were raised as working class Catholics. I have described the similar experience Margaret Beckett and I shared as children. Many of us had received demeaning welfare handouts. Our education had equipped us with profound guilt that inspired reforming zeal.

By late 1990 I felt that I was imprisoned inside a shrinking cage. Enviously I watched fellow MPs delve into the exciting worlds of environment, health and defence. Issues on which I had some knowledge and a head full of ideas that were fighting to get out.

There seemed to be few challengers for my portfolio of Social Security. Other MPs were glad someone else was doing it. There were consolations. In 1989 I fought a ferocious campaign on the fraud of personal pensions. Of the rare oral Prime Minister's Questions that I had, most were to ask Margaret Thatcher about the mis-selling of the pensions.

I reported Barclays and then the Midland Bank to the Advertising Standards Authority for the dishonest way they were advertising their pensions. The journalists were unmoved. This was simple left-wing exaggeration. Thatcher once told me I was a 'socialist, simply against choice'. It was at least five years later that the enormity of the scandal was properly exposed. About six million victims had been mis-sold pensions. When it was happening, shouting from the rooftops by the frontbench team attracted little attention.

One of the only times when my efforts enjoyed national publicity was a pure fluke. In January 1989, as an opposition, we had engineered a debate on the miserly cold weather payments. Our hope was that freezing weather would give the subject topicality. Luck was against us. It was the warmest January for decades. No one was interested until mild-mannered Tory government minister Peter Lloyd answered an impromptu question from Alice Mahon. He was denying the need for extra payments in cold weather. 'Elderly people should buy warmer clothing. It need not be expensive. Good bargains can be found in jumble sales,' Peter advised.

The remark was made at midnight and I was sitting on the front bench with Robin Cook. All the reporters had gone home. The fax machine I shared with the M4 group served its purpose. Throughout the early hours it relayed the message 'Atrocious, patronising, but revealing – Tory jumble sale answer to hypothermia'.

The wall-to-wall coverage the tabloids gave the news rivalled an earlier gaffe by Edwina Currie. She had urged the elderly to knit bobble hats to keep warm. This was a thrilling drama and a small victory. I nominally led the debate but Robin Cook was by my side selflessly feeding me ammunition. Opposition could be fun. The streamlined scheme for a new system of cold weather payments which I advocated that night was introduced a year later by the Tories. It followed the traditional reaction of governments to new ideas. First ignore them. Then say they are impractical. Later say they are too expensive. Finally introduce them and claim them as your own.

I resisted the temptation to crow and played the traditional role of an opposition. When you get what you want, denounce it as not enough. Politics is a disreputable trade.

Tony Lynes was my ever-present inspiration. But the burden of parliamentary frontbench work was a thief of time. My arthritis had hit a severe patch. One of the jobs of frontbenchers was to travel to constituency party meetings throughout the country. I turned down most invitations. One I attended in Newcastle left me exhausted. The Labour Party seemed determined to turn its back on its record of great social welfare achievement. A reshuffle had robbed the social security team of Robin Cook and Margaret Beckett. This dwarfed our party's ambitions. Was this my future? From shadow minister to minister for social security? I could be trapped for years in exhausting work for a government with little appetite for the fundamental reforms that would give me personal satisfaction. From the back benches, I could speak the truth and campaign.

Although my wife Sam and Tony Lynes strongly advised against, I decided to resign. At the end of October 1990, just as Neil Kinnock was drawing up his shadow team for the new year, I wrote to him, 'Please do not consider my name for the new team. I am grateful for the chance of serving with some of the great parliamentarians of my generation. Now is the time to concentrate from the back benches on some of the many other interests I have.'

Neil insisted on sending me a letter back. He wrote:

> I completely understand your reasons for your decision – although Michael [Meacher] and I will be very sorry to lose you from the Front Bench team where your experience, ideas and hard work have been greatly valued.
>
> I know that you will continue to show great commitment and effectiveness both in your Constituency and in Parliament and, naturally, your policy development ideas will, as ever, be welcome.

A kind gesture from Neil. Had I made a mistake? Probably. But there was no going back. My political future was firmly on the back benches for the rest of my parliamentary career. It seemed the right idea at the time because I was feeling unable to cope with my health problems and the weakening conviction in Labour's policies. They were too much to overcome. Then I received the most humbling letter I have ever had in my life.

I gather that you chose to leave the frontbench. I was very impressed by the original research you did this summer and whilst I understand very well the frustration of rarely being able to speak, yet being expected to do the drudgery, I am very sorry that you are no longer there.

I do hope things go well with you.

It was from David Blunkett.

There were consolations. Freedom from the slavery of frontbench duties allowed me to indulge my interest in foreign affairs. There is well-founded cynicism about MPs' jaunts. They have been widely abused by the parliamentary Gullivers and Marco Polos. The travel gluttons are swiftly identified. At the drop of a hat they will jet off to a luxury sunny tourist trap to selflessly serve the cause of their constituents and international harmony.

One Labour MP, David Young, was de-selected by his local party in Bolton because they did not see enough of him. He protested to the *Guardian* that this was unjust. The *Guardian* could not resist pointing out that, when they contacted him, he returned the call from his hotel room in Katmandu.

A combination of insatiable curiosity, gregariousness and an interest in languages equips me for fruitful foreign travel. I specialise in dangerous, cold countries in winter. As it turned out, my visits were usually before or just after revolutions. There are two advantages. Revolutions are times of concentrated magnetism in history. The cold weather, combined with the threat of bloodshed, is a formidable disincentive to fellow MPs. So the competition for places on my itinerary was thin.

Hungary was still under the Russian yoke when I first visited. A demonstration in Budapest was protesting against the suffering in neighbouring Romania, where Ceauşescu was bulldozing ancient villages into large pits and replacing them with utility blocks of flats that lacked indoor sanitation. Strict political balance is maintained on delegations abroad. A week trapped in a ghetto of English-speakers in a foreign land brings MPs of opposing parties into closer contact than usual. The consequence is to strike up lifelong friendships or enmities. By the end of the Hungary trip, fellow Labour MP John Home-Robertson and I were barely on speaking terms with the two Tories who had continually provoked us. At a press conference the Tory leader of the delegation spoke vacuously to the press. 'What a wonderful Parliament you have. So well behaved . . . No, no we have no views on Ceauşescu. An internal matter, y'know.'

Incensed, I gave the television cameras exactly what they wanted 'Ceauşescu? . . . A mediaeval tyrant oppressing his own people and a linguistic minority. The Hungarian Parliament? . . . This is a dead parliament. You have just approved a Chernobyl-style nuclear power station and no one has complained.' The television station gleefully broadcast my remarks. It was just what the journalists were waiting to hear. The items provoked friendly letters and prolonged contact with a few progressive Hungarians.

Similar problems were anticipated when I toured the pre-revolution Baltic States with David Owen and Tory MP Mark Wolfson in 1990. I had been warned that David was disagreeable and tetchy. But he was charm itself throughout our visit. He spent large chunks of time trying to persuade me to intervene on his behalf with Neil Kinnock. Surprisingly he had never had a conversation with Neil. He wanted Labour not to put up candidates against the last two surviving Social Democrat MPs at the coming 1992 election. It was futile. No Labour leader has the power to tell local parties to stand candidates down, especially in winnable seats. The plea suggested that David Owen did not fully understand Labour Party grassroots.

To a Welshman the Baltics have special attractions. Three unique languages trying to survive against a big brother neighbour that speaks a world language. Latvia has a smaller population than Scotland, and Estonia a smaller one than Wales. They had been colonised, invaded three times and were the reluctant 'near abroad' of the Soviet Empire. A few months before we arrived, Lithuania had made its faltering declaration of independence. All three states were fearful of the future. In the January of

1991 demonstrators were shot in Vilnius and Riga. Vivid film by Latvian film maker Juris Podnieks appeared on television all over the world.

In the Commons I had asked John Major, in an oral question, to send British MPs to stand side by side with our Baltic counterparts in their besieged parliaments. President Landsbergis telephoned my office in Parliament asking for the World Service to broadcast more emergency programmes in Lithuanian. The domestic media had been silenced and many Lithuanians had no knowledge of what was happening. At that time, there was no contact between the Baltic parliaments and Westminster. John Major earned my gratitude. He discovered a pot of money that he used to send three of us there. It is called the Unconventional Diplomacy Fund. Never before, or since, have I found any mention of this fund. Did he invent it?

We were briefed by the Foreign Office and directed to report to Foreign Secretary Douglas Hurd when we returned. My companions were Scottish Nationalist Margaret Ewing and Russian-speaking Conservative Quentin Davies. The three parliaments were barricaded and defended by young men with hunting rifles. A dozen people had already been killed at the television station in Vilnius and two of Podnieks's cameramen had been shot in Riga. There was intense fear and uncertainty. If the Russian special troops attacked they would overwhelm the barricades in minutes and certainly kill their poorly armed defenders.

It was in Vilnius that the bravest act I have ever witnessed occurred. Quentin Davies marched across a line that said 'Keep Off' in Russian and Lithuanian. Margaret Ewing and I meekly followed, watched by a disbelieving crowd of Lithuanians. On that same spot, a fortnight earlier, the Russians had killed half a dozen demonstrators. Quentin harangued two soldiers on an armoured personnel carrier blocking the entrance to the radio station. 'Why don't you go home?' he asked the Red Army squaddie. The soldier replied that he would love to go home. 'I'm from Kazakhstan. Who wants to be here in Vilnius in January?' But he had to guard the station against thieves. 'No. No. You're the thieves,' Quentin helpfully explained. The soldier waved his Kalashnikov at us and suggested that it would be a good idea for us to go home. He was very persuasive. We retreated. Rapidly.

The incident cheered up the troubled Lithuanians. In a couple of subsequent visits in 1994 and 2008, I saw the extraordinarily rapid progress made in the three Baltic states. They are transformed, self-confident and visibly prosperous. There is still residual fear of Russian rouble hegemony, but independence has firmly taken root. The improvements in life are concrete and, I hope, permanent.

On one occasion I managed to combine an official parliamentary trip with a holiday. It was a planned two-day visit to convince Icelanders not to restart whaling. It developed into the best holiday I have ever had. Rhodri Morgan and I decided that this was a chance not to miss. Julie Morgan and Sam came along and we tagged a week's holiday on to the Council of Europe visit. We yomped around Iceland in a 4x4. It was August. Yes, it was cold. Yes, it snowed. Yes, it was a wonderland of wild dramatic landscape, much of it untouched by civilisation. We tried to convince the Icelanders that resumption of whaling would be counter-productive. They could lose more than they would gain. A consumer boycott, for animal welfare reasons, of their other fishing products was a real possibility. We might have had an effect. They did not restart.

Surprisingly, the Icelanders sell the whale meat to the Japanese. They do not eat it themselves. But they eat many other unexpected *fruits de mer*. Hartfisch is a traditional staple food. It is tasteless and has the texture of finger nail clippings or the skin sloughed off by snakes. Mixed with butter and subjected to prolonged energetic chewing it becomes more or less edible. Politely we chewed the hartfisch. Other delights we resisted. They judge skate to be inedible until it has been anointed with urine and buried in the ground for four weeks to allow it to reach its state of delicious perfection. I wrote about this trip in my newspaper column. One item caused more interest than any of the portentous and deeply serious facts I had written about for years: the price of beer in Iceland was £7.16 a pint.

The parliamentary timetable often eclipses momentous international events. The drama of the fall of Ceaușescu coincided with the fizzling out of parliamentary business before a Christmas recess. I made the only speech on the subject – at 1.15 a.m. on 20 December 1989. I quoted

Ceaușescu as saying that he would introduce reforms in Romania 'only when the beech tree bears apples and reeds bear lily flowers'. The minister William Waldegrave in replying was characteristically generous. I had previously asked him to beef up broadcasts in Romanian. The BBC was the most trusted voice in the whole of the Soviet Empire. Waldegrave said he had gone to John Tusa of the World Service and we now have extra broadcasts in the Romanian language. Unfortunately I cannot claim that the increase was a major influence in the revolution. They began only in the week of the fall of Ceaușescu!

A fortnight later I was flying to Bucharest with the leader of the Peasant Party, exiled millionaire Ion Ratziu. He had hired a plane to fly journalists to the Romanian capital. As political ballast, Father of the House Bernard Braine and I had been invited. Ratziu was hoping to be elected president, in gratitude for his work in London on behalf of Free Romanians Abroad. Bucharest was unforgettably exciting. The frozen streets were packed with demonstrators who were still excited and volatile. Rumours of new shootings by the Securitate swept the city. Bernard and I placed flowers on the three shrines that had been hastily set up in the places where large groups of students had been killed two weeks earlier.

I hastily learnt a sentence in Romanian. In order to say something fresh I roughly translated the words (in Welsh) on the war memorial in Newport: *I'n Dewrion. Eu henwau perarogli sydd.* A Romanian-speaker roughly translated from English into Romanian, every word of which had a romance language root: *Bravilor nostri eroi* (To our brave heroes), *dulce va fi* (sweet will be) *memoria nomenlor lor* (the memory of their names). In the middle of the desert of incomprehensible Slav languages was a Romance oasis full of words that were immediately familiar to speakers of Latin and Welsh.

Ratziu was rejected as president in the subsequent election. The voters did not like his English accent and his bow tie. One told me he did not vote for him because 'he never sliced salami with us'. That was a reference to the semi-edible meat, fur and horn mixture forced on Romanians by Ceaușescu, which Ratziu did not have to suffer in his millionaire life in Britain.

Later that year, we had a character-forming family holiday in the Black Sea resort of Mamaia and in the mountains at Poiana Braşov. It was a fine demonstration of the power of the mind to obliterate the rough edges to Eastern Bloc tourism. My interest in Romania continued with other official visits. In 1996 I had a wonderful weekend there lecturing to young Romanian politicians. It is deeply satisfying to follow the – albeit faltering – progress of this beautiful country out of its epoch of oppression.

I went to Bulgaria to monitor their first election. It was unique in that no party was keen to win and inherit guaranteed economic turmoil. The choice was between the former Communist red party and a blue coalition that included all opposition groups from fascists to ecologists.

Townspeople, and young people generally, were voting blue. The Army and the peasants were voting red. One elderly voter on a farm explained her choice: 'We don't want the blues, they are the ones with beards from Sofia who want to let the criminals out of jail. We remember what it was like when they were in government before.' Closer questioning revealed that 'before' was in the 1930s. 'They were no good then,' she explained, 'we had no proper roads or washing machines.' As diligent observers, we questioned everyone. But we had a peculiar difficulty. Bulgarians nod their heads when they mean no and shake them vigorously from side to side when they mean yes. The translation given to us, alongside the seemingly contradictory head movements, incited disbelief.

The election was scrupulously fair. Some of Bulgaria's newly minted election rules were better than our own. At a great meeting of the dozens of international observers, the message was of an entirely fair election. One American group, determined to earn their corn, quibbled that they thought there was intimidation. They quoted as evidence the fact that 'flowers were on display on the tables of all the polling booths. *Red* flowers.' Another observer said that there was similar evidence of bias where he was at Varna: 'Above every single polling station, throughout the day, the sky was blue.'

Part III

Unbending knee

16

Peacenik's wars

The early 1980s were the most dangerous years the planet has experienced. Two frail fingers controlled the nuclear button that could have wiped all life from the planet sixty times over. Historian E. P. Thompson said that Andropov, the Soviet leader, who was on a life support machine, was 'effectively dead from the neck down' and President Reagan had long been 'dead from the neck up'.

The peace issue dwarfed all others. Did anything else matter if all earthly life was to end? Many Conservative MPs still believe that their 'toughness' in escalating the nuclear arms race forced the Soviet Union to back down. They believe that stance precipitated the collapse of communism. There is another explanation. History will judge that communism was undermined by the material success of the West. The bleak failures of Eastern Europe were exposed by mass communications, especially satellite television. The luxurious wealth of the West and grey destitution of the East destroyed the credibility of the communist system.

My devotion to the cause of nuclear disarmament was all-consuming at that time. It meshed easily into my involvement in the anti-nuclear power movement. With Newport friends Les and Judi James, I had linked up in April 1980 with organic farmer Peter Segar and environmentalists Hugh and Mag Richards to found the Welsh Anti-Nuclear Alliance (WANA). The Welsh Anti-Nuclear Campaign would have been a better title but the acronym was problematic.

WANA was a respite from my work as a councillor. It was pure joy to co-operate with people who were driven by unselfish idealistic convictions, free from ambition for office or civic regard. WANA was incredibly successful. A tiny group of bright people measurably changed public opinion in Wales on nuclear power. The campaign to persuade all Welsh local authorities to declare themselves to be 'nuclear-free zones' was brilliantly conceived and executed. WANA was also profitable, through selling badges and car stickers. A rare achievement for a protest group.

CND was waking from its long hibernation and the Nuclear Free Wales movement became interwoven with the peace movement. The campaign concentrated on the eight county councils. Achieving a clean sweep of these would enable us to claim that the democratic representatives of all Welsh people were in favour of a nuclear-free Wales. It would have been impossible to get the support of all the district councils or all the MPs because a proportion of them were Tory. We were confident that we could get the support of all the Labour county councils before moving on to tackle the independent ones.

Seven counties adopted WANA's cause. In 1981 Clwyd became the final piece of the jigsaw. Our claim was that, when Clwyd agreed, a whole country had declared itself 'nuclear free'. I was due at Clwyd County Hall in Mold as press officer for WANA on the historic day.

I never made it. It was a freezing February morning; I had trouble with my overheating ten-year-old Datsun. Precious time was lost replacing an engine hose with frozen fingers at a roadside service station. Trying to make up time I drove too fast. I hit a patch of ice a few miles from Hereford. I braked and the car slid across the road out of control. More braking did not help. I sideswiped a car that was coming in the opposite direction. My car turned over end to end at least twice. There was no time for fear. The emotions I felt were surprise and curiosity as the car thudded and spun.

When it stopped, it took a few moments for me to realise that the car was upside down. The engine was still running. The only other sound was the glugging of an escaping liquid. I was frightened. Was it petrol? I expected the 'whoosh' of an explosion at any second. Afterwards I discovered it was water pouring from the Winchester bottle I had used to top up my overheating engine. The doors would not open; it was also darker than it should have been. The car was wedged on its roof in a ditch, the doors jammed against the sides. I kicked the windows in an effort to smash my way out. That did not work. I searched in vain for something to smash the glass. Happily one of the mechanical winders worked and I wound down a window to create a space big enough for me to crawl out. In front of me were the feet of a bystander. 'Christ, he's alive,' he said.

Then and now my feelings about the incident are detached, as though it happened to someone else. My car was towed away to its final resting place. I was relieved not to be sharing its fate. I was warned that, given the lack of immediate shock and upset, I would invariably suffer a delayed reaction a few days later. Nothing happened. I had too many other things on my mind. There was a noticeable, probably permanent, influence on my driving. I often accumulate a queue of cars behind me on country roads.

Clwyd's nuclear-free declaration was a world news event. The then leader of Cardiff City Council, Bob Morgan, told me he heard about it on Russian television in his hotel bedroom in Moscow. It was major item in the USA. I featured on the front page of *Asahi Shimbun*, a Japanese newspaper with the world's biggest circulation. Yet the news squeezed in only as the final item of that evening's Welsh language TV bulletin. Wales was nearer the truth in its assessment that county councils, even acting in unison, did not make foreign policy or even national energy policy. Exploiting hype is at the heart of successful campaigning. WANA was intent on squeezing the last drop of benefit from this propaganda coup.

Peter Segar, Plaid Cymru leader Dafydd Wigley and I took the news to the European Parliament where contact was made with other countries' anti-nuclear groups. An Alsatian peace group named Les Artisans de la Paix handsomely entertained us overnight. They had a seemingly endless supply of champagne. There was a shortage of chairs and I spent a long, semi-sober evening sitting on a floor discussing the fate of the planet with Dafydd.

In 1981 a peace camp was set up at a US base at Caerwent on the outskirts of Newport. In its six-month life it sucked in vast quantities of the energy of the peace movement in south Wales. The site was on the narrow verge of the main road between Newport and Chepstow at the junction to the base. Later it moved to a large lay-by.

Peace camps were sprouting up in front of nuclear bases all over Britain. The case for believing that Caerwent was a nuclear dump was weak, but there was good evidence that it was being prepared as a site for chemical weapons. A meeting to discuss the wisdom of establishing a peace camp was hijacked by a Rasputin lookalike who rejoiced in the name 'The Beast'. He was tall, black bearded, liberated, smelling of haystacks and permanently clad in a long black overcoat.

Old heads warned against a campaign without an attainable specific aim. How long would a camp last? Could it survive a winter? Would the essential support organisations be sufficiently well organised to keep it going? 'The Beast' announced that regardless of other opinion he intended to set up his tipi on the site in a few days' time. The meeting decided to act immediately in order to dilute the influence of 'The Beast'. His image was fine for recruiting Old Testament prophets but counter-productive for a peace movement seeking allies in middle Wales and England.

The widely acceptable faces of middle-aged, middle-class CND supporters turned up when the camp was struck. They included Mid Glamorgan county councillor Ray Davies, CND leaders Joan Ruddock and John Cox plus Tipi Valley drop-out Brig Oubridge. There were also a couple of dozen assorted young peaceniks from the area. The unstable community had rich potential for both favourable publicity and disasters. Road accidents were certain because the site was a distraction. There were three minor crashes. Thankfully none of the tiny children wandering around the site were hurt. The camp community was made up of the saintly dedicated peaceniks, drop-outs, criminals, civilisation wreckers, sexual predators, a convicted bomber, the insane, new world beatniks and even someone from MI5. The man from MI5 was soon identified and thrown out.

One drop-out vicar, with loathsome personal habits, verbally abused the locals in a Caerwent pub. They attacked the camp and put Councillor

Ray Davies into hospital. The hippies insisted on their right to smoke and cultivate illegal drugs. Drunkenness and sexual licence dominated a great deal of the social life. Thanks to the heroic efforts of leader Nick Fisher, the camp did not destroy itself. When it moved to a safer site, the local authority health inspector declared that it was run in an 'exemplary manner'. Fortunately, a kind media masked the worst excesses of the uncivilised fringes of camp life. A great deal of useful eloquent peace messages emanated from this fragile anarchic village of tipis and caravans.

On Sundays, dozens of peace campaigners turned up at the site and much good work was done in strengthening and reinforcing campaigning zeal. But the inevitable series of internal cascading camp crises continued. Breaking point arrived when 'The Beast', who had been a faithful permanent camp inhabitant, announced that he was organising a pop festival on the site. The event was to be advertised through the networks of new age travellers, peace campers and other alternative lifestyle drop-outs throughout Britain. The full horror of several thousand hippies turning up for a Glastonbury-type festival of noise and drugs in our lay-by was obvious to the rational campers. 'The Beast' never came up with a convincing answer as to how our one chemical toilet would cope with an influx of thousands. An onslaught of prolonged thunderous noise on the neighbouring farms would have incited understandable rage. Six months after it was set up, the camp closed. After an afternoon of balloons, fun and self-congratulation, we left the site. We were relieved of the immense burden of trying to sustain the unsustainable. 'The Beast' in his solitary tipi remained for several weeks. Where is he now? Probably a millionaire stockbroker in the City.

I was never a resident of the camp. But it was a springboard into the media. It gave me a platform for furthering the peace message. Newport CND played a full part in the marathon Greenham Common protest that attracted the attention of the world. In 1982 two million peace protesters marched through Central Park, New York. The USA's Catholic bishops supported them. I took part in the three great London marches. The world had recognised the deadly peril of weapons that could destroy our planet fifty-seven times over. The peace movement changed the world.

I have never relinquished my membership of CND, even though I have been irritated by their occasional unsellable counter-productive pacifist policies. The Stop the War coalition is also adept at damaging the peace case by overstatement but it is far more right than wrong. I have enthusiastically campaigned with it.

For a brief period the instincts of the peace movement and the government were aligned. Tony Blair offered an inspiring vision of a new world order in a speech to Party Conference in 2001. But it went badly awry under the presidency of George W. Bush. Tony brooded on how he could forge a link of trust with the neo-con president who was buttressed by uber-religious groups.

In late March 2003, I wrote to Tony about Iraq:

> Our involvement in Bush's war will increase the likelihood of terrorist attacks. Attacking a Muslim state without achieving a fair settlement of the Palestine–Israeli situation is an affront to Muslims, from our local mosques to the far-flung corners of the world. A pre-emptive attack of the kind we have made on Iraq will only deepen the sense of grievance among Muslims that the Western/Christian/Jewish world is out to oppress them. This will provide a propaganda victory to Osama bin Laden and can only increase his support and the likelihood of more acts of terrorism.
>
> In the Commons you repeated that it is an article of faith to you that Britain and the USA should have a common foreign policy. Fine when there is an American President such as Roosevelt, Eisenhower, Carter or Clinton: disastrous when it is a right wing fundamentalist Republican such as Bush.

The vote on the Iraq War was the foulest episode of the Blair government. It was the whips who won it for Tony. The 139 Labour MPs who voted on a severe three-line whip against British involvement were not enough. There were eighty other Labour MPs who had indicated their worries by their support for amendments and Early Day Motions. They were bribed, bullied and bamboozled into voting for war, or abstaining. I wonder if Tony and the whips ever dwell on the thought that 179 British lives would not have been lost if they had told the truth and desisted from bellicose bullying.

Later Tony pontificated on the merits of 'hard power' and 'soft power' military interventions. He exulted in the merits of deploying 'hard power'. Experience proved otherwise.

It was the 'hard' choice to back Bush's war in Iraq and to invade Helmand province. Hundreds of British soldiers and an uncounted number of Afghans have been killed and little has been gained. It was 'hard' of Israel to invade Lebanon. It was 'soft' to call for a cease-fire. According to a Labour minister that would have been a 'meaningless gesture'. Not for the children buried alive at Qana, the thousands killed and the millions whose homes were bombed to rubble.

It was 'soft power' to use our brilliantly effective troops to save hundreds of thousands of lives in Sierra Leone, Kosovo and Bosnia. If we had not over-committed ourselves in Iraq and Afghanistan, we could have embarked on 'soft' peacekeeping missions in Darfur.

Yes, gains had been made in Iraq and Afghanistan but Bush's mission to turn both countries into Western-style democracies is an impossible one. If we are determined to root out wicked regimes worldwide other countries cry out for interventions. Oppression is not limited to two countries. Chechens, Uzbeks, the peoples of Aceh and Zimbabwe continue to suffer without disturbing the conscience of Western nations.

The 'hard' choice is to throw away £37 billion plus on the vanity virility symbol of Trident. It does not need to be replaced for eighteen years anyway. The 'soft' choice is to concentrate on peacekeeping to ensure there is no repeat of the slaughter of the past decade. Fifty-four of the last fifty-nine world conflicts have been civil wars in which the casualties were mainly women and children. Two million children have been killed and four million maimed.

The need for a fully independent foreign policy diminished with the election of Obama. An increasingly bellicose Bush went down still spoiling for war against Iran and/or Syria. The most intelligent American president since Kennedy renewed hope. If we are permanently doomed to be the dumb ally of the USA, it's encouraging to follow a president with a conscience and a brain.

17

The colonising succubus

How did it all go so wrong? The Iraq War was the culmination of a movement that began life ten years earlier. The despair from a fourth election defeat for Labour was tangible when we met for the opening of the 1992–97 parliament. It was to be the most disillusioning period of my political life. I was close to breaking with Labour and destroying my future in politics.

The requiem for our loss continued for months. How could we have been beaten by Major . . . after the poll tax fiasco? Neil Kinnock had wisely gone. He was mourned as the lost leader. Had he stayed the recriminations would have been mercilessly directed at him. But we were a beaten party. Dull, arid opposition was ours for a further five years. Would any of Labour's values survive? Had four rejections destroyed our faith in ourselves?

The consolation was that solid, reliable John Smith was in Kinnock's place. Hope and pride began to flow back. John was a delight. He was ebullient, wise and good natured. He had a catalogue of wicked humorous stories. Wit was his most penetrating weapon, yet he also conveyed to the public feelings of reliability and trustworthiness. Unlike Neil Kinnock or Tony Blair he regularly dropped in to the Members' tea and dining rooms. No other Labour leader, before or since, would fill an empty seat at the table saying 'Do you mind if I join you?' As leader, John Smith continued to mix on equal terms with fellow MPs.

Hell dawned on 12 May 1994. At the time I did not realise that it was the end of the Labour Party that I had loved all my life. I was in my office preparing a speech when fellow MP John Garrett popped into my office and said, 'John Smith is dead.' There had been no official announcement but the BBC were carrying a story that he was ill. I was booked to welcome a party of visiting children that morning from a Newport school. I could hear my voice breaking as I told them that they had arrived on a day that everyone would remember. There was the mature understanding on their faces that we constantly find surprising in young children.

The Labour Party had been cruelly bereaved. It was a reminder of the premature death of Aneurin Bevan. Labour had been restored and reunited under John. The *Argus* asked me to write a tribute. It was therapeutic to have a task to occupy me on that tear-filled day. I recalled that it was said of John that 'if God wished to announce Armageddon with a view to keeping panic to the minimum, he would have chosen John Smith as his messenger'. His funeral service is a treasured memory, especially the beautiful singing of a psalm in Gaelic. I will always remember his generous advice, a kind word of encouragement, his humour and precious hours of friendship.

No one had previously given a thought to a new leader. Rumours swept through the parliamentary party like a contagion. Within hours of John Smith's death, the name Tony Blair was on everyone's lips. Margaret Beckett was the deputy but was discounted because of her perceived coldness and poor television appeal. Robin Cook was the most able debater but his appearance would allow the media to destroy him as the apparition from the planet Kkcck. John Prescott was liked and trusted, but it would be impossible to teach him to speak English in a logical sequence.

Blair had universal appeal and would win the general election for us. His right-wing views were a disincentive. But the ballast of the traditional Labour Party would, I believed, prevent his swinging too far to the right. I was wrong, of course. Alun Michael was campaigning for Blair. I promised my support. It was difficult to explain to Clare Short that I would not be voting for Margaret Beckett. For any position other than party leader, I would have supported her. She was entitled to be resentful towards me because of all the help that she had given me in the past. She has never shown it.

Blair's election gave Labour a boost in the opinion polls that we held right up to the general election. Suddenly we were new, young and attractive. Labour's star soared to previously undreamt-of heavens of popularity. The prospect of a Labour government was sweet and seductive. But pessimism and self-doubt haunted us. Parties are not rational organisms. Our emotions mainly determine our judgement. Four times we had been tormented with the promise of election victory. Just as we were about to seize it, victory was snatched from us. We were conditioned like Pavlov's dogs to expect endless repetitions of the same sequence of disappointment. Something deep and dark inside me told me we would never win.

My unhappiness with the Blair project deepened. Was he a cuckoo in Labour's nest? Although I am frequently described as left wing, I have never joined the Campaign Group nor was I opposed to the dumping of Clause Four. Old-style nationalisation had been a failure. Most of my working life had been spent in nationalised industries. Nothing of significance had replaced the profit motive as a trigger to efficiency. Nationalisation had spawned bloated Leviathans of inefficiency and self-interest.

But there were treasures from our Labour heritage that had to be cherished. A news report forced my first rupture with Blairism. It claimed that Blair was opting for a grant-maintained school (GMS) for his son. GMSs were grammar schools in all but name. I wrote to Tony and spoke to his Parliamentary Private Secretary, Bruce Grocott, the established line of complaint for a backbencher to use. I wanted assurances that Tony had not used his own position to seek privileged education for his son to attend the Oratory School.

My letter was friendly and tentative: 'Possibly untrue reports today . . . if accurate would undermine our party's educational ideals of non-privileged education . . . The Oratory had sought status for itself at the expense of other schools.' Neil Kinnock did not usually answer such letters. Blair did. But he had not understood the point. He said that 'the Oratory is one of a number of very good state comprehensives my son could attend. We chose it because we believe it will be the right school for him. Labour policy has not changed.'

In the January of 1995 Blair was to speak on education at a meeting of the Parliamentary Labour Party. He was unapologetic. Roy Hattersley made a coded attack on him. My attack on Blair was uncoded. In fairness, I began by paying a sincere tribute to Blair for attracting, by his personality and policies, a record number of members to the Newport West party. I described myself as a 'serial loyalist to Labour Party leaders since Attlee'. Addressing him directly by name, I said his decision was 'inexplicable and unforgivable and that you have betrayed the ideals of our party and undermined the struggle that our party is having in the country. We cannot preach against privilege and then insist on it for our own families.' Tony Blair look shocked. That was the end of the friendly relations that I had enjoyed with him since 1987 when we were both junior shadow ministers.

Having ventilated my views I was content. The rest of the day was packed with meetings and I put the matter to the back of my mind, hoping that Blair might reconsider. Then a friend told me that some of my comments were on Ceefax. It was a sanitised version of the meeting put out by the spin doctors. Their account was positive about Blair's contribution, ignored Hattersley's, but said that I had expressed 'unease' about Blair's decision on the Oratory.

The word 'unease' is not in my vocabulary. My habitual adjectives are far more direct. I was approached by BBC journalist Nicholas Jones. I told him it was a private meeting. He replied that he was a person of integrity and that any conditions I imposed on a statement would be respected. I told him it was still a private meeting, but that I had used more colourful and candid words than 'unease'.

Leaving the chamber later in the afternoon, I was mobbed by about twenty journalists in the Members' Lobby. All had notebooks at the ready. They were hungry for a Labour split story. Loudly and emphatically I repeated that it was a private meeting. It was all useless. Journalists have other ways of building a story. Several talkative MPs had a clearer recollection of what I said than I did. Having heard the same adjectives confirmed by two or three who had been present, the hacks were happy to print the cobbled-together account of what I had said. Late in the evening I confirmed to my trusted pal David Cornock that the version of the journalists was accurate. As the *Western Mail* is late going to press his account was the only one that used quotation marks.

It was a major news item. Some carried imaginative accounts of Blair's shocked features. A whip, Don Dixon, then unidentified by the press, was quoted as saying, 'If Blair does not understand now how he has upset the party, he never fucking will.' There were many unattributed quotations from Labour MPs on the lines of 'It had to be said, but I am glad that I didn't say it'. I braved the tea room at breakfast next morning. No hostility was detected. The chief whip, Derek Foster, warmly praised me and said how difficult it always is to attack a leader. Another senior whip, George Mudie, stopped at my table, looked to the right and the left, and gave me a bear hug. Others with handshakes, smiles and winks signalled their support. They included members of the shadow cabinet. The role of conscience of the party had been bestowed on me. It was to be mine for a long time.

Tony Blair was then suffering unrelenting mockery from the Tories, attacking him for saying one thing and doing another. His defence was unconvincing. But he was trapped when Harriet Harman committed a mortal sin to trump his venial one. Her son was to go to a grammar school. Blair had talked about not buckling under the pressure of political correctness. Harriet spoke of the iron law of parenting and of getting the best for her children. What I said at the next PLP was never leaked to the press. I read out an extract from a letter a 77-year-old constituent of mine sent to Harriet: 'Surely you should know that getting special privileges for your son was a gift to the Tory camp? Why are the hopes and aspirations of millions of ordinary folk secondary to the short-term advantages of your family?'

I suggested to Harriet at another meeting of the PLP that one of the iron laws of Labour was not to secure the best for your children at the price of depriving other children. I told Tony, 'It's fine not to buckle, when you're right, but it is mulish stubbornness not to do so when you're wrong.' I asked them whether they had lost touch, 'isolated in a golden circle of beautiful people, bound together with ties of mutual admiration around their leader'. In reply Blair said he would stand by her. He could not sack her without exposing himself. She should have resigned. Frustrated about what was happening, I wrote a letter to the *Guardian* in code that was impenetrable except to cognoscenti. They published it under the title 'Midwich Socialists':

> I have a nightmare. If an alien force wishes to take over a country, they could grow alien beings in veal crates in public schools, feed them a special diet that made them beautiful and ambitious but stunted their idealism. They then would be placed as an incubus inside a political party that would love and reward them with applause and high office. Sometimes the deception would falter, on an issue such as school choice, and the party may suspect that these beings are aliens in the party, but not of the party. Too late, the Midwich Socialists would get so strong that they would destroy their host party. But it's only a nightmare, isn't it?

Alan Simpson told me he enjoyed the humour. But the situation was not funny. Our party was being colonised by a Thatcherite succubus.

More treasured Labour policies were under siege from the Blairites within. In September shadow minister Kim Howells made the first of two hugely damaging outbursts. He said he did not believe in the 'Balkanisation of Britain, nor paying extra taxes that could result from devolution'. Worst of all was his comment that Labour's enthusiasm for devolution would decline if we won the general election handsomely.

All the Tories' most damaging arguments against devolution were being mouthed by Labour's spokesperson on the constitution. In September 1995 I wrote to Tony Blair emphasising that despite the compromise decision to support a weak assembly for Wales instead of a Scottish-style parliament, no Welsh MP had stepped out of line, until Kim's rant.

In my letter I wrote:

> Kim has done nothing to promote the agreed policy. But he was
> undermining it by echoing Tory propaganda. As I had resigned from
> the frontbench partly because of restrictions it placed on me, I believe
> Kim should take the same step. The choice is to be inside or outside
> the tent. Kim chose the best of both worlds and claims his right to pee
> on our policies from inside the tent.

No reply was ever received. Kim was allowed to continue to rampage,
bewitched by Midwich Socialism. He was continuing his lifelong role as
a banner carrier. There is always someone who wants to elbow their way
to the front of the procession in order to carry the banner. As a student
Kim had been a revolutionary. When he became an NUM official he did
the fashionable thing and joined the Communist Party. The left wing MEP
Llew Smith recalled with bitterness sharing a platform with Kim during
the miners' strike. Kim's contribution was an endless diatribe against
the Labour Party. That did not stop him from joining the party when
parliamentary ambitions stirred. As a born-again New Labour acolyte, he
became newer than anyone else. He was handed the banner of Blairism.

But it was also Blair who was shedding the image that gave him the
leadership of the party. He supported Kim in that the party should no
longer use the word 'socialist'. Kim intrigued his friends even more
by his espousal of what he called 'Christian values'. This was no mere
conversion. It was the full lobotomy.

As Harriet refused to jump I tried to give the party the chance to
push her without an obvious sacking. Not knowing, in early 1996,
when the general election might come, it was possible that the existing
shadow cabinet would never face a vote. If Major went to the country
in the autumn of 1996, the general election would save Harriet. I put a
motion down for the PLP that the shadow cabinet elections should be
in July 1996. I was told that Blair informed the shadow cabinet, 'I am not
shifting the date just because Paul Flynn wants it.' What followed was an
extraordinary display of control freakery in overdrive.

There were compelling reasons for getting the shadow cabinet elections out of the way before the summer recess and the conference season. In the PLP debate I tried to make the case on the grounds of party advantage. The meeting had been rigged by the whips who had organised a mass attendance. When the debate was coming to an end and the vote was due, whips were dispatched to drag trusty Blairites out of committees. This was the pre-pager era. Only trusties were summoned. Usual suspects such as Jean Corston and Chris Mullin were not called to vote. They would probably have supported my motion. The vote was inevitably lost. But that was not the end of the story. My fragile loyalty to New Labour was to be frequently strained.

From the date of Blair's election as Labour leader in July 1994 until polling day in 1997 I was certain of victory. Although I am not a betting man, I took a £100 wager with journalist Peter Oborne that Labour would win the general election with a majority of more than 120.

Two months before the election I had an unexpected shock. It was in the Commons chamber following PM's Question Time. Shadow cabinet member Ron Davies made his way across the back benches to where I was sitting. He whispered confidentially, 'Roy Hughes is standing down.' My celebration was instant and overpowering. I had long dreamed of his disappearance from the Newport East seat. Almost any replacement would be an improvement.

Ron's next comment was intriguing. 'You have always been well disposed towards Alan Howarth, haven't you?' Yes I had. When he crossed the floor I publicly welcomed him and sent him a friendly note. We shared many debates on social security. As a former Tory minister he condemned from their benches the Jobseekers Bill as a recipe for 'seek and ye shall not find'. I was sworn to secrecy. Roy Hughes did not mention the subject at a meeting of the Welsh group of MPs that evening. He had other things on his mind. That night he was off to India to find a few more invaluable facts to help the people of Newport East in the final weeks of his service to them.

The following morning's papers broke the story. They forecast that

Alan Howarth was to be imposed on the seat. Although I was a friend of Alan, imposing him would not be right. I had a word with John Prescott as deputy leader. He said he had agreed that Alan Howarth could break the rule and become a Labour candidate even though he had not been a member of the party for two years. But he assured me, 'There is a condition that he is never imposed on a constituency.'

That seemed reasonable but I was not prepared for the subtleties of New Labour candidate-fixing. There was to be a selection. But it was cleverly engineered with techniques that were to become familiar later. All strong local candidates, including future Welsh Assembly Member Rosemary Butler, future minister Kevin Brennan and local trade unionist Mike Smith, were eliminated from the shortlist of four selected by a panel in London under Blairite control. Only Alan Howarth had a chance of being selected. The other three on the shortlist were doomed. Local man Reg Kelly had twice bravely challenged Roy Hughes as the sitting MP. That had left him with many constituency enemies. Bryan Davies had lost the neighbouring Newport West seat in 1983 and then failed to be reselected for 1987. Newport East would not have their neighbours' cast-offs thrust on them. Future MP Helen Jones kept asking, 'What the hell am I doing here? Why was I shortlisted?' 'Because you're the token woman candidate' was the answer no one wanted to give her.

The big beasts of Newport Council and the Newport East party were summoned to meet Tony Blair. They were told that Howarth was best for the party. The constituency that had given twenty-five years of loyalty to Roy Hughes had a Hobson's choice. Alan Howarth was selected with a large majority, to the astonishment of Roy Hughes himself. He had predicted that Newport East would never pick a former Tory.

Roy later revealed that, after he had hinted that he was prepared to stand down, 'they came at me like elephants'. Of course, there was a peerage in the deal for the future Lord Islwyn as the price for abandoning his local party and constituents. Well-founded local and national cynicism was expressed. Arthur Scargill offered himself as a Socialist Labour Party candidate at the election in May 1997. My antagonism to the New Labour stitch-up was eclipsed by my contempt for the dishonest impossibilist promises of Scargill. My fear was that a substantial vote for Arthur would split the Labour vote and allow the Tories to win. He had to be resisted.

Even though I had an election to win in my own constituency, I attended all Scargill's public meetings. I asked him whether he accepted any responsibility for the collapse of the mining industry under his presidency. He lived in a dream world that had no discernible link with real politics. Like Mrs Merton he brought his own audience with him to public meetings. A few were genuine local voters. Most were well-known members of south Wales's far-left groups. Theological differences among the left-wing sects ensured that most of those disagreed with Arthur's Socialist Labour Party. At one meeting he called me a liar and said that not all Labour MPs were against him. By a hair's breadth he saved his deposit. But he lost his temper with journalists at the election count. 'You've ignored me throughout the campaign; I'll ignore you now.' The result was humiliating and his graceless speech was booed.

On the other side of Newport, we were enjoying an incredible fun-filled campaign. If the entire Newport West party and I had gone off on holiday for the 1997 election campaign we would have still won a resounding victory. Agent David Mayer and secretary Mark Whitcutt crafted another skilful campaign. But it was the Tory candidate Peter Clarke who secured our record-breaking victory.

A few days after he was adopted I raised a point of order in the Commons about an article that Peter had written in the Scottish edition of the *Sunday Times*:

> Madam Speaker. Erskine May makes clear your powers to summon here those who besmirch the good names of members. Have you read the attack on the Secretary of State for Wales [William Hague] in which he was unfairly described as deluded and simple? For his fine work in bringing 6,000 Korean jobs to Wales he was accused of pimping for Britain? Will you now call to the bar of the House and insist on an apology from the Conservative candidate for Newport West?

In retrospect Peter was correct in much of his criticism of Hague. But he had committed the political mortal sin of being right too early. There were better things to come from the colourful Mr Clarke. He had been a candidate before. Standing in East Lothian in 1987 he advocated declaring war on South Africa, the privatisation of police and fire brigades, lowering the school leaving age to twelve, ending all dole or social security payments, the abolition of all local councils, a tax on golf and the demolition of all unsold council houses. He said that 'General Pinochet must be our inspiration' and that 'Enoch Powell is the greatest Welshman of all time'. He described Mrs Thatcher's conduct on the Anglo-Irish Agreement as treacherous and foolish and threatened to stand as an Orangeman's candidate in East Lothian. He also volunteered to serve in the American cavalry. They rejected him.

There was only one public election debate, at St Mark's Church in the heart of Newport. Arthur Scargill was one of the speakers. Arthur's plan to double pensions on the first Thursday of a Socialist government seemed measured and reasonable compared with Clarke's novel remedy. His answer to pensioner poverty was 'to ship all the pensioners to Eritrea'. The audience was white faced with shock. Future Monmouth Tory MP David Davies was in the audience and recalls the trauma of disbelief he suffered. Peter kindly explained to us that we were not thinking laterally. Living in Newport on £60 a week was poverty. In Eritrea pensioners on the same income could afford the best mud hut in the village or the finest meal of locusts that money could buy.

He rang me a week before the poll asking me out to dinner on the evening before polling day. Gently I explained that my hard-working canvassers would not understand if I was wining and dining the Tory candidate while they were slaving away knocking on doors. He moaned that life was unbearable in the Conservative Party office, 'surrounded by octogenarian ladies reminiscing about canvassing for Stanley Baldwin'.

In Wales on Sunday 27 April, four days before polling day, Peter Clarke complained that he had been the victim of menacing phone calls. They were the latest in a series of incidents since he'd helped fund a manifesto produced by Scottish Conservative Students that advocated a relaxation of the incest laws. *Wales on Sunday* quoted his saying, 'Malicious and unfounded allegations that I am a paedophile have followed me around ever since. The reason I am standing in Newport is that I am barred from standing in Scotland, where I am from, because of these malicious allegations.' My campaign team read *Wales on Sunday* at our routine meeting on 27 April. Many of our team decamped for the rest of the week to the marginal seat of Monmouth.

The Labour majority doubled in Newport West to 14,800. The Tories suffered their lowest vote since 1925. Monmouth was gained from Tory Roger Evans. Thanks, Peter. In spite of my impassioned entreaties, Newport Tories never again selected Peter Clarke as my opponent. For the next two elections in 2001 and 2005 the choice was a local doctor. The Tory slogan was that he was 'a real Doctor not a Spin Doctor'. It was cruelly graffitied with the words 'So was Doctor Shipman'.

I had another stroke of luck in 2001 with a phone call from one of my heroes, the playwright David Hare. He wanted to write an article about my campaign. Stage struck but appreciative, I assured him that my campaign was so relaxed that there was nothing to write about. Of course, I would be very happy to meet him and show him the joys of Newport. His piece in the *Daily Telegraph* was very kind and flattering. It was titled 'The laid-back passion of a Labour MP who thinks for himself'. He wrote:

> I've always thought 'colourful backbencher' the two most heart-sinking words in the English language. Hear them and at once you see a whisky-breathed racist from club-land or a woman in a pleated skirt who wants to bring back hanging, and, yes, she would be willing to tie the noose herself.
>
> When I contacted Paul Flynn, author of *Commons Knowledge* and Labour member for Newport West since 1987, to ask if I may watch him campaign in his constituency, he has to explain that he doesn't actually campaign in the normal sense of the word.
>
> His office, for instance, is in his front room, and is operated chiefly from an Apple Mac. 'Most campaigning is the politics of futility. The

great majority have made up their mind. I refuse to insult them by pretending that three words from me are going to have an effect.

'Charles Kennedy is flying up and down the country preaching about the environment from a jet plane. How hypocritical can you get? I prefer to send everyone a brief letter – I don't mention New Labour, ours is a free-standing campaign – and I tell them that, if they want to know more, they can read the half-million words on my website.

'To the young I say, "Look, twenty Chartists died in John Frost Square in Newport, trying to set up a republic. Doesn't matter who you vote for. Just vote."'

Flynn's approach, at once passionate – he's wonderful on Star Wars – and laid back, may well be shaped by his 14,537 majority. But his independence of mind goes back to the age of 10, when he campaigned in his home town of Cardiff in the 1945 election for Jim Callaghan.

His formative crisis with New Labour came over Tony Blair and Harriet Harman's choice of schools for their children. 'It's a lack of understanding of what the party felt. It's the lack of real instinct. Same with pensions. People have paid their dues all their lives, they've paid their contribution at the rate of inflation for 50 years. But then their pension comes at a derisory level, which doesn't reflect what they've put in. You can't get across to Blair that they don't then want the stigma of having to fill in forms, going cap in hand for income support. You can't get it across because it's not his own experience.

'So, yes, over the school thing, I did think of packing in politics. I asked myself the question: is there enough difference between us and the Tories? And the surprise has been, yes there is.

'I've been pleased. The minimum wage. Whatever the taxes are called, they've been beneficial. There's been a real redistribution of wealth, though of course we're not allowed to say so. The rich have stayed rich – they always do – but the bottom 10 per cent have increased their income by 12 per cent.'

The Prime Minister, Flynn says, could have avoided all the worst humiliations of the past four years if he had listened to his own backbenchers. Only one per cent of them favoured the Dome, and even fewer backed the 75p pension rise and the attempt to rig devolution with place-men.

But, surely, I say, this must only add to the frustration? What are the concrete achievements? 'Well, we did stop the Mode of Trial Bill, which would have limited the right to trial by jury. I am pleased to say Bob Marshall-Andrews completely outwitted Jack Straw intellectually in debate.'

As we walk round the lovely village of Caerleon-on-Usk, I tell Flynn that, for my sake, he must put his principles aside and approach an actual voter. The chosen victim admits reluctantly that he's going to vote Lib Dem. 'Good for you,' Flynn says. 'They're very good people.'

Reluctantly, I take colourful backbenchers off my hate list. The election?

People say it must be a busy time for you, I say. 'No, I'm looking forward to it for a rest. I'll sleep in my own bed. I don't have to listen to Eric Forth talking nonsense at four o'clock in the morning.'

A friendly article in the Tory *Telegraph* was an undreamed-of bonus. Although my majority dropped from the heady 14,537, it was still a reassuring, heart-warming 9,304 in the former Tory seat. Thank you, David Hare.

18

Preened by baboons

My childhood roots had bound me inextricably to the Labour Party, but as a Welsh-speaking sixth-former I had been increasingly drawn to the nationalist wing of Labour. There was a lively Irish anti-partition group in Cardiff and there were natural alliances between socialists and Irish and Welsh nationalists. All were represented at a 'Parliament for Wales' rally held in the Castle Grounds in Cardiff in 1951. The march through the streets to the traditional site of the Welsh Parliament, where the Welsh Office was later built, was an inspiration for an idealistic sixteen-year-old. The Labour Party banner under which I marched read '*Senedd i Gymru*' (A Parliament for Wales). It did not read, 'An Assembly for Wales' or 'a Half-arsed Parliament for Wales' or even 'Elcos for the People'.

In a century and a half of Welsh history, Welsh politicians would promise to fight for Welsh autonomy when campaigning in Wales. All betrayed Wales once they got to Westminster. In hindsight, I recognise that we devolutionists have lost out twice. We feared that a new referendum would repeat the calamity of 1979. Then the polls had pointed towards a victory but devolution was buried by a four to one vote against. A deal was now done. The parliamentary Welsh devolutionists settled for a half-arsed parliament in exchange for a promise that it would not be subject to a referendum that might again have delivered no parliament. An embryo parliament was better than nothing. We were to be double crossed.

On a Wednesday morning towards the end of June 1996 a bombshell burst. There were a few newspaper stories that Blair was to announce a new policy of holding referendums on devolution. The previous evening there had been a meeting of the Welsh group of Labour MPs. Our leader, Ron Davies, left early to see Blair. Ron had recently vehemently denied that there would be a referendum on Wales.

On the Wednesday morning I faxed Tony Blair with the message that, if it were true that there was to be a new referendum on Welsh devolution, my loyalty to him and to New Labour would be at an end. I accused him of naked hypocrisy and opportunism. At 11.30 there was a meeting of the Parliamentary Labour Party addressed by Blair. In a question I made the same point, demanding that if the *Independent* newspaper knew about the referendum, why didn't the PLP? Blair refused to reply and said through the chairman (Doug Hoyle) that there would be an announcement later that day.

Ron Davies spent the evening performing cartwheels before the media trying to convince them that it was his idea. Their derision was understandable. It was one of the most severe blows of my political life. Like the dozen other 'Parliament for Wales' supporters among Welsh Labour MPs I felt personally betrayed. We had agreed an unsatisfactory compromise to accept a 'half-parliament' on the condition that it would be part of the manifesto, not subject to another consultation.

Now, without any discussion with Welsh frontbenchers, MPs or party groups, the policy had been dumped. Wales was ripe to be divided again by those who played on every difference of language or geography. It would be the people of Wales against the Welsh establishments again. In the 1979 referendum, Labour was divided, they ruled.

For more than a century the hopes of Wales had been sabotaged by English politicians, by our own Welsh quislings seduced by Westminster, or by internal jealousies. Who had betrayed Wales this time? Was it the voices of the anti-devolutionist MPs who were close to Blair? Whatever the truth, the lesson was that Blair had contempt for the mass of Welsh and Scottish MPs and for our shadow secretary of state, Ron Davies. There had to be some protest. John McAllion, the best of the Scottish frontbench team, resigned. Had Ron Davies resigned, whoever replaced him would not have been an improvement. So disturbed was Blair's judgement it could have been the candidate from hell, the anti-devolutionist Kim Howells.

At my request I had a meeting with the Chief Whip, Donald Dewar, to discuss resigning the whip. That is the ultimate protest. It would have placed me outside of the Labour group in the Commons. Before taking any action, I would debate it with my faithful party members in Newport. Donald and I had an undisturbed hour because England and Germany were playing a football match in which neither of us had a national interest. He was civilised and kind and understood my point of view. He urged me, whatever I did, not to damage the party's interest.

I decided not to make any terminal moves for a week. I would do two interviews with journalists I respected so that I could control the contents – with the *Observer* and Radio Four's *Today* programme. The *Observer* printed the article on their front page, quoting me saying, 'The Labour Party has now travelled to the right of the Liberal Democrats. If we carry in this direction for a year or two we will be to the right of the Tories. I am totally hostile to the concept of New Labour.' It went on to quote me saying that Blair was no longer behaving like the leader of a democratic party, 'he is autocratic and arrogant'.

My interview with James Naughtie was the first item on Monday's *Today* programme after the 7.00 a.m. news. I was told that my answer to his first question lasted two minutes. I did pay tribute to many of Blair's virtues in making Labour electable by removing the fear of Labour from the minds of many voters. On a roll and genuinely angry, I raged on: 'We are producing policy documents which are timid and anaemic. They don't rejoice in the achievements of our party. Because of the fear of upsetting the tabloid press we produce policies that are not radical but reflect the prejudices of the Tory Party. Tony Blair seems to believe that he is omnipotent.'

The interviews became the first item on every radio and television news bulletin. Having settled the strategy I lay low in my office and refused further interviews. Television crews begged me to leave the building so that they could take walking shots of me. If I had done that, they would have tried to interview me. The effect would have multiplied the publicity. In any case, I avoid limping shots of my uncertain arthritic gait.

Ron Davies came across to my office as an emissary from Blair. He said that he had never seen Blair so angry. I told him that I had done all I intended to do and I would not give any more interviews. I did not want the party to spend its energy in possibly protracted expulsion procedures, and that I had already written out my resignation from the Parliamentary Labour Party. I invited him to pass it on to the Chief Whip. But it was still my intention to stand in the general election in some capacity. Ron said that expulsion from the party was the nuclear option and that it need not come to that.

Publicity is impossible to control and depends on other news. That Monday happened to be a light news day. Steve Bell's cartoon in the *Guardian* next morning showed Blair as Louis XIV saying, 'Autocratic, Moi?' It was upsetting that my actions were causing the party so much damage. The genie was now out of the bottle and it had grown into a monstrous uncontrollable beast. I still hoped it might do some good in restraining Blair from future excesses.

The party machine moved into top gear to destroy my views. Ron Davies said that my claim that he was given a 'resign or accept' option was a complete fabrication. Implausibly he said he had prior knowledge of the decision. The only defence I could make to the accusation that I was a liar was to throw the charge back at Ron. That would lengthen the row and deepen the hurt. Anyway, I had given an undertaking of silence. Later I was to learn that Ron's veracity was malleable. But for the moment, I trusted him.

A researcher in the party's London headquarters told me the only activity that day was to urge Blairites in all corners of the country to write letters to the papers condemning me. That was borne out – letters to me personally divided ten to one in my favour, letters to the paper split five to one in Blair's favour. *Newsnight* carried an item on it. Friend and foe in the lobby told me that my constituency chairman (the future Welsh Assembly minister John Griffiths) 'did you proud'.

The only way I knew to survive the torment of such a day was to wrap the nerve endings up in work. Matthew Parris in *The Times* entertainingly described my entrance into the chamber:

> His arrival triggered strange and ambiguous body language in colleagues, some shifting uneasily, others attempting frightened little pats to his shoulder or half-snuggles-up in his direction. Anthropologists studying such behaviour among baboons would note this tangle of admiration and anxiety, concluding that we were witnessing tentative early approaches to a junior ape who had dared challenge an unpopular but feared senior.

Tony Blair called a meeting of Welsh MPs exactly a week after he had announced the decision. It was a dreadful experience. A few did speak to Tony Blair as though he were an equal colleague, principally Denzil Davies, Ann Clwyd and Ted Rowlands. The majority addressed him as a minor deity. The baboons were preening the leader. It was the only time since the devolution referendum of 1979 that I felt such a sense of shame.

Who were these grovelling lickspittles? I had long respected most of my fellow Welsh MPs as tough resourceful characters. They have all fought their way to Parliament. Here they were, star-struck, seduced, cowardly and grovelling. The elected representatives of the people of Wales had been dealt a contemptuous insult. There was little fight left in most of them. Had they all had their backbones removed? Their plea was, 'Yes. You have just walked over us, Tony, would you like us to lie down, so that you can do it again?' Once again, shame was the spur to undo the injustice that my party had visited on my country.

So many were not thinking of their country, their constituency or the values of the party that had sustained their election. Their minds were on places in the Lords, office in the next government or gifts of major and minor patronage. It was good to escape the shadow cabinet room and the stench of sycophantic hypocrisy. I longed to breathe fresh clean air. I looked forward to returning to the Newport party where we spoke the truth to one another. The key body in any constituency Labour

Party is the General Management Committee. Newport West's GMC was unique. It met every fortnight, more frequently than any of the 650 other constituencies in Britain. This was an advantage because I had reported fully to them my increasing disillusionment with New Labour and disintegrating relations with Blair.

All party members are entitled to attend its meetings. At the Friday meeting about a hundred members turned up. I was upset and anxious. What I had to say was the most important message I have ever given to them. I reminded them of the promise I made when they first selected me, that I would never deceive them and always tell them the truth. I told them, 'I believe we will win the next election, but we will lose the party.'

Some members had come to bury me. At least one aspirant replacement candidate had been drumming up support. A senior respected figure in the party, my saintly mentor Aubrey Hames was genuinely upset and told me so. The great majority spoke with warmth and understanding. Newport West is a very close family. This was the best of the many evenings in my life when I was grateful to represent my comrades in Newport West.

Shadow cabinet elections were duly held in July 1996 and Blair had a plan to restrict the candidates to the Blair slate to avoid any divisive election. For the first time ever I decided to stand. By chance I bumped into Blair on the terrace. 'Ask him to vote for you,' said Ron Davies. I did, reminding Blair that I had supported him for leader. 'What are you standing for?' he asked, genuinely puzzled. It was the first he had heard that anyone was out to spoil his plans. The terrace of the Commons in the summer is a very public place. Stories of the encounter were soon winging their way around the Commons and into newspaper diaries.

Other names were then put forward. The week before the vote I spoke against the increase in MPs' salaries. With Chris Mullin and Alan Simpson, I moved that MPs' wages should be linked to the level of the basic pension. If pensioners got a 1 per cent rise, so should MPs. If MPs had 28 per cent so should pensioners. That would certainly concentrate the attention of MPs on the shrinking total of the basic pension. Great idea, but not one to win me support from my fellow MPs. Having sought to reduce wages and challenge Blair's decision to avoid a vote, I was not optimistic about my likely tally.

My most reliable friend and adviser Sam said, 'Prepare yourself for a result that will be somewhere between humiliation and total humiliation.' I put out a press release explaining why I was standing for the shadow cabinet and saying that any votes I received beyond two I would regard as a triumph.

The result was a great relief, possibly a minor victory, with sixty-one votes. Ann Clwyd was nearly elected with ninety votes but most losing challengers scored thirty or forty. My close friend Nick Ainger, who had previously told me I was courting ignominy, agreed the result was a temporary draw in my battle with Blair.

The September 1997 referendum approved an assembly for Wales by the smallest of margins. It was not the parliament we had yearned for, but it was the beginning of one. I endured a tormenting night in a BBC Wales studio commenting on the referendum result. The company of future Lleferydd (Speaker) of the Welsh Assembly Dafydd Elis Thomas and the future leader of the Welsh Lib Dems Kirsty Williams was stimulating and comradely. The 'No to the Assembly' vote maintained a lead through the long, bleak hours of the night. As dawn broke the Carmarthen result arrived. It gave the 'Yes' campaign a slender lead. Our studio was suffused with happiness. There were tears, laughter and hugs. Shame was replaced by pride.

The celebrations were brief. Dark days were ahead. What followed became a titanic struggle for the leadership of the Welsh nation. Starting with a walk on the wild side, it involved good people behaving badly, one-legged ducks, seismic election defeats, mass treachery and rigged votes, and ended with a biblical confession.

The two gladiators were both good ethical politicians who have been friends of mine for forty years. Alun Michael is an incurable do-gooder, high on detail, low on humour. He is earnest, predictable, irrationally ambitious, tetchy when provoked, a workaholic and a serial father (five children). At 3.00 one morning I was woken up by the sound of hammering from Alun's bedroom in the flat we shared. He was building a desk, because he had 'no other time to do it'.

Rhodri Morgan is a unique political phenomenon. Ideas, jokes and solutions Catherine-wheel off in a shower of iridescent brilliance. To Tony Blair, he was an unguided rocket: too unpredictable, too untidy, too original, too clever and far too Welsh.

The most wounding lesson in Welsh history is the treachery of our past leaders. Over the last 150 years, a succession of politicians left Wales for London with the promise of home rule on their lips. Seduced by Westminster and the trappings of power, none had delivered. Now, for the first time since the fifteenth century, we were about to have our own ruling body on the soil of our own country. Who would lead the nation ... Llywelyn Ein Llyw Olaf, Owen Glyndwr, Robert Owen, Emrys ap Iwan, Aneurin Bevan and, now, Rhodri or Alun?

I was in a hotel in Tel Aviv watching a group of Hungarian folk dancers when the warning thunderbolt struck. My wife Sam announced, 'Sky TV says Alun Michael is Secretary of State for Wales following the demise of Ron Davies.'

'He's dead?' I spluttered.

'No, it's probably worse than that', Sam replied.

I snorted in disbelief at the news reports, 'Gay sex? Ron, gay?' This is a man I had known as a close and trusted friend for twenty years. Heterosexual sex, possibly. But not homosexual. Even in the fetid testosterone-overloaded world of Westminster, I never heard any serious accusations that Ron was playing away from home. The story as reported was that Ron 'was out strolling on Clapham Common. He met a Rastafarian stranger. Ron, the Secretary of State for Wales, found much to talk about with someone whose job was acquiring boys and women for clients. They went for a meal and spent the next two hours together.'

Ron said there was no sex or drugs involved. Huh? Then he was robbed and now he had lost his job. Tough on crime and the victims of crime? The accepted wisdom in announcing bad news is 'Tell it soon, tell it all, tell it truthfully'. Ron did not get beyond telling it soon.

The settled Welsh political landscape heaved and became

unrecognisable. This was to be Welsh Labour's foulest hour. Another leader for the Assembly had to be found and New Labour decided that Alun Michael was to be the chosen one. They refined fresh principles for the coming stitch-up. These were the basic nostrums:

- Truth is the opinion of the majority and changes daily.
- A promise is infinitely malleable.
- Rights are the servants of expediency.
- Knowledge, intelligence and originality are diversions from the truth.
- Election results are decided by leaders, not electorates.
- Everything can be bought, including loyalty and faith.
- A pledge is for elections, not for a full term.
- Love of democracy is the enemy of efficiency.
- Select the desired outcome and adjust your principles to achieve it.
- Election cheating is no gamble: winners write history.
- The wages of sin are bounteous and sometimes paid in ermine.
- The loyalty that is most admirable is loyalty to superiors.
- Between error and truth, chaos and order, sin and virtue, lies the Third Way.

In September 1998 Ron Davies as Blair's Secretary of State for Wales stood and won the leadership of the Welsh Assembly-in-waiting, against Rhodri Morgan. The electorate comprised Welsh Labour Party members, unions, affiliated organisations, and Labour Assembly candidates, MPs and MEPs.

I had supported Ron, as the architect of Welsh devolution. After Ron's catastrophic 'walk on the wild side', Rhodri was my choice against Alun Michael. I had always liked and admired Alun. As an old friend, I had been pleased that he had landed his dream job at the Home Office. But the job of leader of the Welsh Assembly would have been a move for the worse for Alun. I pleaded with him to change his mind and not stand for the leadership.

Tony Blair had the unchallenged right to appoint Alun to his cabinet. But he had no right to appoint the Labour leader in Wales. That is the job of the people of Wales. 'It's a process called devolution,' I helpfully reminded Alun. The Welsh group of Labour MPs was already seething because of Tony Blair's autocratic behaviour. A fine Welsh Office minister, Win Griffiths, had been peremptorily sacked. Two Welsh MEPs had been dumped in favour of an unknown Blair loyalist who had been rejected by his English constituency. Was Blair about to anoint Alun in defiance of Welsh opinion?

Newsnight introduced the two protagonists to the nation. Jeremy Paxman asked Rhodri if he was standing as a candidate for the Labour leadership. Rhodri said, 'Does a one-legged duck swim in circles?' Mr Paxman asked, 'Is that the Welsh for yes?' In defence of his comment, Rhodri later added, 'I also understand that the Pope is indeed a Catholic and that the arboreal dwelling creatures of the family *Ursidae* are not known to be users of the flush toilet.'

Paxman's questions to Alun were hostile but reasonable. Alun was tense, argumentative, repetitive and woefully unconvincing. The final image that lodged in the viewers' minds: Alun answered Jeremy's closing 'Thank you, Mr Michael' with a snarling, sarcastic 'AND THANK YOU, TOO!' He tore off his lapel microphone, flung it away and flounced out of the picture.

Proving that one side still had their sense of humour a spoof letter was sent to Peter Hain, 'signed' by Peter Mandelson:

> Tony is worried that Alun is stuck up sludge creek in a leaky coracle. Perhaps you should pass him the barge-pole that you wouldn't touch this job with?
>
> Get rid of the suntan, Pete. Standing next to you, Alun looks even more like a corpse. Rhodri has not only swallowed all this bollocks about democracy, he has persuaded some of the Taffies to do the same. Do your best Pete; otherwise you will make us a laughing stock. As you know, that is *my* job.
>
> Regards, Peter.

Downing Street twitched and fidgeted at the prospect of a Welsh leader whose brain impulses could not be pre-determined into orderly submission to New Labour's nostrums. The party did not have the appetite for a divisive election. I was sparring on Radio 4's *Today* programme with one of Labour's old warhorses, George Wright, the gauleiter of the TGWU in Wales. George had backed a 'Team Ticket' that would put Alun in charge with Rhodri and Wayne David as his deputies. To John Humphrys on the *Today* programme, I argued that a divisive election for the leader of the Labour Group in the Welsh Assembly could be avoided if Rhodri was acknowledged as the choice of the people of Wales. I got my planned soundbite in: 'Alun is London's choice, New Labour; Rhodri is Wales's choice, True Labour.'

Every opinion poll of party members and the public gave Rhodri a huge lead with up to three quarters of the vote. Rhodri had been denied promotion by Blair because he did not fit the New Labour Party mould. Tony Blair's excuse for not making Rhodri a minister in 1997 was that he lacked ministerial experience. Rhodri hit back and told Tony in 10 Downing Street that 'if ministerial experience was the prime qualification, Margaret Beckett should have been sitting in that chair, not you'.

In the collective mind of the national media the image of the contest was beginning to form. Alun was being parachuted into Wales. Alun was Blair's poodle. Rhodri was the Welsh-bred dragon. Rhodri's version sat comfortably with the hacks' accurately cynical view of politics. For perhaps the first time, the Downing Street spinners had been out-spun. Almost all UK national papers carried cartoons depicting the dragon and the parachuted sheep or poodle. The images became indelible.

Alun's campaign team was the payroll vote of Blair acolytes and union leaders with hopes of gongs or places in the Lords. They combined the worst bullying tactics of old Labour trade union bosses with the power-greed of New Labour control-freakery. The stitchers were threading their needles. It was not a single stitch-up, more a vast blanket woven from thousands of minor stitch-ups, weaved together in every corner of Wales. A large number of union staff, computers and fax machines were beavering away to serve their favourite son. Even though Rhodri had clever resourceful staff, his was a penny-farthing operation compared with Alun's lavishly staffed and funded Rolls-Royce. Rules had been agreed to ensure that an internal Labour election was contested on a fair basis. The rules were shamelessly and repeatedly violated.

Both *Dispatches* and *Panorama* featured the hapless George Wright floundering on why he intended to cast 100 per cent of his members' votes for Alun when a poll proved that 75 per cent of them supported Rhodri. George had not attempted to achieve even the North Korean mockery of democracy. In his case, it was not one member, one vote, but one member, 53,000 votes. George was that one member. Alun was amassing a rotten borough pile of votes from the 'Fixers and Riggers Unions'.

The media backed the colourful Rhodri rather than the anaemic Alun. Only the Blair groupies on the *Daily Mirror* disagreed. They came up with an odd argument in favour of Alun.

> What sort of an Assembly do you think Wales should have? Should it be simply a talking shop? Or should it be a proper working body, which tackles the problems of the Welsh people? On that basis there is only one answer – ALUN MICHAEL.

That is code for 'Alun does not speak as well as Rhodri'. To avoid a talking shop, select the poorest speaker.

University professor Kevin Morgan and lobbyist Leighton Andrews stated their preferences in the *Western Mail*. Kevin Morgan said trying to impose Alun without a vote proved that 'the patronage state is alive' in Wales. 'Devolution is worthless', he suggested, 'if it doesn't allow us to make our choice of leader without fear, favour and pressure from London.' Reflecting an opinion poll result that reported that Rhodri would swell Labour's vote by 9 per cent, Kevin argued that 'Rhodri has the capacity to enthuse and mobilise the Labour Party and the wider electorate'.

Leighton Andrews's curious article tried to smother the campaign with a layer of induced boredom. Rhodri was accused of the sin of originality for his one-legged duck joke. Leighton displayed his own genius as a trail-blazingly original wordsmith by climaxing his praise of Alun with the battle cry 'Nobody does it better'.

Alun had a major problem and I decided to make it worse. He was not a candidate for any Welsh Assembly seat. This was pretty crucial when you hoped to be leader of the new Assembly. The closed panel was reopened for Alun. I and a few others jumped in. In Scotland the party debarred left-winger Dennis Canavan from the list. He stood as an independent and won. A victory for an independent was a shock to the main parties. It was a warning that many old loyalties were crumbling. Wales was soon to experience the wrath of the voters.

Originally, I had decided not to stand for the Assembly. I sought a nomination now only to stop Alun. I announced that I would stand in any constituency where Alun offered himself as a candidate. My hope was to expose his woeful level of support among grassroots members. Personal preferences aside, I was confident that if the choice was between me as True Labour and Alun as New Labour, True Labour would win.

It was a gamble. I could have lost my Westminster seat and become an AM for a part of Wales distant from my beloved Newport. Alun side-stepped democracy and did not offer himself in any constituency seat. He relied on the patronage of the party machine for one of the top-up list seats.

Peter Hain was maniacally optimistic two days before the Assembly election. He handed out hostages to fortune like Smarties at a children's party. No hyperbole was left unsaid. 'The poll is a crushing blow to the other parties,' Peter burbled. 'If the results turn out as we expect it will be seen as a remarkable achievement.' It was certainly going to be remarkable. The next day, Peter was still in triumphalist mood. The day's results were going to be a 'major triumph for the Labour Party'. He was about to learn that twenty-four hours is an eternity in politics.

When the results were announced, all expert forecasts were exposed as follies. Even the *Guardian*'s insightful Matthew Engel had prophesied that 'if Wayne David were to lose the Rhondda, it would be a political earthquake that would bust the seismograph'.

Wayne David had abandoned his Euro meal ticket for life and walked away from the biggest majority in the northern hemisphere to try his luck in the Rhondda. No risk really because, at the previous general election, the Rhondda had the second biggest Labour majority in the UK. A rumour now rippled across Wales. Wayne David was reputed to have uttered, to a consenting friend in private, the chilling words 'I've just lost the Rhondda'.

On the morning of Friday 7 May, Wales Labour fielded three stalwarts of the stitch-up to comment on the results on television as they were announced: Peter Hain, Don Touhig and Glenys Kinnock. These programmes are the modern equivalent to the mediaeval Inquisition. The torture is subtler but more public. The merciless eye of the camera relays to millions all tear-filled eyes, each quivering lip and every downcast face.

Ron Davies was troubled by his slashed majority. But by the time the news came from other pulverised Welsh valley constituencies, Ron's result looked triumphant. Rhodri beamed angelically. Cardiff West had awarded him a vast bouquet of votes – his previously marginal seat had given him the biggest Labour majority in Wales. Perhaps the most eloquent statement of the whole day was the intake of breath by Glenys at the news that Labour had indeed lost the Rhondda. Don Touhig was on mission impossible in dredging up a comforting interpretation of the loss of his own constituency seat of Islwyn by his researcher, Shane Williams.

Wayne David, pale and shocked, was stoical and emotionless. Bookmakers had been offering 20-1 against a Plaid win in Rhondda. The swing there was more than 30 per cent. Torfaen and Llanelli had also astonishingly been lost. No spinning or shape-shifting could obscure the awful truth. A 15–20 per cent swing to Plaid in all seats and Labour's lowest share of the vote since 1983. This was Doomsday, a catastrophe for Labour. Would New Labour now accept that they had done something wrong?

The three television pundits floundered at first. A sane response to these horror results would have been to run sobbing from the set. No, no. Peter Hain was the first to recover. 'I've warned for over a year', said Peter, 'that the Labour Party in Wales shouldn't be complacent about this election.' Welsh broadcaster Betsan Powys deployed some penetrative irony when, with a fetching smile, she asked Peter Hain, 'So, you're losing out of the goodness of your own hearts, then, are you?'

In the following two days, Peter refined his self-justifying alibi. The only consolation was the 'election' of Alun through the assisted places PR scheme. It was a victory bought at high cost. Two Labour seats had been sacrificed to Plaid. In the opening lines of his speech to the Labour Party Conference at Bournemouth in September, Alun described himself as the 'First Ever Democratically Elected Leader of Wales'. Elected? Yes. Democratically? No.

The St David's Hotel in Cardiff was the scene of that leadership result. In the first section, of party members, Rhodri had won 64.4 per cent to Alun's 35.6 per cent. That was the only genuinely democratic vote. Among unions and affiliated organisations Alun won, with 64 per cent to Rhodri's 36 per cent. In the third section, of MPs, MEPS and aspirant Assembly candidates, Alun had 58 per cent to Rhodri's 42 per cent. All unions that had conducted one-member one-vote ballots had voted for Rhodri. Even in the outrageously stuffed third sector he polled a creditable 42 per cent.

Rhodri was hearing the figures for the first time. He was shocked by how close they were to claims made by Alun's camp a week earlier. He was convinced that he had been double-crossed again. He looked relaxed and said, 'I have not won this contest. I don't feel like a loser. A runner-up? Yes. A loser? Never.'

A fire alarm went off and Rhodri joked that it was those one-legged ducks. The laughter had a nervous edge. We were living the dreaded nightmare. Rhodri's friends seethed. We were six weeks away from the election for the first Welsh Assembly. An iron rule of politics is that you do not attack your party at election time. Ron Davies put a brave face on it. 'The party is really one large family.' Rather like the mafia in this case.

Rhodri's friends wanted to climb up to the wing on the top of the St David's Hotel and shout in unison across Cardiff Bay 'STITCH-UP!' Instead we burbled pious platitudes. The truth was forbidden. Thinking was treacherous. Our mouths were glued shut. That night, the Labour Party in Wales was ashamed of itself. We had delivered our own catastrophe.

Two days later the Welsh Grand Committee was meeting in Aberaeron. With all the grace that I could sum up I started my speech with 'Congratulations to the member for Cardiff South on winning the election, and warm congratulations to the member for Cardiff West for winning three out of every four democratic votes cast'. Wise heads were bowed waiting for humiliation.

In electoral terms Rhodri was a positive factor; Alun, a negative one. If Rhodri had been leader, it was a statistical certainty that Labour would have won Llanelli, Rhondda, Islwyn and Conwy. That would have given Labour the overall majority in the Assembly that they failed to achieve. Using the election to boost Alun as leader drove voters into the hands of Plaid. How could the fabled electoral skills of New Labour crash so abjectly? The constituencies identified most closely with Rhodri Morgan and Old Labour had the best results. Those nearest to New Labour had suffered the worst. We had campaigned in the winning seats as Old Labour. Would we now rule as Old Labour?

Not a word of remorse or confession of failure came from New Labour's Cardiff bunker. They faked it. When confronted with disaster, convince everyone else it's a triumph. Alun made a rabble-dejecting speech. Oh, for a one-legged duck.

The opening of the Welsh Assembly was unforgettable. The Llandaff Cathedral service and the Cardiff Bay concert were proof that someone had been thinking anew to create two unique, thrilling and joyous events.

But even in the solemnity of the service, the whiff of the stitch-up lingered. Alun's legitimacy as First Secretary was raised. Amazingly, it came from the lips of Alun himself. Was it sabotage or just a cock-up? Alun's bible reading contained a candid confession. The congregation shuddered at the words. Without a stumble or a blush, he read from the gospel of John, Chapter 15: 'You did not choose me. I chose you.' Amen to that.

The legacy of those awful months is a wreckage of dishonoured principles, ruptured friendships, ruined careers, deep mistrust and new, avoidable enmities. Some of the best in the party were disillusioned and left. Others soldiered on with crushed convictions and hope. The bedrock of our faith in the Labour Party was the certainty that we possessed superior ideals and principles to all other parties. Could this still be true after the party itself had trampled down our cherished values?

There are a number of possible explanations. One is the need of the leadership of the party to control every activity in minute detail. It is a version of democratic centralism, practised with the tedious regimentation of far-left sects. Must it be that one person's will dominates every decision, regardless of the destruction that results? If that is so, it had profound implications for the future of New Labour.

Alun's reign as leader of the Welsh Assembly lasted less than a year. He resigned in February 2000 to avoid a vote of no confidence. The issue was irrelevant. Welsh Labour AMs wanted Rhodri. A group of only five AMs, known as the funeral pyre party, still supported Alun. He resigned his assisted places seat and returned full-time to Westminster. It was time for a new book to chronicle the stitch-up before memories faded. It opened with the words 'Only the future is certain, the past is always changing'.

19

Dragon slayer scorched

Parliamentary privilege is a powerful weapon. It led me into my best and worst parliamentary episodes. Two successful. One ruinous.

Before my election in 1987 there was a hint that a closed power station at Rogerstone in my constituency might be reopened. I gave the news a cautious welcome. It meant jobs and it promised the advantage of environmentally friendly clean-burn coal use. That was a grievous error that cost me votes. The power station was atrociously sited at the bottom of a valley, the sides of which were lined with houses. It was old fashioned, noisy and very smoky when it had been run by the electricity board. In the Rogerstone area of Newport, people rejoiced when it was closed. They cursed me when I saw advantages in reopening it.

My efforts at recanting on the power station were not convincing. That was when, in my first year as MP, Mr Angelo Casfikis came into my life. At his request I met him at the House of Commons. He was a plausible charmer but I told him I was now adamant in my opposition. He pressed ahead with plans to reopen Rogerstone. I began my campaign to stop him. Then manna fell from the sky onto my desk in the form of documents literally in a brown envelope. They revealed scandalous details of the life story of Mr Casfikis. There was never any clue to the source of the information. But I believe the civil servants in the Export Credit Guarantee Department were being helpful.

Casfikis had sought to establish his respectability with an article about himself in the *Sunday Times*. It was a foolish reminder from a man with a name as distinctive as the bottom line of an eye chart. His old enemies beat a path to my office. The information was dynamite. Over twenty years, Casfikis had set up dozens of companies. All went into receivership. Yet from most he had arranged a lifeboat company to make a getaway. He was named as responsible for an £11 million company failure of a bottling factory in Nigeria. A search revealed county court debts littered throughout the country from £1,000 in Epsom to £100,000 in Scotland. The Miners' Union confirmed that he had pocketed national insurance and union contributions deducted from the wages of his mining employees at Cwmllynfell and Godregraig. The Insolvency Service had told me that his mines were £80,000 in the red.

Yet Casfikis had enjoyed great encouragement from government energy ministers whom he had seen at least five times. He boasted that he could pick up a telephone and see a minister within two hours. That's far better access than MPs have. He also had serious backers who were prepared to put up millions to reopen the power station.

In the brief time allowed for an oral question, and under privilege, I described him as 'a man of straw, a business leper to be shunned'. Angelo was unconcerned. He was still bullish about his plans to reopen the station. I applied for parliamentary time to unload my long inventory of his life of serial deception and theft. The 1987 Tory government were still encouraging him, as their first chance to start a new generation of privatised electricity companies.

The Speaker gave me a full half-hour in the chamber in a Friday Adjournment debate. I rang Casfikis to warn him and to give him a chance to refute any of the dirt I had on him. He refused to talk to me but his female assistant said, 'If you mention his conviction for fraud, for which he was heavily fined, would you mention that others were involved in the crime?' I did exactly that, in those precise words. Before she informed me of it I had no knowledge of the fraud conviction. More manna.

The debate was reported with glee by local television. HTV Wales had organised, with my help, a map to illustrate the various parts of the world where he had left his trail of fraud. The *Argus* was fairly generous to

Casfikis. They reported all my allegations, but also his mock indignation and hurt because he had been attacked under privilege. There was no other way. Had I not acted, a clapped-out polluting power station would now be blighting the lives of thousands of my constituents.

My past sins were forgiven in Rogerstone. Copies of the Hansard of the adjournment debate were posted in all the local pubs and clubs. The murky details were relished. From an early error I reached the scale of a mini-hero when Casfikis left Britain. Two years later the twin dominating cooling towers of the power station were dynamited and fell thundering to the ground. The industrial wasteland has gone. The area is now transformed into the very attractive Foxgloves suburb made up of hundreds of new homes, shops and community facilities. Parliamentary privilege had served its purpose.

There was a new dragon to be slain. Researchers from a Welsh current affairs programme *Taro Naw* had long been following the extraordinary business career of Brian Walker. It took some believing. There was incredulity and merriment when I listed his misfortunes in an Early Day Motion (EDM) in Parliament. He was preparing to open a children's Fundome in the heart of my constituency. I asked whether his past safety record proved that he was suitable to have children put into his care. Nine previous companies of his had gone into liquidation. Four of the premises where they were housed had been destroyed by fire. He had debts of more than £1 million from previous ventures and £50,000 was owed to firms in my constituency for the Fundome.

An elderly couple had a flat in premises that he was converting. The husband was nearly blind and he told me how they had been bullied and harassed by Brian Walker to vacate their flat. He twice promised to defend himself against my accusations at press conferences that he called. The press turned up and so did I. But there was no sign of Brian Walker. The Fundome venture was visibly crumbling. It was to be officially opened by the Mayor of Newport. He was grateful to me for sparing him the embarrassment.

Only once did I meet Walker. He produced a semi-literate leaflet denouncing me during the 1992 general election. He confronted me while I was speaking in John Frost Square, brandishing his leaflet and staining the air with whisky fumes. My minder Noel Trigg, a former professional boxing champion, skilfully diverted him by demanding, 'Why didn't you pay the boxers in that promotion you ran?' It worked. Walker was thrown on the defensive. Eight months later he was declared bankrupt and banned from running a business for eleven years. He left Newport.

It was a decade later that I next used privilege. It was morally uplifting but financially disastrous. It started well with an EDM, which enjoyed wide media and MP support including the signature of Vince Cable.

> That this House is appalled by the further impoverishment of victims of endowment mis-selling; applauds the guidance freely available from *Which?* and the Financial Services Authority (FSA) on compensation claims; regrets that the spokesperson for one company failed to mention these free services in her broadcasts last week, nor did she explain that those using her company's services would lose out in commission charges of 21 per cent of any compensation gained; and is alarmed that companies, not controlled by the FSA, are again exploiting endowment victims with excessive charges for services of little or no value.

I had long campaigned against rip-offs in the financial world including endowment mortgages, pension mis-selling, ambulance-chasers and debt-bundling frauds. While I was fireproof in what I said in Parliament, I was open to be sued for what I said outside. A comment attributed to me in a specialist newspaper named *Money Management* went a little beyond the wording of the EDM. It had a tiny circulation of about 5,000 people who were all financially well informed and unlikely to be seeking advice. That was the alleged libel. The firm involved claimed that a wholly accurate comment I made about 'firms charging up to 50 per cent' applied to them. It did not. I had always made clear that companies clawed back *between* 10 per cent and 50 per cent.

Charges of up to 15 per cent were defined as reasonable by *Which?*. The companies I criticised charged between 20 per cent and 50 per cent for advice that was freely available from the websites of *Which?* and the FSA. Those who had already been fleeced through their poor value endowment mortgages were losing large chunks of their compensation for advice that was hardly worth the price of a stamp.

One company, which is no longer trading, set their legal hounds on me. Part of their complaint was reasonable. It was about a couple of sentences on my website that could have been misinterpreted. I removed them immediately. I had better things to do with my time than to engage in a fruitless row.

Then they demanded an apology for the EDM and comments in *Money Management*. I was not responsible for the latter and I suggested that they sue the *Financial Times*, which published *Money Management*. For months I did not treat their threats of legal action seriously. After all, I had done nothing wrong. But their letters were persistent and increasingly strident. I sought legal advice from a solicitor with Labour Party connections. Unfortunately I was not aware that MPs are covered with insurance for legal costs in cases of this kind for sums up to £25,000. Engaging an outside firm invalidated any claim for help from the Commons fund. That proved to be a very expensive oversight.

Convinced of my innocence, I refused to back down. In my judgement, this was an attempt to kill a wholly justified campaign against the exploitation of those who are financially unsophisticated. My solicitor and barrister gave me some encouragement and a few worries. I was advised that I had an 80 per cent chance of winning if the case went to court. But there was no guarantee. It depended on the disposition of the judge and other uncontrollable factors. I could lose. Then the costs could be enormous and I and my family would be ruined.

For a couple of months I did not take the threat seriously. A week before the 2005 general election the news that I was being sued for £300,000 damages was splashed over my local paper. The source of the story was not identified. The motive was certainly to embarrass me and damage my chance of re-election. It may have worked because my majority slumped. The paper printed my defence. It was not helpful. Dirt sticks.

I was still looking forward to my day in court. The issue was clear-cut and I was battling on the side of people who had suffered large financial losses. My solicitors gave me an estimate of costs. They told me I was unfortunate in that the company's solicitors had a reputation for being aggressive and ruthless. My solicitors appeared out of their depth and demoralised against a firm with a ferocious reputation in pursuing writs. Costs were building up rapidly. For sending half a dozen letters each, my solicitors' costs were about £5,000; the other company's were £20,000.

The dire warning was that if the case went to court the cost would rise dramatically, up to half a million, perhaps a million, pounds. I am not a gambler. The costs were being racked up at a rate of £2,000–£5,000 every week. I threw in the towel when they reached £44,000. It was the only way of ending the nightmare. Of course there was no significant damage to the company, although their initial claim was for £300,000. The sum they finally agreed in damages was a relatively trivial £1,000. It was my silence they were seeking. This was pressure by costs. Mine were £10,000. Theirs were £34,000. That was a total bill for me of £45,000.

The Commons authorities and the Inland Revenue accepted that my costs were wholly, exclusively and necessarily incurred through legitimate parliamentary campaigning. That paid my defence costs. It did not help with the damages and the company's costs but the Inland Revenue helped with some of those. I have never regretted my stand although I would handle it in a different way next time. These risks go with the parliamentary territory. I had been burnt but I am proud of the stand I took. The publicity spread the message that ambulance-chasing firms were charging excessively for their services.

I wrote to all MPs warning them of our vulnerability. The value of privilege would be diminished if we could be silenced by the threat of crippling court costs. Dozens wrote back. Many had suffered attempts to silence them with libel threat charges. In spite of the present money-grabbing image of MPs, I have a long list of MPs who lost large sums of money in pursuit of courageous and worthy aims. Some MPs were successful. Many were not.

There have been some changes since. All MPs are now aware of the pitfalls. Parliamentary privilege must be defended. I remain satisfied that I stood up to the pressure for as long as was reasonably possible. Any political damage is long gone, as my constituents now fully understand the situation. All I lost was money. No one should be in politics if their main goal is financial. I emerged from the ordeal poorer, but with my integrity intact and my head held high.

20

Not when, but why

My guru Tony Wright helpfully defined MPs as the Whys and the Whens. The Whens are obsessed with when they will get a job, go on a trip, be recognised as leaders. The Whys seek out the truth and remedies for reform. Campaigns are at the heart of the work of the Whys. The variety of subjects is unpredictable and incredible. From the trivial to the momentous, eliminating injustices informs the backbencher's workload.

The arrest of duck feeders, boxing brain damage, passports for pets, exploitative salespeople, shortage of foxes, nuclear cons, parasites' parasites, greedy farmers, drug-peddlers, lying charities, financial confidence tricksters and even a possible inducement to a party leader have aroused my wrath. I have raged in Latin, Middle English and Welsh to right wrongs. Campaigns have an honoured history. But where are the modern Sidney Silvermans, Peter Freemans or Leo Abses? They challenged the injustices of their days. It was courageous to oppose capital punishment in the 1940s or homophobia in the 1960s. The major reforms of the future will come from the back benches and not from the redtop-enslaved frontbenchers.

A campaign must be capable of practical solution by Parliament and be likely to engage significant public sympathy. The campaigning backbencher is a slayer of dragons or an uplifter of the dispossessed or a boost to the sum of human happiness/safety/ecstasy. In my first week in Parliament I put down an Early Day Motion seeking the use of Welsh in the Welsh Grand Committee. It was supported by about fifty MPs including Keith Vaz and Ken Livingstone. In the spirit of conciliation, I mentioned the need for quality translation equipment. But the wrath of some Cymraeg-phobic Welsh MPs was stirred. Neath MP Donald Coleman was then chair of the Welsh Grand. He rarely spoke in the chamber. He reversed the habit of many MPs of missing the opening prayers and then attending debates. Donald habitually attended prayers and then absented himself until the final vote. He denounced my EDM in a point of order, saying that the English-speaking constituents of south Wales MPs would not know what their MPs are talking about. To drive the point home about the parliamentary status of Welsh as a sub-prime language, I took to starting a speech in Welsh on St David's Day and continuing until stopped by the Speaker's 'Order! Order!'

One afternoon I was provoked by the Conservative Chester MP, Gyles Brandreth. As I was leaving the chamber I heard him start to move a Ten Minute Rule bill with the words 'English is the mother tongue of all members of this House and has been for 2,000 years'. Instinctively I shouted, 'Rubbish!' The Speaker beckoned to me. 'Do you want to oppose this?' Betty Boothroyd whispered. I explained to her that all I wanted was a few minutes to make a point. I begged her not to react to the first few sentences of what I was about to say.

She duly called me, and I began: 'Whan that Aprille with his schoures soote, the droughte of March yperced to the roote.'

'Order! Order!' Betty interrupted. 'The honourable gentleman knows that the only language allowed in this House is English.'

'Thank you, Madam Speaker,' I grovelled, 'but the language I am speaking is the language of Chaucer and it is English.' The point I was making is that a language that is incomprehensible to almost every member of the House is permitted, but the living language of Wales is forbidden in the only Parliament that Wales then had.

Although I could never trace the record of it, Paul Murphy insists that Gladstone once addressed the House in Latin, quoting pages from the works of Horace. If Latin is OK, why not Welsh? I tried it. In February 1996 I had an adjournment debate on the safety of Channel ferries, dubbed 'Roll On, Roll Over' boats. From my schooldays I remembered Julius Caesar's account of his Channel crossing to invade Britain in 55 BC. He made four journeys back and forth with 800 boats and did not lose a single vessel. Two thousand years ago he had a better record than P&O. I tried this quote: '*Uti ex tanto navium numero tot navigationibus neque ut neque superiore anno ullo omnini navis . . .*'

The deputy Speaker Harold Walker was staring aimlessly into space. I ploughed on waiting to be stopped by him so that I could make my point about Welsh. He never stopped me and I ran out of quotation. Point made. Hansard faithfully recorded the Latin. It confirms the suspicion that deputy Speakers rarely listen to debates. They have mind control that teleports them mentally out of the dreary chamber into more agreeable places.

Success eventually came from an unexpected direction. When William Hague was secretary of state he wanted the Welsh Grand Committee to meet in Wales. He believed that the Conservative Party had gained political advantage in Scotland by having their Grand Committee visit towns which are rarely reached by the Conservative propaganda machine.

I immediately raised with Hague that it would be an outrage to take an English-only committee to Wales, especially to Welsh-speaking Wales. 'In this chamber', I said, 'Welsh has the status of riotous behaviour or spitting on the floor, members are expelled for speaking it. We cannot export the Commons' language phobia to Wales.'

Hague recognised the strength of the argument. But many of my Labour colleagues were unimpressed. A rare meeting of the Welsh Parliamentary Party discussed the arrangements. This body of all MPs had not met for a decade. I again raised the importance of bilingualism. The authorities of the House of Commons were sceptical. They did not believe it was possible to ask a question in one language and be answered in another. Shadow Welsh Secretary Ron Davies generously allowed me to table the appropriate amendments to change the Commons English-only rule. A little archaic Norman-French is used for ceremonies. Now, a living language other than English was to be permitted in the British Parliament for the first time ever.

I was not the only instigator of this campaign. Plaid's Dafydd Wigley raised it before I became an MP. The meeting of the Welsh Grand at Mold in June 1997 heard the glorious Welsh of freshly elected Betty Williams and Gareth Thomas in addition to me and the four Plaid Cymru MPs. The skilled translators of Gwynedd Council ensured that the process was trouble free, to the astonishment of the Commons staff. It was a thrilling and moving advance from the linguistic intolerance of the past. Sadly the committee no longer ventures outside of Westminster.

My next campaign aroused interest throughout the UK and leapfrogged the Atlantic. The case against bull bars on 4x4 vehicles was a powerful one. Great safety gains were made when vehicle fronts were designed to deflect objects away from them, or crumple so the vehicle takes the impact of the crash, not the object hit. Bull bars reverse that progress. They concentrate and multiply the force of a collision at the level of a child's head or vital organs. They serve no useful purpose on public roads. But they were once loved as a macho fashion accessory. This was a heartfelt, energetic campaign in which I tried everything – including shroud-waving.

An eleven-year-old girl in Wiltshire had been hit by a bar. The bull bar bracket broke. She lived for four days, then died of her injuries. The bar made the difference between life and death. I approached the family gently. The mother was an eloquent, strong and touching witness to the wanton folly of these killers. The campaign went national. Particularly telling was the coverage on BBC TV's children's show *Newsround*. I urged children to persuade their parents to remove them.

In a four-hour debate for my bill on a Friday, unexpected voices were raised. Arch-Tory Olga Maitland spoke warmly and knowledgeably in support. The minister Steve Norris also spoke in support. Then, the kick in the teeth. He destroyed the bill by talking it out. But it was not stopping there.

The campaign attracted Euro-wide support. Bull bars became naff and unfashionable on jeep vehicles. But bar manufacturers continued to tell drivers of mid-engined vans that they were at risk and needed them. An unexpected independent voice weighed up our campaign. Keith Lockwood of Vauxhall Motors wrote in February 1997:

Discounting the role and impact of House of Commons backbenchers is naive and short-sighted. We only have to study the impact one backbencher had on the behaviour of the British motor industry on the bull-bar issue. It would be true to say that whilst Vauxhall acted quicker than most, the whole automobile sector has now moved to tackle the problem without a single new law being passed. Media opinion has also turned against the use of these products. Advertising too! The backbencher took a lead. Industry followed. Powerful stuff for a mere backbencher.

An unexpected spin-off was a call from the American campaigning consumer site. A journalist was interested in the campaign and wrote an article in the *Mother Jones* magazine. They called them 'killer grilles' and campaigned against their use on SUVs. UK legislative failure here was translated into a modest safety success through the parliamentary megaphone of publicity. European legislation followed and the manufacture and sale of bull bars is now prohibited.

Talking sense on illegal drugs is politically dangerous. But for every constituency vote I have lost by advocating pragmatic policies over the years, I have probably gained one from the cognoscenti. Being 'controversial' means most people agree with what you say about twenty years after you've said it. I have learnt patience. It's a great incentive to continue living.

One of the most difficult judgements in politics is how far policies can be removed from public perceptions. Many politicians are content to follow the lowest common denominator of popular opinions. The *Daily Mail* will tell them what to think. American congressmen have budgets to assess their voters' views with private polling on all major topics. Slavishly following every whim, intolerance and bigotry of electors is rewarded with permanent incumbency. Hack British MPs pride themselves on knowing what the man in the bus queue wants and then demanding it. A computer could do that more reliably than a human being.

Politicians have a duty to lead and challenge the inanities of popular prejudice and the redtop press. The least we should do is to point in fresh directions. Being too far in advance of public opinion invites accusations of eccentricity, dottiness or insanity. Decriminalising drugs was widely misinterpreted as a policy to make damaging drugs more widely available – to be sold like sweets at the corner shops.

That I am critical of all drug use has been rarely reported. The *Guardian* always preceded my plea for the legalisation of cannabis for medicinal use with the words 'Paul Flynn, who suffers from severe arthritis'. The clear implication is that I wanted to dose myself up with drugs.

The mythology of illegal drugs has terrified the older generation. They fear that youngsters who use cannabis will end up with a needle in their arm, dead in a dark alley. The chances of that happening are as likely as a social drinker becoming an alcoholic, and for the same reasons. Nowadays the majority of young people have tried an illegal drug. A tiny number migrate to hard drugs. They are more likely to do that under prohibition. Generations of young people are being criminalised. They have no choice but to use the illegal market for their inevitable experiments in soft drugs use. The same market pushes the hard drugs that ensnare and kill.

Prohibition of drugs rarely works, especially where there is a ready supply and huge profits to be made. The evil drug trade is a many-headed beast. Cut one head off and two others grow in its place. Profits drive the increased use. In the USA, switching from an illegal alcohol market to a legal one in the 1930s shut down the 'speakeasies', cut alcohol deaths and robbed the gangsters of their profits.

When we were in opposition, before 1997, the party was neurotically cowardly. My fellow Welsh MP Alun Michael saw my approach as damaging to Labour's interest. He expressed his view with some vehemence in 1994 in a debate which Tony Banks and I led. His then boss on the home affairs team, Tony Blair, was more relaxed. We deliberately did not press our motion to a vote. We all said in our speeches that decriminalisation was not Labour Party policy, to avoid any electoral damage. The debate was unique in my parliamentary experience. Minds were changed. Two north of England MPs and a Scottish one announced they had changed their opinion in our favour

My father James Flynn (facing the camera) training for the job that nearly cost him his life.

My soldier brother Terry cuts a homecoming cake, next to his wife Lilian, young sister Mary and my brother Mike in 'Lefty' hat; below them my mother and stepfather, Bill Rosien.

St Patrick's pupil, Grangetown,
Cardiff, age six.

St Illtyd's grammar school boy,
age twelve.

St Patrick's scholarship class, 1945.
Only eight went to grammar schools, including me – a class dunce.

Victory in 1987. *Left to right* agent David Mayer, Sam Flynn, PF, defeated Tory MP Mark Robinson.

Newport West was a key marginal seat in 1987, favoured with the Labour Party campaigning bus.

Four new MPs sing 'The Red Flag' at Newport station: *left to right* Alun Michael, Paul Murphy, PF, Rhodri Morgan. (*South Wales Argus*)

Comradely relations are rampant among Newport's MPs, PF and Jessica Morden (*centre*), and Assembly members, Rosemary Butler and John Griffiths (*not pictured*).

Campaigning against pit closures. Tony Blair was shocked to hear
that Rowan Williams was faithful to all Labour policies –
as interpreted by the Newport West party.

A 2009 visit
to the British
war cemetery
at Ploegsteert,
Flanders, where my
father was shot and
captured in 1918.

My daughter, Rachel, aged fifteen, at our Christchurch Road home.

My son James, his partner Libby Golledge and my granddaughter Abigail at Wookey Hole, 2010.

My father-in-law Doug Cumpstone, my stepdaughter Natalie, stepson Alex and granddaughter Elsie, 2009.

My three grandchildren: *left to right* Abigail, Max Biaggi, Elsie Allen.

Sam, with surprise painting by constituent Kevin Ruall.
(Western Mail and Echo)

in the course of the debate. It was the first time that they had heard the case for decriminalisation.

The best chance of reducing drug harm is to collapse the present illegal, irresponsible and armed black market by replacing it with a legal market that can be rigorously policed, regulated and controlled. There is a gulf of misunderstanding between the generations. Young people say that illegal drugs are their drugs of choice and that the smoking and drinking drugs of the middle aged are more addictive and lethal. MPs preach at young people: 'Don't do drugs.' Possibly from one of the nineteen bars in the Commons, with a whisky in one hand, a cigarette in the other and a couple of paracetamols in their top pocket.

Changing perceptions is not easy. In 2009 we were told by Labour minister Bill Rammell that we must sort out the Afghan drugs problem because '95 per cent of the heroin in Britain comes from Afghanistan'. Your point, Bill? These are the exact words used by Tony Blair in 2001. After eight years and hundreds of British deaths there has been only one change: the price of heroin on the streets of Britain is the cheapest ever because of over-supply.

Eight years of total abject failure to influence heroin production in Afghanistan has not disturbed a brain cell inside the placid heads of our government ministers. Everything will come out right in the end. It's all routine really. Just keep on babbling idiocies and the drugs will one day disappear. Some time at the end of the rainbow, laughing Afghans will tend their carrots and potatoes and the streets of London will be drug free.

It's all la-la land. The squeezed-balloon example of Colombia is forgotten. Billions of American dollars and bloody drugs wars squeezed the Colombian drugs only for it to balloon in Peru and Bolivia. If Afghan drug production was eliminated, the heroin trade would increase in north Pakistan, Burma, Tajikistan and Kazakhstan. The whole vast region would be Colombified.

Embedded in the public consciousness is the belief that the policies that work are those that call for tough solutions, and it is very difficult to replace that idea even with examples of the success of intelligent policies.

The American anti-drug education programmes (DART) have flopped. The UK's 1998 Operation Charlie is a forgotten absurdity. Ignored is the most impressive anti-drugs policy success in Portugal. In five years from 2001, de-penalisation cut drugs deaths by 50 per cent and achieved massive savings in criminal justice costs. The Portuguese government acted with great courage against almost universal public and press hostility.

Sadly, my twenty years of campaigning have delivered few perceptible effects on drugs laws. But there is new hope. There have been two tentative pragmatic reforms. The Tories allowed needle exchanges and David Blunkett sensibly downgraded cannabis from B to C classification. The hysterics and prohibitionists said that there would be a vast increase in use. The opposite happened. Cannabis use fell. Not because of the new category but because of changing tastes and fashions. That is always the main determinant in drug use. The percentage of young Britons who have smoked cannabis declined from 20 per cent in 2000 to 15.6 per cent in 2007. There is a steady downward trend in the popularity of cannabis amongst British teenagers. It follows changing attitudes towards cigarette smoking and the smoking ban.

In a wholly evidence-free act of populist prejudice, Jacqui Smith in 2009 put cannabis back into classification B. That increased the maximum jail sentence for those caught in possession of cannabis from two to five years. Even though the UK does not have a single prison that is free from the use of cannabis, heroin and cocaine. In as a cannabis user . . . out as a heroin addict.

Regrettably, in 2009 in an outbreak of pre-election tension the Commons returned to old ways. Home Secretary Alan Johnson sacked Professor Nutt (chairman of the Advisory Council on the Misuse of Drugs) for being caught in possession of an intelligent idea. Science was lynched. Virtually all knowledgeable opinion was outraged. Political parties are in an arms race to out-tough each other on drugs. There are rational voices. The splendid drugs reform group Transform and Ben Goldacre of *Bad Science* fame provided Parliament with a refreshing antidote against Alan Johnson's prejudice-rich evidence-free sacking of David Nutt. Good sense will prevail.

In recent years I have sought common ground between the countries of the Council of Europe on drugs. Sweden will never adopt Dutch policies, nor will the UK imitate Switzerland. But there is common ground on which we all agree. The international Red Cross movement and the Senlis Council think-tank are campaigning for a European Convention on drugs. The convention would shift policy from expensive failing criminal justice remedies to practical evidence-based harm reduction ones. Campaigning for the convention is my main anti-drugs activity. I have presented the case at international events at Strasbourg, St Petersburg, Rome and Warsaw.

More than 150 national Red Cross and Red Crescent movements are signed up to a convention. The organisation has ninety-seven million members and volunteers worldwide. Their founding motto is 'Use the knowledge of science and warmth of human compassion'. Progress is painfully slow but the Council of Europe has approved the convention with support from Conservative and Liberal Democrat MPs. The British government sent a supportive brief to a debate in Strasbourg and the final vote was unanimous. My previous attempts to change drugs policy in the Council of Europe have failed because of organised opposition from Sweden and some of the former Communist bloc countries.

I am now convinced that there will be a European Convention on Drugs by 2011. At best it could reduce the scourge of drug harm for populations of more than 800 million people. My years of work will not win me votes in a general election but completing the convention is a principal spur for me to continue in office in the next parliament.

The need for reform was tragically brought home to me in 2007. Two constituents of mine were released from prison a few months apart. Both had entered prison as heroin addicts and came out clean. They were in their early twenties. The woman lived for a week. The man lived for a day. Abstinence from drugs had left them vulnerable to their customary doses. In official statistics they are registered as prison drugs successes. Officially, their stories end on the days of their release from prison in Cardiff. I have sat with the parents and accepted my share of the blame for the failure of the political system to protect their loved ones. Had they been addicts in Portugal or the Netherlands, they would probably still be alive. This is the terrible cost of political cowardice.

Legal drugs was another of my campaigning bug-bears. One of the great myths of Western society is that there is a drug for every pain, grief and shock. Our bodies are miraculously resourceful in creating their own painkillers. The brain manufactures a chemical identical to the active substance in cannabis. Our random highs of unexpected pleasure are free and legal. For centuries, humankind has withstood the onslaught of pain without drugs or surgery. Of course, there have been many miraculous lifesaving and life-improving advances in pharmacology and surgery. But drugs should be our last, not our first, resort. I admire a man who underwent a vasectomy without anaesthetic, or discomfort. It is not stoicism or courage, simply a technique we can all use by playing mind tricks that deny pain the attention it does not deserve. In a dentist's chair, I maintain my peace of mind by mentally composing my next speech. When sleep is blocked by pain, always magnified by the small hours, rest comes by imagining I am reading a document written in management-speak or listening to a speech by John Major.

I first met my lifelong companion – arthritis – when I was nine. It has been an irritation and an inspiration. I leapt out of bed and fell over. The pain was new and severe, but transitory. Occasionally I had difficulty in walking. Rheumatic fever was suspected. At that time it was a dreaded childhood illness that returned as heart trouble in later life. But I had escaped that. Rheumatism was diagnosed and I was fed a pink medicine. It had no noticeable effect.

Bone ache intermittently nagged me gently until I reached my mid-thirties. Then it got nasty, especially in my hands. Rheumatoid arthritis was the new posh diagnosis. Pain and exhaustion were frequent month-long episodes. I devised tools to operate the choke on my car. Techniques were learnt to avoid using my hands. Leaning on them with my shoulders opened doors. Elbows can operate staplers. There were no alternatives to some tasks, including many in my job at Llanwern steelworks.

The problems were not constant. The beast was a cyclic visitor. Sometimes merciful, often treacherous. My cynicism about the value of medical intervention was at an embryonic stage. I took the odd painkiller when I could not sleep. The deterioration in my mobility worsened. Problems were spreading all over my body: feet, knees, hips, hands, arms, shoulders and neck. The prospect of increasing infirmity was a worry. In 1974 my hands were closing and I could not fully open them. Arthritis nodules appeared on the backs of my hands and elbows. My consultant insisted on injecting steroids into my hands. The pain was excruciating and I bellowed like a stuck pig. Mercifully he did one hand only and asked me to return for the other one to be tortured six months later. It seemed to work. But at the end of six months I could not remember which hand he had treated. There was no noticeable difference.

Being knowledgeable about the side effects of steroids I refused further injections. The consultant threatened a wheelchair as a real possibility in six months' time if I persisted in refusing steroids. He was a convinced believer in the value of modern anti-arthritis treatment. 'Years ago', he told me, 'there were dozens of wheelchairs in the waiting room. Now there are none.' I stopped taking the tablets and visiting the consultant. There was a swift and long-lasting improvement in my condition. Coincidence? Probably. Without reason or discernible pattern it disappears for months and then returns.

Arthritis determined my retirement from my job in the laboratories at Llanwern steelworks but its intermittent nature did not stop Newport West party from selecting me as their candidate in 1987. My family cheerfully decided that PPC (Prospective Parliamentary Candidate), in my case, meant Poor Pathetic Cripple. There was a perverse bonus in Parliament. When the beast was active, my walking gait was irregular. I limped and stumbled, at worst I ricocheted from one side of a corridor to the other. If I had the slightest smell on alcohol on my breath, a fair conclusion was that I was staggering drunk. Such reputations are easily gained in Parliament, very damaging and impossible to shake off. I announced when I first arrived in Parliament that I would not drink alcohol there. Everyone quickly understood why I walked in that funny way. My life was too full to allow an irritating disease much attention. The best distraction from the construct of pain is work and worry.

Workaholics have no spare brain capacity to dwell on pain. Almost everything else is more immediate and demanding.

I have studiously avoided making my parliamentary role a platform for solving my personal problems. But it would be a waste not to use my unusual personal experience of dealing with arthritis without medical intervention. It's appalling that some children with arthritis are being conditioned for a life of supine acceptance of pain and drug dependence. There are alternatives. Many arthritics have had lives of great achievement. Role models are more inspiring than relying on lifelong prescriptions. I once wrote an optimistic letter to a child with arthritis which was published in a children's magazine.

> Pain is a lonely experience that cannot be shared. Mine has become more bearable. Our bodies and brains get used to the constant nagging. The best medicine I know is work, exercise or other activity that occupies our full attention.
>
> My good luck is having a very full life with many interests. The anxiety of keeping up with pressing tasks is a wonderful distraction. They push pain into the back of our minds. I am looking forward to passing the age of 75 working hard as an MP. Arthritis will certainly still be nagging away, but I have the advantage of a special knowledge and sympathy with others whose lives are similarly affected. The lesson is that we must strive to make the disease our servant not our master.

The commentator Andrew Roth concluded perceptively in a biographical note, 'Perhaps the rheumatoid arthritis, which makes Paul Flynn limp, makes it difficult for him to bend the knee in deference to New Labour.'

Personal and political interests overlapped in 1993 when I was preparing to have hip and knee operations. Having discovered a racket in the overselling of hip prostheses, I secured an adjournment debate. I sought advice from a distinguished orthopaedic surgeon, Michael Freeman, who carried out the world's first knee operation. The conversation strayed on to my own planned operation. My visitor shook his head sadly. 'Can you do your job as an MP adequately?' he asked. Probably over-compensating, I have always been hyperactive, with a record-breaking parliamentary workload. 'Then cancel the operation. You're too young at fifty-eight. Work out when you are going to die and have the operation ten years before then.' At that time, one in ten hip operations had to be revised or, as the surgeon invitingly put it, 'the wreckage has to be cleared up'.

As I was planning to live beyond sixty-eight, I cancelled the operations. It was a good decision. Within weeks, my health mysteriously and wonderfully improved. I was almost pain-free for the next two years. Many hail the value of surgery. My experience was of a health boost by not taking the tablets and avoiding men with knives. My parliamentary debate was on the commercial imperatives that were driving the increase in hip operations. There were more than thirty different replacement hips hawked around by profit-greedy companies. One was different from the others because it was blue.

My scepticism has convinced me that there are two categories of medicinal drugs: those that have dangerous side-effects, and those whose dangerous side-effects have yet to be discovered. For decades my body was a drug-free zone. A later collapse for a different reason made some drugs unavoidable.

My disagreement with the pharmaceutical industry continued with new allies and enemies. Friends include the resourceful journalists Ben Goldacre and Sarah Boseley, worthy charities like Mind who are untainted by pharma gold and original thinkers like Dorothy Rowe and Charles Medawar. There were also the free-thinking MPs David Hinchliffe and Ian Gibson. Among the new enemies were the pharmaceutical lobbyists, pharma-dependent charities and some MPs who are on the pharmas' payroll. GlaxoSmithkline displayed their fangs with a letter to selected MPs. It warned that I was a threat to the jobs of their constituents.

Charles Medawar's book *Medicines out of Control* was scientific affirmation of the case against the excesses of the pharmaceutical companies. I nagged the chairman of the Commons Health Committee,

David Hinchliffe, to investigate the danger of medicinal drugs. I sent copies of Medawar's splendid book to all committee members and waylaid them in the cafeterias and on the terrace. Hinchliffe not only held a thorough investigation but he invited me to give evidence. In an act of unselfishness and generosity rare in parliamentary circles he let me do the prized *Today* interview when his select committee's excellent report was published in 2005.

The Health Committee backed almost all Medawar's claims. They accepted that medicines contributed enormously to the health of the nation, but warned that the use of drugs was getting out of control. They confirmed that adverse drug reactions were responsible for 5 per cent of all hospital admissions. Too many drugs are being prescribed to patients before the full side-effects are known. Drug firms had become increasingly focused on marketing and some GPs had been too easily influenced by promotions. The committee also recommended an overhaul of the regulatory system in a bid to keep the pharmaceutical industry in check.

The committee said that negative clinical trial results were being suppressed and positive results were not adequately designed. Promotion of medicines to doctors and patients led to the over-prescription of drugs, citing painkillers such as Cox-2 inhibitors, which have been linked to heart problems. A few months later proof of the value of the Health Committee's conclusions came in what the American Drugs Regulator called the 'single greatest drug safety catastrophe in the history of the world'. The Cox-2 inhibitor drug Vioxx had caused 140,000 strokes and heart attacks. The UK's defective yellow card system failed to detect more than a dozen adverse reactions. The MHRA, Britain's regulatory body, is financed and dominated by the drugs companies and was again proved to be woefully inadequate.

Surely now a major reform would come. But the government's reaction was supine. Health minister Lord Warner poured cold water on the select committee's report. He weakly denied that the industry and government were too close. He claimed that the government had an effective and proper working relationship with the pharmaceutical industry.

In 2008 Lord Warner appeared before the Public Administration Select

Committee (PASC) in our inquiry into former ministers' jobs. He has taken on a range of advisory roles including one with a pharmaceutical company and four other bodies linked to his previous role as health minister. The committee were worried that ministers were hawking their contacts and influence to the highest bidders. I was strongly of the view that the decisions of ministers when in office might be distorted by the possibility of lucrative consultancies when their ministerial careers ended. In answer to a question of mine Lord Warner said, 'I gave up income to become a minister; I reduced my income when I was employed as a minister, so I had a reasonable expectation that I would quite like to re-establish my income at a reasonable level after I ceased to be a minister. I still have not returned it to the level it was before I was a minister.'

PASC expressed its strong concern that with rules so loosely and variously interpreted, former ministers appear to be able to use with impunity the contacts they built up as public servants to further private interests. This is another predictable episode in the story of major scandals exposed and weak half-hearted remedies enacted. There are many other pharma dragons to be slain.

The increasing use of mammals in drugs-testing, despite new Labour's promise to phase them out, is one. It is a scandal which requires radical attention. Thousands of mammals are sacrificed until they give the 'correct' laboratory results, leading in some cases to disasters when the drugs are tried on patients. Animal models have rarely been scientifically validated. It is a forgotten salutary lesson that thalidomide was fully tested on animals, including pregnant rabbits, without showing any adverse side effect. Retrials on a particular strain of rabbit reproduced the birth deformities suffered by human babies. It's a shame that Labour's government has made so little progress in eliminating outdated, dangerous and cruel research methods.

The most damaging and intransigent example of drug overuse is that of anti-psychotics in residential homes to keep elderly patients docile. Millions of defenceless people end their final days in drug-induced misery and confusion.

The campaigns to popularise depression as a serious mass illness afflicting twenty-five million Britons have succeeded. Hundreds of thousands are now dependent on drugs that can create violent adverse reactions including a doubling of some birth defects. A campaign in America to convince parents that their children suffer from the fairly recently invented malady attention deficit hyperactivity disorder (ADHD) has resulted in 5 per cent of American children taking regular doses of amphetamine-type drugs. Some have dubbed this a 'chemical holocaust'. One bumper sticker reads, 'Ritalin, so much easier than parenting.' This is drug-pushing on a gigantic scale.

It has a long history. Every patient of Sigmund Freud was prescribed the 'harmless beneficial' drug he took himself and foisted on his family and friends. It was cocaine. Later bromide, benzodiazepines, tricyclics and now SSRIs have been promoted as miracle drugs. From cocaine to SSRIs, all have been guaranteed not to create dependency. They all did.

The pharmas have grown fat and rich on valuable new products but also on their snake oil remedies. Society has been over-medicalised. The propaganda war is uneven because the industries' tentacles of power are all-embracing. But reforms will come when the insistent voices of writers, academics and politicians are heard.

The scandals of the money scams are endless. Many of the 1990s mortgage sharks had graduated from selling personal pensions in the 1980s. The business was merciless. Without a blush, these thieves in pin-striped suits cheated their customers with a smile.

Selling personal pensions in the 1980s was hugely profitable. At least six million people were wrongly advised to leave good occupational or SERPS schemes. Some of these pensions were sold over the phone in a quarter of an hour. Many policy-holders were reluctantly compensated later. Firms that moved with the speed of a striking cobra in selling pensions slowed down to the pace of an arthritic sloth in compensating victims.

Helping young people to leave care was a campaign which benefited from my experience as a local councillor. I visited Bolton and north London to see good examples of after-care treatment. I sent copies of an adjournment debate in December 1995 to outsiders, including Princess Diana. She had previously expressed an interest in the subject. Diana sent me her 'warm good wishes' and commended parts of the debate. The letter was not marked 'Confidential' and I released it to the press. There was little response until Reuters later in the day put out their version of the story, 'Princess backs Labour MP in attack on Government'. The story went nuclear.

Reuters were wrong. In all campaigns I enlisted support from all parties. That is the only way to succeed. Tory Roger Sims and Lib Dem Diana Maddox both supported my debate. It was unfortunate that the very valuable backing of royalty was misunderstood. But it did increase the attention that the original debate received by several thousand per cent.

As a republican I have always had a healthy cynicism about charities cosying up to the royals. Sometimes it's mutual support, allowing royals to justify their existence because of charity work. Part of Diana's popularity sprang from her association with unfashionable causes that focused on the neglected and despised. It was entirely sensible for a republican to exploit a royal's popularity to serve a good cause.

Many campaigns did not succeed and are still being pursued. Among my many other crusades was one to introduce Daylight Saving so that the hours of daylight are matched to the times when most people are awake. The reduction in road deaths would rival those that followed legislation on seat belts, the breathalyzer and speed cameras. Daylight reform was sabotaged because of sectional interests, among others that of the post office workers, voiced by Peter Hain.

A campaign to make St David's Day a bank holiday had support from all the eight old county councils in Wales after I wrote to them in 1996. John Major gave the idea the brush-off with a one-word reply.

I campaigned to improve the 999 service after a confused cost-cutting reorganisation sent fire engines to Newport (Gwent) instead of to Newport (Pembrokeshire) and vice versa. The fight was distinguished by a piece of public relations by BT that was a television classic. I was waiting to be interviewed in London when I heard that a BT manager had walked out on his interview just after telling the interviewer on air to get stuffed.

One of the oddest of parliamentary responsibilities is surveillance of the Church of England. As the Church in Wales was disestablished, running the Church in England is an unwelcome burden for Welsh MPs. But it is part of the warp and weft of parliamentary life. Diligent backbenchers must seize all opportunities. Tony Banks and I were the top in asking questions of the Church Commissioners. Blood sports on Church land and investment in the arms trade were my bugbears.

Regularly I have hurled animal-friendly texts from Isaiah and Hosea at the luckless MP answering for a Church that preaches charity for one species only. On the arms trade the Church had eccentric guidelines that allowed them to invest in any company as long as no more than 30 per cent of its production was in arms. So it's OK to invest in GEC. They are big-time merchants of death producing millions of deadly weapons, but they also make other things. But not OK to invest a penny in a small firm making nothing but £30,000-worth of hand grenade pins.

I produced a spoof press release from the Archbishop of Canterbury announcing the 30 per cent threshold of sinning. I wrote:

> As a practical, attainable religion for our times Christians would in future be allowed to sin for 30 per cent of the time as long as they were virtuous at other times. No longer need anyone strive to do the impossible and obey the full ten commandments. Seven would be enough and three could be ignored. Free choice would be given in the selection. His Grace added that he hoped that not many would deny themselves the chance to covet their neighbour's ox in exchange for rampant adultery.

By a stroke of luck, one of our most original contemporary writers, Dr Dorothy Rowe, noticed the story. She used it in her thoughtful book *The Real Meaning of Money* published in 1997. It neatly illustrated how morality is relative to most religions.

One bizarre incident gave me the chance to defend a group of my constituents and side-swipe police grovelling to foxhunters. A group of a dozen ramblers from Caerleon in my constituency were arrested. They were caught feeding ducks. I was a mite disbelieving when I first heard the complaint. Further investigation revealed the group had paused on their journey to the Brecon Beacons for a snack at a village duck pond. Some did indeed feed the ducks.

The Dyfed-Powys Police arrested them and imprisoned them for five hours. That sort of thing can ruin a whole day out. Their solicitor in his claim for compensation for them said the rural police are always 'keen to arrest people if there is a fox hunt nearby'. The group were not involved in any protest but the police assumed on the basis of no evidence that they were hunt saboteurs.

I can vouch for their innocence. I know all of the hunt protesters in my constituency and I am married to one of them. The police were forced to apologise and the ramblers were each compensated with £2,000. I published details of this fascinating incident in an Early Day Motion. I expressed the hope that the police would behave with similar diligence against the foxhunters indulging in illegal activities when a hunting ban came.

The police are hyper-sensitised to rural crime. A police inspector told me that one evening there was a battle in urban Newport between Jamaicans and Somalis. Shots were fired and a man was attacked with a sword. The same evening there were complaints that children were making excessive noise playing football in one of Newport's rural villages. The police had five calls from the village and none relating to the outbreak of urban warfare.

Another example of distorted priorities was the way we treat travelling animals. Public opinion had been fed a myth about the danger from rabid animals. In 2000 it was true to say that in the previous twenty-five years there had not been one single case of an animal going through quarantine with rabies, but thirteen people had come in with rabies. It would be more rational to put holidaymakers into the nearest prison when they arrived from abroad rather than imprisoning animals in quarantine. As a precursor for the introduction of passports for pets, I had a Ten Minute Rule bill to tidy up the law and introduce enforceable regulations on quarantine. I was not optimistic because only thirteen Ten Minute Rule bills had reached the statute book in the previous thirty years.

It was to be a surreal experience. The late Alan Clark demonstrated that his love of animals matched his love of women. In the committee stage of the bill he said:

> Hitherto, I have argued that rabies is a dreadful disease, that we have had to pay the price for keeping our country free of it. Many constituents drew my attention to the horrendous experiences that their pets have suffered in quarantine kennels. That led me to inquire what level of supervision or powers of intervention were vested in the authorities. The answer was practically none. I am completely converted to the argument that the bill will relieve animals of a great deal of hardship. It is incumbent on the House to get it on to the statute book as soon as possible.

At the third reading of the bill I was alarmed to see that the late Eric Forth intended to speak. He was in favour of more quarantine and had been got at by the quarantine owners who were lobbying against improved standards for animals, which would increase their costs. Ten Minute Rule bills have a fragile existence that can be blown away by a stroppy backbencher. The malevolent or bloody-minded MP can talk them out with a filibuster or simply 'object' and destroy a worthy bill. Remarkably Eric backed the bill. I did not understand why. In order not to disturb the vulnerable irrational unanimity, I made an uncharacteristically short speech. The bill became the fourteenth Ten Minute Rule bill in thirty years to become law. Passports for pets legislation followed.

However, in the same year there was to be no unanimity on a bill aimed at reducing boxing injuries. The bill reflected new evidence of brain damage caused by boxing. Repeated blows to the head destroy brain cells that are never replaced. The damage is imperceptible and cumulative. It results in early senility. It was what the boxing fraternity once called 'punch drunk'. We do not use such a crude term for Muhammad Ali's health problems.

The sport already bans blows below the belt. What the boxer has above his neck is at least as important and vulnerable as what he has below his waist. While all sports are dangerous, boxers can receive hundreds of blows to the head in a single bout. It is almost as damaging as using a person's head as a football. One neurosurgeon claimed that 80 per cent of all boxers have brain scarring as a result of the cumulative effects of blows. My bill sought to outlaw blows to the head. It ran out of time, but the subject surfaced again in 2009, remarkably as an equality issue. Women boxers won the same right as males to have their brains damaged in the Olympic Games. This time there was a great deal of public support for the objections I raised. How many women find the prospect of black eyes, cauliflower ears and broken noses attractive? A barbarity shared is a barbarity doubled.

Another issue that arises regularly is the legality of khat and similar recreational drugs. The demand for a ban is evidence free. The legal prohibition of almost every drug has resulted in increased use and harm. Prohibition of alcohol in the USA created an empire of crime. Britain's harsh anti-heroin and cocaine laws of 1971 boosted the total of addicts from 1,000 to 280,000. Prohibiting the cultural drug of Somali and Yemeni communities would drive a dangerous wedge between them and the police. A legal market would go subterranean as an irresponsible criminal market pushing khat of unknown purity and strength to new users. The burden of work for the police, courts and prisons would be increased. Until now governments of all parties have heeded the arguments of pragmatism on khat. But for how long? The bigots are in full cry.

There is a long historical justification for a Newport MP to champion republican views. In 1839 there was a Chartist rising in Newport. Some of the leaders were charged with treason for attempting to set up a republic. Republicans are permitted to take the MP's oath preceded by conditions. Mine is, 'As a convinced Republican and under protest. . .'.

The royal tentacles even spread to the powers of MPs to get rid of them. My Elected Head of State (Referendums) Bill sought a referendum following the death or abdication of the present monarch. The questions on the ballot would be:

> Do you agree that on the death or abdication of Her Majesty Queen Elizabeth no one should succeed her as sovereign and head of state and the future heads of state should be elected? Yes/No

> If future heads of state in this country were to be elected, do you think that they should be elected by members of both Houses of Parliament or by a popular vote?

The bill raised interesting constitutional precedents. It needed the approval of the Queen before it could proceed from first to second reading. I had to send two copies to Buckingham Palace. The Queen could have stopped the bill in its tracks. I received a letter from the Palace saying, 'Her Majesty was prepared to put her prerogative at the disposal of Parliament for the purposes of the bill.' A member of the Privy Council had to be present in the Commons chamber to signal the Queen's approval. David Mellor fulfilled that task. It would have been interesting if she had said no.

Royalty was once the national pride for the majority of people. In the 1990s, the young royals and the hangers-on became a national embarrassment, mocked throughout the world. In the past foreigners wound us up by telling jokes about bad weather or queues; now it's jokes about toe-sucking or talking to plants.

We are a grown-up country. We should be equal as citizens, and not downgraded as subjects. Two decades ago the crowds stood twenty deep in the streets when the Queen's parade passed by to open Parliament. Now some people line the pavement. Most of them are waiting to cross the road. Life for a modern royal is like living in a monastery with glass walls, never being allowed to let their hair down and permanently working to justify their own existence. If might have been better for them if my bill had been successful or Windsor PLC announced it was going out of business.

That was only my second letter to the Queen. I had written some twenty years ago and applied for the vacant job as Lord Lieutenant of Gwent. I asked her for a job description and details of qualifications. Was it absolutely essential to be male, white, an ex-officer in the army, a freemason and rich enough to do a full-time job that pays no wages? Sadly my application was unsuccessful. Possibly because I am so short that the sword would drag along the ground. Perhaps there were other reasons why a shift-worker in a steelworks did not get the job of being the Queen's representative in Gwent.

It is a central role of parliamentarians to work with charities. However, some of them invite rejection with their exaggerated, foolish claims. Often the motive is empire-building for the charity itself. One of many examples was a stunt by the homeless charity, Crisis. They sent all MPs an expensive cardboard house plastered with alleged facts. I challenged them by changing the 'facts' to 'myths'.

MYTH: Most homeless charities need donations.
FACT: Some homeless charities are so rich they indulge themselves in useless expensive gimmicks.

MYTH: Government policies on rough sleepers have had little effect.
FACT: The Rough Sleepers Unit has reduced rough sleepers in five years from 3,000 to 700.

MYTH: Most rough sleepers have not been offered acceptable housing.
FACT: Almost all rough sleepers have previously been in two or three acceptable housing situations.

MYTH: There is an increased need for homeless charities.
FACT: The over-provision of homeless charities has forced them to expand the definition of hidden homelessness into areas in which the soup and blanket providers have little or no expertise.

MYTH: Anyone living in overcrowded, imperfect housing without a fitted kitchen or patio is homeless.
FACT: Homeless people are people without homes.

MYTH: Homeless charities deserve support.
FACT: Homeless charities are often solutions in search of problems.

MYTH Homeless charities exist to aid the homeless.
FACT: Homeless charities' main pre-occupations are inventing crises and defending their empires.

MYTH: Homelessness is at its highest level since 1997.
FACT: The total without shelter or a roof is at its lowest level since 1997.

MYTH: People sleep rough because they have no housing.
FACT: People sleep rough because of alcohol or drug addiction, mental ill-health or the effects of institutionalisation in the armed services, prisons or care homes.

Crisis had the grace to admit that my answers to their propaganda prompted them to rethink their claims.

As a person of mature years I am greatly irritated by the repeated myth-mongering and the patronising attitude of charities for the elderly. Off target, one repeatedly claims that '25,000 elderly people die of cold each winter'. It is a good campaign rallying cry but it is not true. I have asked them to provide details of twenty-five people who have died of cold in any recent winter. No evidence has been forthcoming. Thanks to twenty years of improving heating and insulation, deaths from cold are extremely rare. Excess winter deaths arise from many causes.

Tens of thousands of old people end their days in a drug-induced haze of misery and confusion. But in spite of my repeated entreaties to them, few charities for the elderly are interested. The key commandment of the Backbencher's Ten is 'Neglect the rich, the obsessed and the tabloids, and seek out the silent voices' (see pages 231–2). There are no voices complaining that one in five admissions of the elderly to hospital are caused by the misuse of medicines. Investigations in England and Scotland found that between 54 per cent and 88 per cent of the prescriptions of powerful neuroleptic drugs to elderly residents in homes were not needed, and were wrongly prescribed.

It is a heartbreaking story. Whenever I raise the issue in Parliament MPs approach me and tell me that what I have described also happened to one of their relatives. The stories are very similar. Frail but lively people were turned into zombies after short periods in residential homes.

Neuroleptic drugs are often prescribed, not because of medical conditions, but because it is much easier to run a home of the passive and supine rather than the lively and argumentative. The results for the elderly residents are catastrophic. There is a campaign to eliminate elder abuse. In 2009 the scandal was discovered by the government. They reported that the drugs were useless or damaging to 150,000 of the 180,000 of those who are prescribed neuroleptics; 1,800 die prematurely.

I relish invitations to address groups of elderly people. This is the best time ever to be a mature citizen. Life is far more enjoyable in every way than that which our parents and grandparents endured. Our pensions are more generous than our children and grandchildren can expect. We are healthier, more agile and richer than any other generation. Age Concern should accentuate the positive and change its name to Age Celebration.

My roots in a working-class family have given me a lifelong contempt for those who exploit the poor. Before we heard of sub-prime mortgages we had non-status mortgages. One organisation, the City Mortgage Corporation, was condemned by the Office of Fair Trading for its oppressive interest rates and redemption charges which inflicted life-long debt on its clients. It loaned to those who could not get high-street mortgages. When they fell into debt the company seized the homes. In EDMs I called on William Hague to return the £20,000 these loan sharks had given him to finance his campaign for election as the Tory leader. He never responded.

Another odious group descended on my consistency offering to help the newly redundant. Named Hoopers Employment Law Publicity Ltd, they offered to arrange publicity for tribunal cases at a cost of £570.50 per worker. The publicity could not be guaranteed and would probably be of no value. The claim was that wide publicity would ensure a favourable result in compensation for those who had lost their jobs. The splendid Newport Citizens Advice Bureau was already providing good guidance and representation to the forty workers involved at no cost. A sharply worded EDM sent the group packing from Newport.

Although they rarely admit it, foxhunters like killing animals. Hunting a live quarry and the twisted depraved pleasure of the kill is the only element that differentiates fox-killing from drag-hunting. In a debate on St Valentine's Day 1992 I asked the late Sir Michael Colvin why the hunts did not drop the cruelty and change to hunting a trail. He compared the sensation of following a trail, rather than following a live quarry, to the difference between a proper romantic clinch and 'kissing your sister'. Another comparison he made was that it was like making love without a climax. The thrill of the kill is their turn-on.

A recent excuse is that the ban is an infringement of personal liberty. That's not new. Banning slavery, stopping six-year-olds going down the mines, ending wife beating and criminalising cruelty to domestic animals all interfered with some people's freedom. The rabid hunters will not accept the will of the people expressed in ten democratic votes in the Commons in favour of a hunting ban.

The mask slipped when Simon Hart, Chief Executive of the Countryside Alliance, wrote that his organisation would be 'ridiculed in Parliament' on the publication of a letter sent by the Masters of Fox Hounds Association to 800 hunt masters. It warned of the nationwide 'shortage of foxes' and urged landowners to breed more foxes to 'solve the problem'. It was a pleasure to publish the letter, which did not disappoint. Ridicule was heaped on the hunters' heads in large dollops. Here was proof that foxhunting is unconnected with pest control but serves only the sadistic pleasure gained from the protracted torment and death of small mammals. 'Put the cruelty back into hunting' will not be a popular cause in future elections. 'Make Cruelty History' is a potent slogan, especially when 'Cruel' and 'tory' are printed in blue.

Nuclear power is probably the world's longest running successful confidence trick. It's a ruinously expensive, dangerous technological blind alley that cannot deal with the crisis of global warming. Only renewables and conservation can do that. Both major parties in the Commons have been seduced by the blandishments of the new-nuclear persuaders. Why? I asked the Tory spokesman in 2009. What changed his party's policy to making nuclear a first resort instead of a last resort? Was it the £93 billion to clean up old nuclear that the taxpayers must pay? Or was it because no nuclear power station has ever been delivered on budget or on time? Or perhaps the fact that the only new-nuclear power station in the world, in Finland, is three years late in construction and €2 billion over price? The nuclear delusion is deeply and seriously mad.

More proof that the majority of the people can be fooled most of time is the continuing fantasy that British farmers are poor. I did a programme for the Welsh-language channel, S4C. I wanted it titled 'In Search of a Poor Farmer'. One of the farm unions produced 'a poor farmer'. After three days of talking, visiting his farm and examining his accounts I told him that the only way that nearly all of my constituents could match his lifestyle would be by winning the national lottery. A distinguished Welsh wildlife journalist, Iolo Williams, was pilloried for saying that he had never met a poor farmer. You are not meant to notice that, Iolo. The poverty propaganda has been widely swallowed. It is topped up with regular whinging that is regurgitated by an uncritical media.

Every tiny drop in farm income is reported as a national calamity. The nation indulges in a mass sob-in. Unreported was the news that cereal farmers in England saw an increase of 70 per cent in average income in 2006/07 and a further increase of 45 per cent in 2007/08. Yet there is never any respite for the average family that is forced to pay £580 a year in farm tax subsidies. Meanwhile much of the wealth of the nation is owned by the asset-wealthy farmers who can easily afford to elevate themselves out of the dependency culture.

In 2007 a case of disputed ownership of land created havoc in the village of Peterstone Wentloog in my constituency. Mark Roberts, who described himself as the Lord Marcher of Trelech (the media called him

'Lord Extortion'), sent on New Year's Day a bombshell through the post to forty families. It demanded 9 per cent of the value of their homes in return for permission to have vehicular access to their own property, access that they had enjoyed all their lives. Litigation was threatened if they did not speedily accede to the demand.

The sums were between £19,000 and £45,000. A caution was placed, through the Land Registry, on their homes making them unsellable. The legal position was an incomprehensible morass. Ancient titles were being misused to revive the feudal injustices of the middle ages. Swift action by my Welsh Assembly colleague Rosemary Butler introduced secondary, retrospective legislation that cut the maximum claim from 9 per cent to 2 per cent. Extortion of this kind may be legal, but it is unethical, unprincipled, cruel and immoral.

The Peterstone Wentloog group joined other scammed villages in an appeal to the House of Lords. They overturned a previous decision on which Mark Roberts's claim was made. The village has been fumigated, the parasites wiped out. Sadly they have a nasty habit of returning.

The media has always been generous in reporting my parliamentary activities. Unfortunately my relations with my local newspaper crashed to a new low in 1994. My personal friendship with the editor Steve Hoselitz had weathered many storms. I frequently exchanged background information with him in a relationship of trust that was never ruptured. He never divulged to me the serious debasement of standards that was about to happen to the *Argus*. Others did.

New proprietors in 1993 were planning to send the paper downmarket. They invented a mythical Gwent family on which dummy editions of the paper were evaluated. Most of the members of Family Gwent were unemployed layabouts who spent the day drinking lager or watching porn videos in their lives of idleness and crime. Hoselitz always had high ideals for the *Argus*. At Westminster the paper enjoyed a good reputation. A previous editor even ran a Friday arts page and a regular feature on local history. Breaking point was reached for some staff with an exercise on how far downmarket they could go before turning off Family Gwent. One feature would ask readers to match the faces of local notables with photographs of their posteriors. Understandably, Gwent's great and good were reluctant to expose their behinds for the *Argus* photographer. Senior staff had to suffer the embarrassment. A procession followed the photographer into the gents' toilet. The flashes intrigued the staff. To the background of office tittering very senior people took their turns. Possibly connected with this episode was a change of editor. My 'Commons Knowledge' column was then filling a half of a broadsheet page and was well illustrated with photographs. The new editor told me he wanted 'less politics' in the column and more humour. Humour was there in abundance. I did not feel up to writing a column on gardening or knitting. Politics is what MPs do.

He decided to 'rest' the column for a few weeks. The Cardiff-based *South Wales Echo* were trying to elbow their way into Newport at that time. They offered cheap advertising in order to attack the *Argus*'s circulation. They asked me to write a column for them. My intention was to write for both papers. The new *Argus* editor disagreed.

The *Echo* was welcoming but changed the column to 'First Reading'; it then became 'Flynn on Friday'. Although the *Echo* is not read by many of my constituents, it had the largest circulation in the most influential heart of Wales. It is a legendary journal for anyone who is 'Cardiff bred'.

Losing the *Argus* column blocked my main channel of communication with constituents. It was an impetus to find others. My book *Commons Knowledge*, with the same name as the column, was part of the spin-off. I also upped my profile in the national media, especially in broadcasting. My website and blog now provide wide instantaneous access at a time when newspaper standards and readerships are falling. Never before have MPs enjoyed such brilliant instruments to contact and serve constituents.

21

Afghanistan denial

The UK's subservience to American foreign policy is a Blairite legacy. Harold Wilson kept the UK out of Vietnam. On Iraq, Afghanistan and Iran we have surrendered our independence to the Bush/Cheney/Rumsfeld neo-con line. In 2009, the pressures on President Obama determine our options. The first black American President, and one with the middle name Hussein, is constrained in his ability to defy military advice. The rednecks will destroy him if he appears to be weak in challenging the perceived threat from Muslim groups.

In Afghanistan, the dream of rapid rough justice became a screaming nightmare. Support for the invasion of Afghanistan in 2001 by America and Nato was almost universal in the Commons. I objected to the foolish aim to end the heroin trade. It was doomed to fail for exactly the same reasons that the prolonged battle to make Colombia drug-free failed.

The West intervened in the civil war on the side of the loathsome northern warlords against the loathsome Taliban. The Taliban melted back into the villages in response to the mighty Western war machine. The mission failed in its primary objective and justification of capturing Osama bin Laden, the instigator of 9/11. But it was otherwise reasonably successful in dragging some Afghans out of the mediaeval oppression of the Taliban. Later Blair lost the Midas touch he had deployed in Bosnia and Sierra Leone. He blessed the bellicose invasion of Helmand province. From March 2006 onwards the enfolding predictable hell of Afghanistan has been my primary parliamentary preoccupation.

In an oral answer to me at Prime Minister's Questions he defended the Helmand mission and John Reid's foolish hope that the mission would last three years 'without a shot being fired'. It's always easier to repeat an old lie than reveal a new truth. There was no vote on the Helmand deployment, but there was a Westminster Hall debate in March 2006. Mine was the only voice raised in opposition. Then only seven British soldiers had died since 2001 – five in accidents. I tried to update Tennyson: 'Bush to the left of them, Blair to the right of them, Hollered and thundered, Theirs not to reason why, Theirs but to do and die, Into the valley of the shadow of death, Into the mouth of Helmand, Drove the five thousand.'

In December 2009 the death toll eventually doubled the 118 killed in the charge of the Light Brigade. The accuracy of my Cassandra warning and my solitary campaign convinces me I have a continuing individual role to play in Parliament. It drives me on to a new election a decade after retirement age. Politicians of both main parties were trapped in denial. They refused to confront the deep futility of the war in Afghanistan. It's more comfortable to tilt at the windmills of peripheral issues. In 2008, fellow European countries were howled at for dodging their share of the burden. In 2009 refuge was sought in the myths that more troops and helicopters were solutions.

The media serve up delusional pap from embedded journalists. The key issues are the ugly truths of Karzai's corruption, his evil human rights record, the atrocities of his police and army, plus the barbaric oppression of our warlord allies. Politicians blaming foreigners or each other are on comfortable ground. It's easier than thinking.

One unembedded Reuters reporter revealed the hatred that the people of Helmand have for Karzai's police. The message from an elder in the newly liberated Pankela village in Helmand was clear. 'For God's sake do not bring back the Afghan police. The police stop people driving on motorcycles, beat them and take their money,' said Mohammad Gul. He pointed to two compounds where pre-teen children had been abducted by police to be used for the local practice of *bachabazi*, or sex with pre-pubescent boys. If the boys were out in the fields, the police would come and rape them, he said. 'You can go to any police base and you will see these boys.'

'When the Taliban arrived in the village ten months ago and drove the police out, local people rejoiced,' said Mohammad Rasul, an elderly farmer. 'The Taliban never bothered us.'

The BBC's correspondent David Loyn has said that 60 per cent of Afghan police are addicted to heroin and many of them are deeply involved in facilitating the drug trade. Few are paid and most are Uzbek remnants of the loathed Northern Alliance. They enrich themselves by theft and extortion. A quarter of the police and army desert every year. They are mercenaries on hire to the highest bidders.

British lives were lost to maintain Karzai as president. His record on human rights includes his refusal to pardon a young man sentenced to twenty years in prison for accessing an internet article on women's rights, while pardoning a group of young men guilty of gang-raping a thirteen-year-old girl. Malalai Joya, a suspended Afghan woman MP and human rights prize-winner, said that the rights of women in Afghanistan were worse under Karzai than under the Taliban.

Of the $25 billion of aid poured into Afghanistan, only $5 billion reached its intended recipients. The increase in the number of new Afghan millionaires and billionaires in Kabul includes members of President Karzai's family. Meanwhile poverty is deepening among other Afghanis. After eight years of generous Western aid, Afghanistan had the world's third highest child mortality rate and the world's second highest maternity mortality rate.

The debate in Western countries in 2008–09 repeated the canard of the Vietnam wars in its naive belief in more boots on the ground. More troops meant more targets for Taliban bombs and more deaths. More helicopters could mean that British casualties would be reported not as single deaths but in groups of thirties and forties.

In 2001 an ebullient member of the Russian Duma thumped me on the back and gave me his mock congratulations. 'You Brits are very clever.

You have captured Afghanistan. We Russians did that in six days. We were there for ten years. We spent billions of roubles, killed a million Afghanis and lost 15,000 of our soldiers. When we ran out, there were 30,000 Mujahaddin in the hills around Kabul. It will happen to you.'

President Obama is fearful of the illusion of victory. His surge of troops in 2010 was one face of his Janus policy to appease the military. Naming a possible exit date was the other face that he hoped would confound the belief in a war without end. He hopes that a deal can be struck to consolidate the few gains made and avoid the bloodbath of the panic retreat of the Americans from Saigon. Public opinion in America and Europe will not tolerate indefinitely the pointless slaughter of our soldiers. Clinging to myths is a deadly distraction. On a visit to the Pentagon in 2008, a military strategist explained that 'popular insurgents always win against alien invading forces'.

Parliamentary life is reliably unpredictable. Labour MPs who revolted against the three-line whip on Iraq have been slow to react to the tragedy of Helmand. I was astonished to read a House of Commons briefing that reported that all the EDMs opposing our Afghan policy were in my name. So were most of the debates. Tam Dalyell is a parliamentary hero for his persistence. I was conscious that my obsession with Helmand was trying for my friends. The expressions on their faces when I mentioned the subject were similar to that on Tam's wife's face when he mentioned the *Belgrano*. Inflicting boredom is an essential weapon in the political armoury. The message does not change. It has to be endlessly repeated.

Having tried all other parliamentary avenues of protest I tried a new one. At first it was successful. But Speaker Bercow put a stop to it. To bring home the consequences of our decision, I listed in EDMs the names of all the British fatalities in Iraq and Afghanistan. There is a maximum limit of 250 words for a single EDM. The wording was straightforward; 'That this House salutes the bravery of the armed forces serving in Iraq and records with sorrow the deaths of Private Craig Barber, of 2nd Battalion The Royal Welsh, aged 20 from Ogmore Vale ...'

By 2009, the death toll had extended to 179 in Iraq, which required ten EDMs. Along with the Afghan names the list spread over eight pages of the daily EDMs list. It was encouraging that there were five Tory MPs in the total of fifty-three who signed. There is a practice that the wording of all EDMs mentioned at Business Questions is reprinted in Hansard. During a business question, I mentioned the numbers of all the EDMs. Hansard printed the names in only the first of the EDMs. There were no precedents to this novel gagging procedure that I could use to get round it.

I tried another tack with some trepidation. A woman demonstrator had been arrested at the Cenotaph for reading the names of the British fallen in Iraq. The pretext was one of the unintended consequences of anti-terrorism legislation. Only time, however, could stop a reading in Parliament. Our speeches are usually limited to ten minutes. I was apprehensive at the possibility of giving offence by fumbling or mispronouncing a name. Even worse would be running out of time and omitting names. Reading the ranks and names would take too long. I used a names-only list which could be read with a respectful pause between each name within eight minutes.

In a debate on the need for an inquiry into the Iraq War, I said:

> The most insistent voices calling for an inquiry are those of the loved ones of the fallen. They want to believe that their loved ones died in a noble cause. Others are haunted by the possibility that their loved ones died in vain. Perhaps the most appropriate way that we can face up to the results of our decisions would be now to recall and honour the names of the fallen ...

All the media reports spoke of the House being 'silenced'. There is a special intense silence that all experienced speakers recognise from an audience when their full interest is captured. Hearing the litany of the dead and recalling their faces and the suffering of their loved ones is moving. A few months later I read a list of the Afghan war dead.

Between my two readings Speaker Bercow had been controversially elected. I strongly backed his campaign with media interviews and my blog. He demonstrated his independence by telling me by letter that future readings of names would not be allowed. He said that the use of the names for the purpose of advancing an argument was not appropriate and would no longer be permitted.

It was a possibility that the Speaker had been pressurised by government ministers who were discomfited by the readings. I had no appetite for a row with the Speaker or any intention of repeating the readings. I accepted the ruling without demur. There are many other ways to pursue the campaign. In the recess of 2009 I did several interviews on national television. One on *Newsnight* produced a large mailbag, all supportive. Even my anti-politics local paper reported fairly on my campaign to end the futile slaughter.

The Western world has drifted into the perilous delusion of the omnipotence of our military might. Nations with oppressive governments we first threaten, then apply sanctions to, and thirdly invade. In Iraq the overall consequences were dreadful for Iraqis. Poor Afghans are likely to suffer ultimately for our invasion. On Iran, threats are being made against a president suspected of election rigging while cooperation in Afghanistan is with a president who rigged his election. Meanwhile, British foreign policy is no more independent than that of Texas or California.

Afghans have a saying that 'Truth is like the sun. When it rises it is impossible to hide it.' It is having a slow dawn in the British Parliament.

Part IV

Staggering to optimism

22

'You knows it'

It's perilous for an MP of pensionable age to be seen cavorting with a hot rock band. Dignity has to be secured with both hands. Some distance must be maintained from the excesses of the young. I advanced into territory where most rational MPs fear to tread.

In 1996 the *New York Times* named Newport the 'New Seattle'. The word spread . . . worldwide. The fact that few of the then current wave of Welsh pop bands actually came from Newport seemed to be incidental. Any place with one nightclub, a couple of musicians and an imaginative journalist could be the focus for the next groovy vibe. Yes, it was almost entirely hype and luck that an American journalist picked Newport for world attention. So what? It was favourable hype about my constituency. My duty was to milk it. It balanced unfavourable calumnies about my patch.

Without a blush I tabled an Early Day Motion asking the Commons to 'applaud the prophetic article in the *New York Times* that hailed Newport, Gwent, as the home of an exceptionally vibrant musical life which is likely to become the new Seattle through a growing recognition of the top quality of Newport groups including the 6oft Dolls, Flyscreen, Dererro, Novocaine, Rollerco, Give Me Memphis, 2$ Hooker, Armstrong, Membo Jet, Disco, Five Darrens, Jester, Ninja, Swerve and Choke Teens'.

I was entirely dependent on my young staff to inform me. I subsequently found that at least one of the groups did not exist. 2$ Hooker was the invention of my stepdaughter Natalie. Within a week 2$ Hooker was mentioned in the *New Musical Express*. Natalie's father was a serious keyboard player who had been playing the clubs in south Wales for twenty years. Not once had his group Musical Box been mentioned in *NME*. I attempted to lecture the listeners to the *Today* programme on the intricacies of modern rock. My colleagues were understandably aghast. Correctly they were unconvinced of my knowledge of hip-hop.

In a vox pop the *Today* reporter sought views on the deserted wet Sunday streets of Newport. By luck he interviewed my stepdaughter's best friend. She recommended 2$ Hooker as her favourite. A myth was born. Invitations rolled in for this non-existent group to perform. Fiction almost became fact. Benefits did come from the dream of the New Seattle. Some talented local groups gained from the hysteria. The image of Newport gained an extra sparkle and glamour.

Nearly a decade later another phenomenon hit the city. Goldie Lookin Chain (GLC) is a rap group. Their toilet-mouthed lyrics are anarchic, outrageous and often very funny. As musicians they had the minor inconvenience that none of them could play a musical instrument. Nor could any of them sing very well. But they caught the attention of the nation. It was their wild undiluted hype and chutzpah. They were plastered all over the media. Success in this business is determined by publicity combined with some talent. In GLC's case it was 90 per cent publicity, 8 per cent original humour and 2 per cent talent.

They copied photographs from my website of local worthies. I was featured holding a spliff about a yard long. Two of their members became minor television personalities: Eggsy and Maggot charmed Anne Robinson and the *Big Brother* audience. GLC did amazingly well at the Tsunami concert at the Millennium Stadium. The line-up included some of the best groups in world. The day-long concert was televised worldwide. They were at the height of their publicity binge. The crowd loved them, undeterred by their minuscule musical talent. Later they toured Japan. There were local websites there competing to interpret the words of GLC songs as though they had the authority of Shakespeare or Holy Writ.

GLC named me as their spiritual father and the source of their inspiration. I pontificated in a few media interviews in a similar mocking vein. I took care to put some distance between me and their music, and especially their words. My campaign to legalise medicinal cannabis was given a wider interpretation by the band than I ever intended. I urged them to make good use of their fame to expand into environmental messages. They did, but without the same success. Their fans missed the irresistible outrageous obscenity.

The two Newport MPs and Newport Friends of Earth stood shoulder to shoulder with GLC rappers to lobby for action on climate change. It was the Big Ask campaign to encourage the government to do its fair share in reducing carbon emissions. What a team! The cheek and exuberance of GLC, the powerful message of Friends of the Earth, plus two MPs were united in the fight for a strong Climate Change Bill. Not a bad way to interest young people in the great issue of the day.

23

Dear Queen

All human, animal and divine life is in MPs' casebooks. The deserving, the greedy, the obsessed, the downtrodden, the sad and especially the mad all seek help. An infinite amount of time can be devoted to a single case. Some simple requests can be dispatched with a phone call or a letter. Others seeking a change in the law may need a decade's work.

Those who email, write, phone or attend surgeries are predominantly the well informed, the articulate or the obsessed. The downcast and the illiterate are often silent. But their problems are usually the most deserving of MPs' time. All MPs ask themselves whether their time is being monopolised by the unworthy.

There is a great temptation to placate the loud complainers rather than to seek out the silent voices. The admirable Tony Banks came to loathe constituency work. He rejoiced when his ennoblement freed him of an unsatisfying chore. He described constituency work as 'intellectually numbing and tedious in the extreme'. It is years of the same cases, with just the faces and people changing. Some see their tasks as those of a high-powered social worker. To other MPs it is the justification for their existence. Tony was inundated with hopeless, dishonest cases from people who could not vote. His neglect of bread-and-butter work liberated him to campaign brilliantly on the champagne issues as the advocate of good causes of national importance.

For good or ill MPs choose their own priorities. But the public still see MPs as their channel for righting wrongs. Shortly after I was first elected I had a call from a constituent in a hotel in Milan. Her husband had died an hour earlier. She did not know what to do. I put her in touch with consular staff who were helpful. Many constituents trust and depend on their MPs in times of crisis. That is a worthy and honourable responsibility.

Recently an 89-year-old widow, Mrs Avery, rang me about a relatively small problem. The jobsworths on her community council had returned her rent and ordered her to quit the allotment she had tended for thirty years. Her offence was that she was growing too many flowers in the plot of land immediately behind her back window. I wrote to the council asking them to use a bit of common sense. There was no reply. Mrs Avery rang me again on a Friday. She expected the bulldozer to arrive on Monday to clear the flowers she had planted in defiance of the vegetable-only rules. No one at the council was answering their phone. Their chairman told the press, 'Rules are rules.'

I set the dogs of the national press on the case with photographs and details of the lady's heroic war record. I put down a Commons motion ridiculing the decision. There was a howl of tabloid rage. I had a shoal of supportive messages, some from the USA. A Facebook support group was set up. The council was shamed into climbing down.

Winning a reputation as a dragon slayer has its drawbacks. Many with impossibilist grievances are magnetically attracted to MPs. They can be a pestilential nuisance. Former MP Gareth Wardell, the MP for Gowerton, had a splendid solution for the many complaints for which no power in heaven or earth can help. After exhausting all the usual channels he sent the details to Buckingham Palace with a note: 'Your Majesty, I would like you to exercise your Royal Prerogative in ensuring that Mrs Jones's gate is repaired / Mr Williams's perpetual motion machine is patented / Mr Davies's dustbin is emptied twice a week.'

Six months later an answer came back from the Palace explaining that 'Her Majesty has carefully considered the matter and reluctantly decided that this is not a matter on which she feels able to exercise her Royal

Prerogative'. Gareth earned the devotion of his flock. He did not succeed. But he had taken the complaint to the very top.

One highly intelligent constituent plagued my office for years. At our first meeting at a constituency surgery he removed his scarf and tied it around my neck because I looked cold. His problems were complex and convincing. He took to calling regularly at my home and passing on complaints that he had gathered from all over Wales. Every media interview I did was followed by his detailed written critique. He tested the patience of staff with interminable phone calls about insoluble crises, real and imagined. We were all saddened when he died suddenly. There was relief that none of us had recently rebuked him for wasting our time.

A change from the usual routine was a telephone call from someone who described himself as the King of Baluchistan. He wanted a new passport and was insulted by the suggestion that he should join the queue at Lunar House. 'Would you ask the Queen of England to stand in a queue?' he fumed. Careful checks proved that the bearded man with a green prayer cap was indeed a king and a constituent of mine. His Royal Highness Khan Suleman Daud, the thirty-fifth Khan of Kalat, was an asylum seeker. I asked the Home Office if they had a special section devoted to kings. Alas not.

A wholly unjustifiable amount of MPs' time is taken up with immigration cases. Our unhelpful laws invite wasteful evasions and deception. Individuals who could make useful contributions to society wait in idleness for endless litigation and appeals. Widespread abuse demotivates staff and distracts them from essential work.

As legislators we MPs have incompetently added to our burden of frustrating work with the misbegotten complexities of the Child Support Agency (CSA) and the tax credit system. My staff sigh. A CSA case is for life, not just for Christmas.

All MPs have their share of strange people. Margaret Beckett had one who complained that he was having troubles from the waves. 'What waves?' she asked innocently.

He was shocked at her ignorance. 'The waves from the television set, of course. They are entering my head and turning my brains to jelly.'

Margaret was up to the challenge. 'Have you tried Wellington boots?' Her constituent was puzzled. 'No, I haven't.'

'Well,' she helpfully explained, 'it's an established scientific fact that if you wear Wellington boots while watching television, the waves cannot reach you.' As a trained scientist Margaret speaks with convincing authority. She has never seen the no-doubt satisfied constituent again.

MPs' letters often have a galvanic effect in opening doors that are firmly shut to constituents. In many cases all that is on offer is advice. But it's of value to a listening ear that allows angry or neglected constituents to ventilate. One of the suggestions that emerged from the anti-MP neurosis of 2009 was the proposal that MPs who did not meet 'minimum commitments' to their constituents could be fined. No part of the proposal included protection for MPs assailed by constituents with insatiable demands. Constituents or their parties can sack bad MPs. That is a much better discipline than a tick box questionnaire on the complex job of a parliamentarian.

24

Shrinking family

Fear of the death of my mother haunted my childhood. It was the worst thing that could ever happen to me. By 1992 I had been inoculated and protected by other grief. My mother's final years were saddened by divorce from Bill Rosien. They'd had little in common with each other for a long period before then. The house in Penarth Road, which had been our family home for more than forty years, was sold. She happily moved to a comfortable ground-floor council flat elsewhere in Grangetown.

Her life then was her children, grandchildren and great-grandchildren. Terry and Lilian had three fine boys, Derek, Terry and Colin. My mother relished holidays with them in their idyllic seaside home of Aberporth. My sister Mary had married a workmate of mine, Bryan Wedlake, and had two boys, Anthony and Martyn. The elder boy, Anthony, distinguished himself as a Militant firebrand. He was one of only two Militants in Wales to be expelled from the Labour Party.

My brother Mike and his wife Maureen produced three children, Angela, Michael and Therese. There are now nine grown-up grandchildren for the doting grandparents. Mike had a long, hard-working but enjoyable spell as a Cardiff councillor in which he chaired the committee that ran Cardiff Castle. In my sixties, I greatly envied his clutch of grandchildren.

My brother Terry's death at the age of fifty-seven came with brutal suddenness in 1988. His health was robust when he was young. He was a reasonable amateur boxer. He taught my brother Mike and me how to throw a straight punch, a skill that I have rarely needed. His health was ruined by the many years he spent working abroad in Saudi Arabia and the Philippines. He always did jobs that paid well but which never made full demands on his intelligence and abilities. He was also a lifelong chain smoker.

I travelled to Cardiff to tell my mother that he had died. Sam and my stepchildren, Alex and Natalie, came with me. My mother recognised when she opened the door to us that something had happened. 'Who is it?' she sobbed. When we told her she said, 'He had the look of death about him.' I had not seen it. He was thin and grey. But he was also quick witted and active. I had no idea that death was imminent. Terry had the great luck of the love and companionship of a marvellous wife and a family of three sons and three grandchildren. He was buried during a winter gale in the cemetery high on the hill above Aberporth overlooking the sea. His life was unfulfilled. He had missed out on many of the good things that he deserved.

The loss of Terry was a dreadful blow to my mother. She had a mild stroke about a year before her own death. She was arthritic but still active, mentally sharp and alert until the end. She was taken into Llandough Hospital where I saw her the day before she died. My brother Mike and his wife Maureen were with her on the final night.

It was not what I expected as a child. There was grief. But it was the resigned sadness of the inevitable, not the savage shock of an untimely death. I had anticipated the event so many thousand times that the reality was kinder than the feared nightmare. My mother's death left an empty space at the heart of the family. Shortly afterwards, Sam's mother Elsie died. We had grown into a close family, bound together with new bonds, plus a shared working-class background and loyalty to the Labour Party. Elsie was a highly intelligent woman and a model mother and grandmother. An aunt of Sam had a lingering death with Alzheimer's. There were signs that Elsie might have endured a similar torment. Mercifully she did not.

My sister Mary's death cast its shadow two years earlier. This was my little sister. I remembered her being born in 1940, five years younger than me. I shared the delight of my mother and brothers in watching her grow up. She had a good life. She was proud of her long, happy marriage. She told me on in October 2005 that she had terminal lung cancer. After initial optimism from doctors, they said that the cancer had spread. It was fist sized. There was nothing they could offer except palliative care and a bit of chemotherapy to reduce the pain. She told me she did it 'the Flynn way' by not complaining. She accepted the inevitable with cheerful determination and a wish that others would co-operate in preparing for the inevitable.

She never told anyone of the doctor's prognosis. We guessed it was a year. She went on an initial trip to Jersey with Bryan. She mapped out what she wanted to do in her final days. There were trips abroad to Sicily and Madeira that she greatly enjoyed. Before the disease was fully diagnosed she had a long visit to Cairo where her son Anthony and his family were living. Mary was fortunate in having a close circle of friends from the Grangetown neighbourhood that she had known since childhood. They had shared their teenage years and the camaraderie of motherhood. Now, in their late sixties, they all still delighted in each other's company.

She brought them and Terry's widow, Lilian, up to the House of Commons for a visit in December 2005. It was the day of David Cameron's debut as party leader. I was determined to make the visit memorable. All were appreciative of the surroundings; the meal was to be as sumptuous as possible. One of her friends said they did not like red wine. Happily, they did like champagne. That was a distinct improvement for everybody. We all knew the significance of the visit but it was not mentioned. The day was animated, full of laughter, shared affection and love.

She remained outwardly strong. Bryan said she sometimes asked him to give her a hug. She was pleased she survived beyond the prognosis date. The final weeks were spent in hospital. She was practical and entertaining. Never once was there any self-pity. But the pain control was not always effective. She was sometimes in distress. Two days before the end she told me, 'I'm ready to go. It's just you buggers that want me to hang on.' She was transferred to a hospice in Penarth. From her bed she could see the sun rise across the Bristol Channel. She delighted in that.

I saw her on the morning when she died. She was sleeping. Eight hours later Bryan rang to tell me it was all over.

A year after the 1987 election which took me to the House of Commons, Sam and I had moved to a potentially very pleasant four-bedroomed house in Newport. It had been imaginatively decorated by the previous residents. Four of the rooms had black ceilings. The walls and carpets were a dazzling crimson. The first impression was of the Texas chainsaw massacre. But the garden was a beautiful tree-lined haven of rest. With redecoration of the internal Chamber of Horrors, the house has become a convenient and happy home for us ever since. In spite of my entreaties that photography is a hobby not a career, both my stepson Alex and my son James became professional photographers. Stepdaughter Natalie is a fully qualified veterinary nurse who is in administrative charge of a large veterinary service. Her son Max Biaggi was born in 2001. She and her husband Peter lived for two years in a cottage in the garden of our family home before buying their own house. Max revived all the joy in the development of new life for Sam and me.

My son James has his own successful business. He is a gifted wildlife and landscape photographer. I am immensely proud of his work. He was settled in beautiful rural Somerset with his partner Libby Golledge. Out of the blue in 2007 James told me that a grandchild was on the way. I gave a great whoop of joy. Aware of the perverse effects of parental advice, I had never mentioned grandparental deprivation. Libby gave birth to Abigail Sarah Flynn on 9 September 2007. My Sundays are now spent driving to their home in Wookey Hole, Somerset to indulge my grandparental pride. In August 2009, Natalie and her new partner, Jamie Allen, presented Sam and me with a new granddaughter blessed with Natalie's grandmother's name, Elsie Rose. There are few rewards life can offer more satisfying than being a grandparent.

Of course, there have been dark days. In 1997 came some of the darkest.

25

'The life you have'

'Oh. Dear God!' I said. The words were knives piercing my brain. 'Breast cancer,' Sam said quietly, in control. She was speaking from Newport. I was in my office in London. Vanessa Elliott, my researcher, ran out of the office; she had read the horror in my voice.

'I am having the operation on 28 November,' said Sam, 'and whatever you say you'd better be there voting for the foxhunting bill on that day or I'll never forgive you.' This is the news that was feared, half-expected but pushed into the 'but it'll never happen' depths of my brain. Sam had told me about a lump a month earlier. The first hospital visit was alarming. She complained to me over the phone that she had been tortured by the hospital staff. 'All the others had two x-rays. I had seven. They were excruciatingly painful. Like you'd feel if you had your testicles squashed.'

'Perhaps they are just being thorough.' I suggested.

'They clocked me. They knew I was married to an MP,' Sam said. 'But there is a way they have of looking at you. The doctor would not commit himself. He said it's very hard to tell the difference.'

We talked of all the people we knew who had been through this and discovered that all they had were cysts. We were mutually deceptive in forgetting three other cases that had come to my advice surgery. One was the wife of a party member. Her GP had told her not to worry about a lump in her breast. There was a long delay. Her operation came too late and she died. Her neighbour suffered an identical fate as the patient of the same doctor. A third case was a mother from outside my constituency who knew she was dying of breast cancer but who wanted to guarantee a place for her daughter in a posh school in my constituency. We wondered at this final grasp at privilege. I sent her a kind reply and did the business for her as far as possible.

I hated being stuck in London miles away from Sam when the news broke. I longed to hold her, stroke her hair, tell her I loved her. 'Don't come home now,' she begged. 'It's Alex's birthday tomorrow. I won't tell him until the day after. If you're home, he'll smell a rat.' I agreed to stay in London until Thursday morning.

Vanessa returned to the office. She understood the news. Only once before had I ever hugged her. That was at the moment of victory on election day. Her tear-filled eyes stared into mine. She sat on the arm of my easy chair and stroked the side of my face. 'It's going to be alright, lots of women have this operation and get over it.' Her affection for Sam and me was real and touching. My dread of the future was all-embracing. There was going to be a long dark tunnel. I did not dare hope for light at the end. I anticipated the pain but not the humour or any positive legacy of the nightmare.

This day had been planned to be a special one. A farewell three-course meal was booked in the Strangers' dining room that evening: Nick Ainger and his researcher, Catherine, plus me, Vanessa and my American Chinese intern, Cecilia Yu, were invited. It was Vanessa and Cecilia's final day in the Commons. How could I get through the evening? This was meant to be a celebration. Could I banish the black thoughts that dominated my mind and make small talk? There was no alternative. I had to stay in London and this was the only night I could give them a thank-you meal.

I had to tell the whips. Things had not being going well with my Welsh whip Jon Owen Jones because I had failed to vote for a recent piece of government legislation. 'Jon, I've had bad news, Sam is ill.' I turned my back on him as my voice broke. I passed on the details. He understood the pain. 'Go home now,' he said, 'forget about everything. We'll expect you when we see you.'

There were lots of hugs and kisses when I arrived home. Sam said, 'I'm sorry to do this to you again.' She was thinking of Rachel. We did the practical things and rewrote our wills. The prognosis was poor. Sam was worried that the operation might be delayed by her catching cold or a consultant being absent. There was anger and despair. This was unjust. Sam, the non-smoker, who never sunbathed, was knowledgeable about nutrition and always kept to a healthy diet. *Why Sam?*

There was an eternal wait, a week and a half before the operation. I was haunted by own words in a recent Commons debate about MRSA. A thousand times we each privately lived through the worst horrors. A bungled operation by a clumsy or incompetent surgeon, an operating theatre infection, poor standards of cleanliness. Was there a flow of clean fresh air in the place where Sam would be exposed, opened up and vulnerable?

I asked Sam to talk about everything. She thanked me but, I believe, she spared me her worst dreads. The breast-cancer counselling nurse was a comfort, likeable and truthful. The best that Sam got out of her visit were pictures of rebuilt breasts. She enjoyed the joke that the carefully reconstructed breast looks better than the one that nature had provided. One patient suggested that it might be a good in the interests of symmetry and aesthetic appearance if she had the other one done. Self-deception is a great morale booster.

The comrades who rang reduced the horrors of isolation. Bettina Strang, wife of MP Gavin, had been through it all and emerged triumphant at the other end. She was a great solace. There was a doubt because she was rushed immediately into hospital and operated on the next day. Was her cancer at a more advanced stage, or was the Scottish Health Service more efficient? The wife of my school friend Mike Bloxsome rang as a twenty-year survivor. Marion's symptoms matched Sam's and she was now hale and hearty.

Separately we imagined the black evil poison growing inside Sam's body. How far would it escape from her breast? Every day was another chance for it to destroy her, to take command, to become unassailable. The operation went well. It was a four and a half hour mastectomy and reconstruction. I obeyed Sam's order to be in Parliament to vote for the hunting ban. When she recovered from the anaesthetic she asked the nurses, not how the operation went but how the hunting bill had fared.

There was touching sympathy from other MPs. Jane Kennedy cheerfully confronted me in the street, quipping that her new broad-brimmed furry hat was really Humphrey the Downing Street cat. I joked back. Then told her about Sam. They were friends. She was upset. With lightning speed she sent a card that found its way to the hospital by the next morning's post with comforting messages from her and Bridget Prentice. Knowing that hospitals are dangerous places, I urged Sam not to spend too much time with other patients. This is vain advice to offer the gregarious Sam who gains deep satisfaction from helping people. The window in her room drew in fresh air that ensured that the germs from the ward were pushed away from her room back into the ward. Was I becoming obsessed? Probably. Then I heard that there had been an MRSA death on her ward.

There was trouble with 'leaks and her bagpipe'. Sam was irritable and bored after nine days in hospital. I helped her wash her hair. It gave her a great psychological boost. She insisted on doing some work. It was time to stuff the 700 constituency Christmas cards into the envelopes. Only she had the knowledge of who had died, who were still partners and who had fallen out of favour in the past year.

Then came bad news. 'I'm afraid I have five nodes that are affected. The doctor said he is putting me on a course of aggressive chemotherapy.' Sam's voice was once again calm, in control. 'My poor Sam,' I spluttered. This sounded like a death sentence. It was certainly months of suffering and humiliation. Hair loss, vomiting, destruction of dignity to my strong, brave, lovely wife. I told Alex and Natalie. I tried to control my emotions. There was no easy way to say that our comfortable happy life was crumbling.

I rushed to the hospital, sat on her bed, held her close and tenderly, my precious, bruised darling. Told her what I had told her a thousand times, that I loved her. Madly. Wildly. Eternally. We were both frightened of the suffering and loss ahead. She said again that she had no bitterness. 'I've had a wonderful life. I've been so lucky. A lovely family, two good husbands. I wanted to look after you and dad when you get old. There'll be nobody to do that.'

Never in the twelve years that I had known her had she showed any selfishness. It was always someone else first: her family, the homeless, the clients of the Samaritans, those people an MP could help. 'I want you to remember me like this. Not as the way that I will be after chemotherapy. I want to know whether this will be my last Christmas.'

Sam played her trump card. She told the nurses that she had recovered well because she was so positive and cheerful. Another day trapped between these four walls and she would start to go backwards, in spirit and in health. Continued imprisonment would be bad medicine.

I had planned to go Westminster for the big vote against Tony Blair's plan to cut benefits to single parents. This was a chance to halt Blair's excesses. On Monday I had been pressed by Sue MacGregor on the *Today* programme to say whether I was going to vote against. I said that I did not believe in threatening and that there were negotiations going on that I hoped would produce a sensible compromise. 'But are you voting against?' said Sue in her best 'I can be as aggressive as John Humphrys' style.

'Well, I certainly am not going to vote for taking money from the poorest people in the country,' I answered.

I was in a spot. The whips had been very good to me. After two weeks' absence, how could I turn up for one vote – against the government? Sam said I could not do it. As always she was right. That day Sam won her escape from hospital.

It was not a day when I was wholly sympathetic to constituents' complaints. One had woken me up at 7.15 a.m. with an urgent life or death crisis that needed immediate action. That was fair. Others were not. One man insisted that the council and everyone was messing him about. The DSS was paying for his house move, the council supplying him with a new house but no one would pay to move his washing machine. A woman rang to say she had no bed. She had left her husband after running up huge debts, then she lived with her new boyfriend, but that did not last. She was immediately given a council flat and was moaning because no one would hand her cash for a bed and curtains. With saint-like restraint, I did not tell the last two to sod off and blame themselves.

The day's balm was applied by our dear friend Shirley Newnham who dropped in with a poinsettia to welcome Sam home. It was a happy day. Sam loved pottering around the house, preparing an enormous stock of ready meals in case she could not look after us during chemotherapy. I shared fully her fear. Going bald was only one of the horrors. We also expected constant nausea, vomiting and feeling like shit.

On offer at the cancer hospital at Velindre was an experimental treatment with a stem cell implant and massive doses of chemotherapy. There was talk of barrier nursing and Sam being kept in a tent. Such was the breakdown in her immune system. Nightmare was being heaped on nightmare. I had a word with Howard Stoate, an MP and working GP. There was a narrowing of the eyes when I mentioned 'five affected nodes'. The Commons Library came up with a very useful note. After all, Sam was a constituent of mine who was seeking advice. It confirmed our belief that the objective evidence was that stem cell implants were experimental with no proof of their value.

It snowed the morning we went to Velindre. A doctor and a nurse explained the offer. He was in his mid-thirties, pleasant and intelligent. Velindre had lost no patients of the seven that had been through the trial there. Another Welsh hospital had lost one. I understood him to say that it involved lethal doses of chemotherapy, which were counteracted by huge doses of other drugs to persuade the cells to get busy and replace those destroyed.

What if the cells did not get busy? A note we were given said that in the first trials 10 per cent of the patients died as a result of the trial. Now it was down to 4 per cent. The consultant said that 20 per cent of the patients never have a recurrence of the cancer when they had no treatment. Sam was visibly alarmed at the ferocity and high risks of the Velindre option.

She agonised for two or three days and decided on the middle option: not the stem cell implant but the more aggressive of the ones available at Newport's Royal Gwent Hospital. There was still a doubt because it was left to a computer to select randomly those on the 'R course', which used chemotherapy chemicals of a more aggressive character. Baldness was a certainty. There had been a string of seven cases where the choice has been for the mild version by the computer. The unscientific law of chance worked, we hoped in Sam's favour. She was put on the 'R course'.

On the day before the chemotherapy started, Sam spoke sadly that this was to be her last period. She was visibly deeply unhappy. 'Not that I'll miss it very much,' she added. 'It's never been fun. But it's very final. Part of life is ending. It is like a small death.'

Our love had been barren. There was one conception in the lovely days when we first got together. I remember the happiness of her smiling face when she told me that she was pregnant a few months after we set up home together. She had warned me of her many previous pregnancies that had never reached full term. I did not dare believe this one would but I wanted it to. Economically we were on the floor, emotionally we were supercharged. Then Sam had a fall and was convinced that she had lost the baby. She was right. She did not conceive again. That dream was dead.

Now she was mentally prepared for her premature menopause. Her mother had few problems so there was little dread. But now all the emotional and physical turmoil of the change of life was piled on top of a mutilating operation, the horrors of chemotherapy and the anxiety of a possibly terminal disease. Sam shaved her hair off. That was the advice of Mo Mowlam. Mo told me that she had had only radiotherapy but she found it very demoralising when her hair started to fall out. Finding piles of it on the pillow in the morning was loathsome. Better to take control and shave it off. Sam agreed. She looked great in her wigs.

None of our worst fears about chemotherapy were realised. A pattern was developing. Great fear followed by mild outcomes. Sam's son Alex shaved his hair off as a solidarity gesture. Sam's father Doug was pleased because before the chop Alex had experimented with dreadlocks. Bald was better. Sam was winning with her well-honed mind over body techniques. She struggled to stay in full control.

The months of chemotherapy and radiotherapy left her overweight, confused and with slurred speech. She was unsteady and had a fall when we were at the National Eisteddfod. But her humour was intact. There were so many falls, she said, that she had recently been on her knees more often than Monica Lewinsky.

Recovery slowly dawned. A sympathetic article in the *Western Mail* by Colette Hume was welcomed by fellow cancer patients. Colette described Sam as 'warm, funny and relaxed'. Sam told of her regret that she did not go to the doctors at the first sign of a swelling and her sadness that she might never see her grandchildren. She said, 'I did shed a tear when I cut my hair off with sheep shears. I looked in the mirror and went, "Sniff, sniff, my hair is gone." Five minutes later I was fine.'

Colette described Sam's attitude as 'startlingly positive, radiating calm and happiness'. Sam was quoted saying, 'I do self-hypnosis every day. I believe in the power of the mind. The *Horizon* television programme claimed that visualising the cancer helped. That's picturing the cancer being attacked.'

Sam continued, 'I'm looking forward to going abroad, and going out at Christmas in a low-cut dress, and putting to bed the idea of poor old Sam. I'm not poor old Sam. I'm very happy Sam. I'm not going to waste a day worrying about the future. Why ruin the life you have?'

As a former Samaritan she welcomed the flood of phone calls and letters that arrived after the publicity. She freely shared her experience, optimism and common sense. They are powerful medicines. Now, thirteen years after the scare, Sam still has residual problems but life has been wonderful. Our worst worries were not realised. We had emerged from the dark into the light.

26

Making of a mini-guru

I was quietly sipping my pint of non-alcoholic beer. Impatiently I was waiting for Ron Davies to finish his drink so we could go out for a meal, when the *Guardian*'s Michael White made a beeline towards me and asked, 'Been invited to the *Spectator* lunch, have you?' I said I had. He told me to make sure that I turned up. Before I could say another word, Merthyr MP Ted Rowlands elbowed his way into the conversation. 'What are you talking about?' He snorted when he heard that it was the Parliamentarians of the Year awards. 'Well, none of our lot will get any of those,' he generously claimed. 'They are all hopeless.'

I exchanged a glance with Michael, who said, 'Well, Robin Cook made a great speech in the debate of the Scott report.' Ted grudgingly agreed and set off on an endless account of an intervention and speech he himself had made during the Falklands War debate. He was in charge of the conversation and he was not going to give way. This was not the first time that Ted had told that story, nor the thousandth. Ron Davies tugged my sleeve. He had finished his pint. It was time to go.

The *Spectator* indulges its sense of humour in the placing of the guests for the meal. I was squeezed between former Tory Transport Secretary John MacGregor and arch-right-wing journalist Paul Johnson. It was a much bigger event than I had expected with a clutch of former Prime Ministers among the guests. As Backbencher of the Year I was expected to make a brief self-deprecatory speech or tell a joke.

This was a rare chance for me to advance some of my causes to a captive audience. A once-in-a-lifetime chance for some useful propaganda. One Tory MP was aghast at what I said and still tells the story that I harangued the assembled dignitaries with a 'communist rant'. A diarist also wrote unkindly about my mould-breaking speech. I have no regrets. What I said was:

> In a country where 10,000 young people each year are thrown out of full-time care into full-time neglect; where power by birth rivals power by election; where caution swamps political conviction; where a man was imprisoned for writing a book about a benign medicine; where the Mother of Parliaments is debauched by commercial lobbyists; where safe defensive driving is challenged by vanity bull-barred offensive driving; where tabloid papers enslave tabloid politics . . . in such a land, there is a need for restless, irreverent, awkward backbenchers who refuse to take no, maybe or, sometimes, even yes for an answer.

Not bad. Six campaigns in less than a minute.

I had long dreamed of writing a book. I had done some preparatory writing on *Commons Knowledge*. I had about 20,000 words lodged on a computer. There were always pressing reasons not to finish it. The *Spectator* award gave me the effrontery to advise newcomers how to do the job. I tentatively approached a few publishers. Mick Felton of Seren rang at Christmas time to say they were interested. It was a frantic rush to assemble 50,000 words that made sense in some semblance of order. The perfect moment for publication would be the day the new backbenchers arrived in Parliament the following year.

I was schizophrenic. Regularly I was haranguing Major, demanding that he 'should go to the country, now! The country is crying for an election.' Secretly I was praying that he would hang on until the last possible date on 1 May so that I could finish what my staff described as 'that bloody book'.

The final version was in Seren's hands about a month before the election. It was published in the House of Commons on 8 May when the largest number of new backbenchers that century began their parliamentary careers. The *Daily Telegraph* bought the rights to reprint 3,000 words. On 6 May, when most MPs were travelling to London by train, their free copies of the *Daily Telegraph* included a full page of the best bits of *Commons Knowledge*.

The book transformed my life. Tony Banks was at the launch in the Commons with many of the new backbenchers. To his surprise, he had been made minister of sport two days earlier. This was his chance to publicly recant. In his foreword to *Commons Knowledge* he had written (in February 1997), 'The chances of Tony Blair asking me to do anything other than shut up and vote are extremely remote.' He had another volte face. He had also written approvingly of my clash with Blair: 'People wince at the memory of the day Paul told Tony Blair where to get off.' At the launch, he said, 'I unreservedly withdraw that remark. What Paul said to the leader was a total disgrace.' Everyone appreciated the need for Banksy's born-again conformity.

I was terrified at the prospect of the book signings in Cardiff and in Newport. My anticipation was of my sitting lonely and forlorn in front of a pyramid of my unsold books. My friends and family rescued me in Cardiff. Members of the Labour Party turned up in Newport. The London specialist political bookshop Politico's reported that *Commons Knowledge* was the political bestseller for the month of May. It had enormous publicity because of the timing of the publication. Many new MPs have told me that after the bullshit they received at the parliamentary induction courses, they turned to my book to find out what really happens.

The strongest reaction – for and against – was provoked by the throw-away guide to the Commons bars that I wrote rapidly as a filler, packed with deliberately prejudiced bile. The bars I praised welcomed me warmly. One regular of Annie's Bar threatened to pluck out my eye for saying that it is 'a hole of comatose decrepitude, filled with old warriors raking over the ashes of dead fires'.

Although sales were not big when compared with other books, the readership included many media people. Some shamelessly stole unattributed bits from it. But their interest meant that I still have calls to comment on all aspects of Commons life. It was unexpected that I would be on radio pontificating about sex in the Commons with Edwina Currie or repeating wicked anecdotes about several MPs on their local radio stations.

The book has a very serious purpose wrapped up in the humour. The Backbencher's Ten Commandments are a plea to honour the importance of the role. Backbenchers are not just failed or never-will-be frontbenchers.

Charter 88 acknowledged the reforming message and invited me to address their conference on modernising Parliament. There were unique opportunities for the backbenchers' intake of 1997. I cherished hopes that this could the parliament when the honourable vocation of the backbencher could be revived.

In the record tally of 417 Labour MPs, there were several undisciplinable groups. These include the over-55s, who had no chance of promotion because of ageism, Glenda Jackson being the exception (armed with her ability plus two Oscars); those who were in their last parliament because of age or a freak 1997 result; those who intelligently judged that their chances of promotion were nil; those who believed their personalities or abilities to be unacceptable to the leadership for promotion; those who valued the causes they espoused above patronage or personal aggrandisement. And those who were later categorised by Tony Wright as the Whys rather than the Whens. The total of all those groups was very substantial.

Twelve years later *Commons Knowledge* is still in print but in need of a rewrite. It was adapted into a radio series. My status as a minor guru of parliamentary procedure continues as a sesame into occasional media pontification. If my Ten Commandments had been followed the expenses scandal would have been avoided.

On occasions, I have resorted to the book to seek my own advice.

The Backbencher's Ten Commandments

Value the role of backbencher as a high calling

Serve the constituents, the weak and neglected

Seek novel remedies and challenge accepted wisdom

Attack opponents only when they are wrong

Never covet a second income, honours or retirement job

Value courage and innovation above popularity

Honour your party and extend its horizons

Use humour and colour to convey serious ideas

Fortify the independence of backbenchers against the executive

Neglect the rich, the obsessed and the tabloids, and seek the silent voices.

27

Losing me

There are two villages on the Thames at Westminster Bridge. One named St Stephen's and the other St Thomas'. The first is a palace, the second a hospital. One is inhabited by thousands of mainly white people speaking one language; the other has thousands of mainly black people speaking dozens of languages. One is beautiful; the other is utilitarian. One is proud, self-regarding and pompous; the other is not.

A twenty-year-long inhabitant of St Stephen's, I was teleported in dreamlike circumstances to St Thomas' by two paramedics named Andy and Peter on a Tuesday night. I had spent the previous twenty minutes admiring the beauty of the lozenges in the ceiling of the Members' dining room from the perfect vantage point, flat on my back on the floor. The kindly Bob Laxton had organised a pillow of folded napkins on which to rest my head.

It was reassuring to hear the voice of physician Richard Taylor, the Independent MP, describing the sagging left side of my face as a transient ischaemic attack. A few minutes earlier, I had joined Bob, Gordon Prentice and Lindsay Hoyle at our usual table in the dining room for our evening meal. They were behaving oddly. I said that the news of the loss of a CD of confidential information meant the end of the government's identity card scheme. Neither understood a word I said. I repeated the comment. Not a glimmer of understanding. They talked amongst themselves as though I was not there. Gordon said mysteriously, 'I'm going to get Howard Stoate or someone to take a look at him.' He then left. Why?

Undeterred by this irrational behaviour, I crossed the dining room floor and tried to fill a plate with a first course. Bob Laxton pointed out that I was trying to load the plate not on the top or the bottom but from the side. Then, calamity. I fell leftwards heavily on the floor. The ceiling lozenges are remarkably beautiful and different on the Labour and Tory halves of the room.

Drifting into my field of vision between the two halves was the face of Lord Darzai. The previous day he had saved the life of Lord Brennan by using the Lords defibrillator on him. A first aid man fitted me with an oxygen mask. There was some banter. Darzai is a surgeon, not a first aid specialist. I was reassured to notice he did not have his scalpels with him. Dr Taylor was explaining to the assembled group that I had written a book he liked very much. Inwardly, I fretted. 'Does he, too, think I am not here? Shouldn't he do something about my face being attacked by these ischaemias, even if they are transient?'

I was wrapped in a crimson blanket, strapped to a chair and wheeled past the Strangers' Bar towards the ambulance. We passed the visibly shocked Keith Hill, who asked, 'Are you all right, Paul?' I couldn't get the oxygen mask off quickly enough to answer, 'On balance, probably not.'

My grip on reality was firmer when I was transferred at St Thomas' from the wheelchair to a hospital trolley. The Accident and Emergency unit at St Thomas' is a nauseous mix of intense dedicated frantic activity with a palpable air of danger and menace. An intensive care cubicle was free. It was speedily cleaned and I was wired up to half a dozen bleeping and throbbing machines. A young doctor called and thoroughly checked the damage that the stroke had done to my body and brain. He told me the protocol was to keep me in a cubicle for three hours and then overnight on the ward for observation. That was comforting.

A noisy patient in the cubicle next door was screaming. It was wordless, loud, threatening and incomprehensible. A posse of security people persuaded him to leave. A soft-voiced nurse from Wicklow named Lenna was my guardian angel, a friendly presence in the midst of the swirling bedlam. I quoted some verses from my childhood about the Wicklow Vale of Avoca. 'There is not in this wide world a Valley so sweet as the vale in whose bosom the sweet waters meet.' It meant nothing to her but a lot to me – my memory had not been wiped empty. Halfway through my three hours, colleagues Lyn Brown, Nia Griffiths and Huw Irranca-Davies visited. Their company was as bracing as a glass of champagne, humorous, optimistic and comradely. It was a welcome intrusion of pleasant normality into the Hieronymus Bosch world into which I had been plunged. Lyn is the successor MP in West Ham to my friend Tony Banks. He had a stroke. A merciless one. Time to count my blessings.

Sam had been gently informed in a telephone message from Bob Laxton of my collapse. She got to the hospital by midnight on the day it happened. As always she was a great comfort and balm. My first endless night at St Thomas' was spent in the emergency ward. It was a horrific nightmare. Arthritic pain has been my constant companion for fifty-five years. But that night it was so severe I became convinced that I had broken my left hip in the fall. My friend Ann Drysdale wrote a masterpiece, *Three-three, Two-two, Five-six*. The title was her husband's hospital number. They could never get his name right. The book contains a haunting evocative account of the sounds that disturb in a hospital at night. The ringing of distant telephones that are never picked up, the low grunting sighs of severe pain, the unanswered geriatric voices calling for their mothers. The following day's X-rays clearly showed the wreckage of my hips but no fractures. I was supplied with crutches to move the short distance from bed to bathroom.

The following day I was conveyed to the Mark Ward stroke unit by two nurses who were new to St Thomas'. One was beautifully black from Vauxhall; the other was beautifully white from Ascot. The tenth floor has a commanding view down the river towards Lambeth Bridge. The other patients in the ward had suffered severely from their strokes. A fine team of good-humoured, highly competent nurses did magnificent work in patiently tending the severely injured. Grace, Onessa, Nana and Josette were models of professionalism and dedication beyond any reasonable call of duty. Although it made sleep almost impossible, they toiled throughout the twenty-four hours to give ease and comfort to their suffering patients. I believed they regarded me as a little difficult because I declined help for my trivial problems compared with the anguish of my neighbours. One of them said with a derogatory sniff that I was 'independent'. I was just trying to cling on to few shreds of dignity. As always, I purred at that description.

On the day after the stroke, I blogged by dictating a few paragraphs to my staff. I amused the press by reminding them of the question which is always asked of a post-stroke patient, 'Do you know the name of the Prime Minister?' Happily I did. The question was dropped during John Major's reign. Even the compos mentis did not know him. Everyone thought Maggie was still in charge.

After two days, St Thomas' had exhausted their repertoire. It was a reassuring experience of the first-class quality of NHS care. Every bit of me had been checked out: arms, legs, nose, fingers, toes, brain. My heart's thumping had been recorded in glorious Technicolor. Most alarming was the ultrasound moving pictures in red and blue (happily mostly red) of the blood swishing and gushing its way from brain to heart along the neck arterial channel. Apparently they can get gunged up and produce clots. I presume then they give them a bit of a de-coke. I did not ask for details. The daunting experience of an MRI scan was like being buried alive in the company of a bellowing and throbbing church organ. I had no residual damage to speak of. But I have to deny myself the joys of running marathons and Morris dancing for the foreseeable future.

The nurses and doctors have devised a series of hilarious practical jokes on patients, ostensibly to ensure that everything works properly. One test is to order patients to bend their arms inwards then waggle them up and down. This is their favourite chicken joke. I was asked to do it four times. Do they secretly video the spectacle and play it back at their Christmas parties? Like all my other bits, my arms were OK. Or as OK as they were before.

Which is not saying much.

28

Pope of Blairism

The Public Administration Select Committee (PASC) is an uninviting title. But it is Parliament's most resourceful, entertaining and independent group. It's made up entirely of free spirits who have sloughed off political ambitions. The personality of the PASC has been shaped by its cerebral chairman, Tony Wright. Wisely he gives free rein to his inspirational crew. They span the political spectrum from an incurably plebeian Marxist to the 323rd in line to the throne.

The saintly Kelvin Hopkins is the robustly Hegelian scourge of New Labour. Ian Liddell-Grainger, aka the Baron of Ayton, is a lofty patrician with views fit for a great-great-great-grandson of Queen Victoria who also happens to own a castle or two. No one planned it but PASC attracts and retains free thinkers. It is the stuff of whips' nightmares.

We are cooing turtledoves to the wise and wonderful, but snarling Rottweilers to the evaders and crooks. Sketch writer Quentin Letts anointed PASC as the current parliament's star committee. He described two members as 'Parliament's saltiest interrogators'. Simon Hoggart said his interrogation by the committee was a conversation between like-minded friends.

No quarter is given to the big beasts. Former minister Richard Caborn was excoriated by the PASC. He was defending his right as former minister to a £70,000 payment as a consultant to the nuclear industry. Letts said, 'By the time Messrs Flynn and Prentice had finished yesterday Caborn must have wished he'd gone into holy orders after leaving ministerial office. PASC have been consistent value for money, pulling apart a succession of crooks, conmen and blue-sky-thinking pseuds.'

In *Commons Knowledge* I pontificated on MPs' lame questioning at select committees. MPs still woefully under-perform. Even we PASC members are not immune to taking our own hobbyhorses out for the occasional gallop. I have offered to never again mention drugs if Kelvin Hopkins and Gordon Prentice never again mention neo-liberalism and foreign-based party donors. It won't happen.

Experience on the Transport Select Committee in the early 1990s taught me that creative discourtesy to witnesses is a positive duty. Then, civil servant witnesses were trained to make their answers as long as possible. Government ministers are also professionally coached before they appear. They undergo dummy sessions with advisers skilled in anticipating questions. One minister answered a simple question of mine by speaking for eleven minutes. He made all his carefully rehearsed points. It is not the function of a select committee to provide ministers with additional platforms for their views.

When witnesses persist in stonewalling, their streams of vacuous verbiage must be interrupted in mid-flow. A word of apology might help before the witness is skewered with sharp, direct and unavoidably discourteous short questions.

My baptism onto my first select committee was in 1992. The Transport Committee was the high point of the career of Conservative railway expert Robert Adley. It tragically contributed to his untimely death. The whips had done a deal to replace the Labour chairman of the committee with the Tory Alan Haselhurst. The hot issue in 1992 was the proposed rail privatisation. Haselhurst was thought to be a Major government stooge who backed privatisation. Robert Adley was an independently minded railway buff.

In a rare but wholly creditable revolt against whips domination, the committee members exercised their own decision. There were three nominations for the post of chairman: Peter Bottomley, Haselhurst and

Adley. Unusually, Bottomley had nominated himself and amassed one vote. The rebel committee elected Adley.

The best-remembered witness was Richard Branson, who was then planning his Virgin Trains. The committee was goaded by his ignorance of railways. He was visibly riled when I suggested his knowledge of railways was on a protozoan level. In answer to a question on how he planned to improve the running of his privatised service, Branson said he would urge his drivers to drive faster. Gwyneth Dunwoody whispered to me, 'Presumably, to overtake the train in front.'

Adley won unanimous committee approval for a splendid report that precisely anticipated all the problems that rail privatisation later encountered. He called it a poll tax on wheels. Getting their retaliation in first, the Tory press viciously denounced Adley in order to nullify his expected anti-privatisation conclusions. Tragically he died of a heart attack on the Sunday before the Wednesday when the report was published. Committee vice-chair, Gwyneth Dunwoody, came close to blaming Conservative party pressure for his death at the age of fifty-seven. She was probably correct. The report still stands as a worthy, visionary memorial to a good MP who rightly braved the wrath of his own party.

In 2009 PASC grilled former premier John Major. He is a born-again parliamentary reformer. He advocated strong independent select committees, led by well-informed possibly eccentric chairs to challenge the executive with alternative policies. Great idea, John. Why did he not accept Adley's wise advice to junk rail privatisation? He claimed the report came after privatisation. It did not. John's advice is 'Do what I say, not what I did'.

There was a gap of seven years until I next had a place on a select committee. This was not unconnected with my advice in *Commons Knowledge* on how to shine on these committees. The whips preferred dull rather than shining MPs while we were in government. And they influence select committee membership.

I had a productive two years on the Environment Audit Committee from 2003 under the brilliant chairmanship of Tory environmentalist, Peter Ainsworth. The work was thorough, objective and commendably science-based. Sadly thousands of hours of painstaking research, which emphatically rejected nuclear power, were dismissed by government and opposition. The Pied Piper of nuclear lobbyists had bewitched them.

With some regrets I changed committees. PASC had outgunned all other committees in penetrating the layers of subterfuge and bureaucracy that mask government action. In welcoming mood, the committee agreed to my suggestion that they look at Finland and Israel's 'committees for the future'. Political horizons are too close. We should be testing all policies and bills against the interests of those living in five, twenty-five and fifty years' time. A striking metaphor for political life is that we live in a saucer. We all look inwardly across it at our own closed world, but we cannot see beyond the horizon, which is the rim of the saucer. That is the date of the next general election.

The result of our probe was a surprise. Contrary to my view that the Finns and Israelis had advanced ideas, the overwhelming evidence was that other countries admired the UK's forward thinking. It was a refreshing conclusion. PASC accepted the force of new evidence. We dropped our previous view that we had been found wanting. This was intellectual dexterity uncommon among politicians suffering the mind paralysis of stultifying fixed views. PASC is for me.

PASC's common purpose is revealing the truth that is often swamped by political sectional interests. One of the unanswered puzzles of New Labour is why PASC's chairman Tony Wright was not offered a job as a minister. He has an abundance of political gifts and he inspires trust. He has led the committee with intelligence, charm, courage and persistence. Some of the Whitehall walls of silence and secrecy have been breached. Others remain unassailable.

I thought I had a landed a small coup when I was seated next to Tony Blair's blue-sky thinker at a Channel Four awards dinner. Lord Birt had been forbidden to give evidence to PASC while he was working for the Number 10 Strategy Unit. 'Now that I've retired,' he told me, 'I can come along.' So we invited him. I was eager to question him on Blair's rejection of the Strategy Unit's well-argued condemnation of current drugs policy. He gave a master class in jargon-clogged obfuscation. The language he used was clearly derived from English, but incomprehensible to PASC members. 'Policy is a sub-set of strategy, with three-to-five-year horizons that improved system outcomes and forward strategy.'

'You wouldn't have a backward strategy, would you?' Tony Wright mocked. The sarcasm was lost on Birt. He ploughed on. 'Some embedded strategies are rooted in incentive structures... conventional performance measurement capability.' Ian Liddell-Grainger asked Birt what he thought 'his three towering achievements at No 10 had been'.

'It is not appropriate that I share with you the insights I gained in government,' Birt purred. PASC is the inquiring select committee. Who else should he share his insights with?

In some desperation I asked, 'If Blairism ever becomes a religious cult, do you think you will be its Pope?' He was mystified; possibly because I was not talking management speak. He said he was a 'great admirer of the Prime Minister'. Later a shell-shocked PASC convalesced with a brief inquiry into official use of jargon.

PASC's main quest is for transparency and accountability through open good government. Parliament should assert itself over a powerful executive. PASC probed prerogative powers, civil service conduct, cash for honours and Ombudsman reports, and even had an inquiry into inquiries.

The vote to join Bush's war still haunts many MPs. Were they bribed, bamboozled and bullied into committing Britain to an illegal war? Some of the bereaved families are tormented by the thought that their loved ones died in vain. Bush's war was certain to happen. But did Britain have to join it? That decision wasted the lives of 179 British soldiers. PASC published a plan for a new style of inquiry that would by-pass the government. Why wait for government to decide when the time is right for a probe into their own guilty behaviour? A Conservative government had avoided an inquiry into Britain's previous worst foreign disaster of Suez, 1956.

Would future governments behave better if they knew their actions were certain to be investigated by an inquiry outside of their control? We had the privilege of hearing the testimony of those principled civil servants who had sacrificed their careers to blow the whistle on the lies that persuaded Parliament to choose war.

What a contrast with the government's feeble, cowardly attempt in 2009 to hold the much-delayed inquiry into Iraq in secret. PASC members ventilated their rage in the chamber and most of us voted against the government. After consulting the great and the good, PASC produced a blueprint for a model procedure. No one in Downing Street appeared to have given it even a glance. The government had previously followed advice from PASC. They were now humiliated because they ignored PASC. The Iraq inquiry is being held in public. It should always have been a decision by Parliament and not by government.

PASC has let me pursue a permanent minor obsession of mine. In the past I have advised MPs that the best way to keep lobbyists from their doors was to send them a standard abusive letter saying, 'Lobbying organisations such as yours are an ugly, anti-democratic and corrupting incubus that haunts the British body politic. Ask your client to directly approach me. Using you as a conduit only adds to their costs for no worthwhile purpose. The quicker your malign presence is expelled from Westminster the sooner the cleansing of the parliamentary stables will begin.'

Lobbying exists to give extra advantages to the already advantaged. They are persuaders for those causes that can afford their fat fees to the detriment of those who cannot. PASC's enquiry into lobbying allowed me to ventilate years of suppressed anger face to face with the snake oil salespeople. The most shameless were Americans. There, corruption and lobbying are opposite sides of the same coin. They were irked when I told them that politicians should file correspondence from them in a file named 'Parasites'. Truth hurts.

The committee produced a tough report. The PR industry was knocked sideways. We called for a compulsory register of their actions. There will be changes but not as radical as the ones that we urged. But 'westward look, the land is bright'. Obama wants a clean break from lobbying which is the sleazy lubricant of Washington.

BBC Parliament has broadcast the subtle delights of select committees to a large public. They are an antidote to the show-business, juvenile posturing of the Commons chamber. At best, they are blissful oases of intelligence and calm where members can work creatively and constructively. May they grow in strength and influence.

So much for my British committee experience. I became a member of the Council of Europe in 1997 even though I was deeply cynical about the institution. It was too popular with MPs who were inveterate Gullivers, alcoholics and freeloaders. The most enthusiastic members were rarely seen in Westminster, more frequently in Room 104, Hôtel de France.

29

Passport to excess

What is the Council of Europe? A watchdog over the Court of Human Rights? A pretext for shameless alcohol-fuelled jaunts? A dynamo for promoting world human rights? A self-regarding indulgence for windbags? The conscience of Europe and a bulwark against oppression? A playground for MPs to behave disgracefully? The most productive networking forum for Europe's MPs? Yes. It's all of these.

In 1991, I met an MP for the first time in the British embassy in Washington. I had never seen him before even though we had both been members of the UK Parliament for four years. Council of Europe members must also serve the Western European Union, so it can be a full-time job attending all the meetings in venues scattered across the planet. Compulsive travellers and air miles addicts can get away with deserting Westminster for half the parliamentary year. Modern technology can keep them in touch with voters in their constituencies as easily from California as from Westminster.

Whips are tolerant. They prefer to have rebellious members abroad, some of us permanently. One of the whips' games is calling selected members back for key votes and leaving possible rebels stranded. Commons rules state that MPs paying for return trips back to the UK will only be reimbursed when the whips have called them back. Rebel MPs will not be invited. They have to pay for their own flights home. It was a key factor in the vital vote on the Iraq War, which coincided with a major event in Athens. All the serious rebels paid for their own flights home. Others were happy to sell their souls or compromise their consciences for a few extra nights in a luxury foreign hotel. An account of this unfair pressure was leaked to the press. Subsequently no member lost money for his or her votes against the war.

It was a pleasant surprise to discover that most COE UK delegates were serious and hard-working. Some were drunks and expenses gluttons who behaved scandalously. But they were irrelevant to the political panjandrum of the COE's progress to promote human rights. Debating and legislating with MPs from forty-seven other countries is a bewildering but rewarding stimulus. There are the repeated absorbing clashes of cultures, ideologies and languages. At best it's an exotic revealing window into alien ideas. At worse, it's a collision with an impenetrable cliff of ignorance and prejudice.

There are often new insights on domestic policies when viewed from abroad. I was once told, 'Your government's policy on asylum seekers is crazy.' My informant told me his constituents are milking our system. 'They rent out their homes for a year, continue to receive social security payments here, then go to Britain and get another income there.'

My informant, Miroslav Ouzký, was not a ranting tabloid bigot. He is a respected liberal MP in the Czech Republic. He is proud that President Havel's velvet revolution created the most benign regime in Czech history. 'No person or race is persecuted here,' Miroslav assured me. He also questioned the motives of those storming the Channel Tunnel. 'To flee from France? A million Britons and many Czechs have happily set up homes in Sarkozy land.'

It's an antidote to our polarised domestic view that either all asylum seekers are victims or none are. Both views are wrong. The UK and the Czech Republic have honourable records in welcoming the victims of persecution and poverty.

I am proud of the abilities, courage and achievements of many British delegates to international bodies. The political and oratorical skills of British MPs are superior to those of all other forty-seven nations of the COE. The House of Commons provides a great apprenticeship to politicians selected for their basic skills, rather than the familial and party patronage that are often essential entry qualifications elsewhere.

My prize for courage goes to Lord Judd for standing up to the abuse, curses and threats from Russians over Chechnya. As Frank Judd, he was a minister in Harold Wilson's government and later ran Oxfam. In Strasbourg he was the truthful voice on the dreadful Russian atrocities in Chechnya. Frank remained steadfast against a united attack from the post-Soviet Commonwealth of Independent States politicians and the Russian media. He was called a liar and accused of taking bribes from the Chechens. While many politicians from Eastern Europe are subtle and of high quality, their politics are still marked by the brutal imprint of their communist past.

The strength of the Council of Europe is the knowledge of members. We meet socially, dine together and know each other's characters intimately. Frank is known to possess saintly integrity beyond the reach of any form of corruption. In Moscow he became a media hate figure. In Chechnya he will be long remembered as a brave politician whose testimony lightened their terrible burdens.

Sadly there have been British delegates with baser ambitions. They have been a disgrace, embarrassingly greedy and out of control. I heard legendary tales of wild living and drunken fights among past delegations. Today's serious MPs are aghast at the excesses of our predecessors, who saw foreign trips as taxpayer-subsidised holidays. Recent reforms have cut drastically the availability of free alcohol in unlimited quantities. The Council of Europe is no place for any MP with a drink problem. Some have got through the net with painful results. There was a predictable, crucifying and embarrassing climax to a competition between two British MPs to discover who could drink the most champagne. The evening was long and unforgettable.

One of the competitors wisely cheated and dumped excess champagne into flowerpots at the reception in the Bois de Boulogne. No doubt to the distress of the tulips. The other kept drinking to excess. He was in a 'confused' state as the bus passed the Etoile en route to a dinner in a splendid French restaurant in Avenue Kléber. More champagne was guzzled. The tally showed a dead heat in the amount drunk. The demeanour of the competitors suggested otherwise. One had consumed a near lethal quantity of alcohol. He was placed at the top table where he babbled incoherently. The event was a dinner for delegates from about twenty countries. There is pressure for reasonably civilised behaviour, especially among foreign colleagues. The reputation of the British is still damaged by this incident, and it happened a decade ago. It was not the idiotic competition or the wild inebriation that left an indelible memory. It was the display of projectile vomiting across the top table. The details are too unpleasant to describe. He slipped into unconsciousness. A doctor was called. The patient was spread-eagled on a couch in an adjoining room with electrodes attached to his nipples. There was a rumour that he had flat-lined.

He was absent at breakfast next morning. Someone had been 'keeping an eye on him' throughout the night but he had disappeared from the hotel at about 6.00 a.m. Later we heard that he had taken the train from Paris to another meeting in Brussels. Not for the first time he had shown remarkable powers of recovery. The rest of the British delegation was humiliated and vengeful. There was no solidarity when the huge bills arrived for the doctor's fee and for cleaning the carpet. No one suggested the usual whip-round. The perpetrator paid in full. To this day, he says that he has no memory of the incident. The rest of us envy his amnesia. There were other incidents that we would all like to forget.

Many social events are unforgettable for other reasons. Liverpool MP Eddie O'Hara stunned his fellow Brits into admiration on a visit to Crete. The après-meeting event was a dinner in a club. The always sober Eddie took over the microphone and told the appreciative audience a joke – in Greek. He followed that with a half an hour singing popular Greek songs in his pleasant light baritone voice. Fellow Europeans were impressed. They are resigned to their view of Brits as monoglot language cretins. Eddie was the brilliant exception. He is also acquainted with ancient Greek. Before he became an MP he was a teacher of teachers. Eddie is unknown in the UK. In Greece, he is a legend.

One leading eloquent British advocate of human rights uses his talents in other directions. An attractive new member of the Council of Europe staff was warm in her appreciation of the kind welcome she had from a British delegate. 'Yesterday he has asked me how I was getting on. Today he brought me some flowers and chocolates. So kind.' She did not know his name. All three of us listening to her story offered to tell her the name of the Lothario. There could be only one contender. A stout defender of women's rights, he toils day and (especially) night to add to the sum of female happiness. His devotion to foreign travel offers a diverse choice of opportunities in building international relationship between the sexes. They also serve who mainly charm and woo.

My main COE initiatives were on the Common Agricultural Policy (CAP), two on drugs and one on smokeless tobacco. My Don Quixote charge against the CAP took on the might of the Euro farming lobby. Initially there was progress. What was formerly a Farming Committee changed to an Environment one. Previously it was a shameless lobby for farming alone, to the neglect of other industries and the third world. I could justly claim that 'for the first time this committee has abandoned its role as a mouthpiece for agricultural big business and is demanding an end to the dependence of Europe's farmers on state charity. Euro subsidies are vast, unjust, self-defeating, and a main cause of environmental damage and poverty in the developing world.'

It was a worthy battle, but the Goliath of the farming mafia was aroused. Thirty-four hostile amendments to my report were submitted by farmer lobbyists. They were debated in the meeting in Santiago de Compostela. Only two were accepted. I could command a majority of the Environment Committee. They agreed with me that Europeans paid twice for the CAP, with taxes and the highest food prices in the world. The cost to the average family is £16 a week. European politicians have been cowardly in buckling to the propaganda and threats of the farming lobby and resisting essential reforms.

My report recommended that the Council of Europe investigate the cost of CAP to the developing world, the taxpayer and consumer, other industries and the economy of the EU and the environment. Two farmer MPs, M. Dupraz from Switzerland and Sig. Gubert from Italy, denounced any attempt to reform the idiocies of Euro farm policies. Although the Swiss are not in the EU, they use the Council of Europe to voice their claims for domestic subsidies. Their handouts are the least defensible. Farmers in new Euro countries get 15 per cent of their income from subsidies; original Euro member countries get 32 per cent, while the Swiss enjoy 72 per cent.

That truth was a novel revelation in a debate that had been swamped by farming interests. Paying 40 per cent of the Euro budget in handouts to millionaire farmers is wasteful and damages the economies of the developing world. When my staff and I wrote the report, we had little hope that it would be accepted by a committee of sixty-four members (including many farmers) from forty-six countries. Our highest hope was to air the issue and expose the scandal to the full glare of European publicity. There were further assaults by the farming lobby when the final decision was made in the hemicycle in Strasbourg. I flattered myself that the trust I had gained from fellow European MPs helped me to defeat the insidious mighty propaganda of the farming lobby. After an uninhibited debate the report was accepted.

The media welcomed the victory and the Council of Ministers purred their approval. They backed the call for a shift in focus to tackle some of the negative effects of the CAP and recognition of the benefits of non-subsidised farming in New Zealand. They acknowledged the role that agriculture can play in promoting rural development, protecting cultural heritage, traditions and the preservation of water, air and soil.

With more than a touch of hyperbole, I was reported as saying in my post-victory euphoria in 2005, 'The CAP is crumbling under the weight of its own waste and absurdity.' If only.

In 2005 it was decided to act against the prime cause of British MPs' bad behaviour – Room 104. For decades the British delegation had used a pleasant three-star hotel in the heart of Strasbourg named the Hôtel de France. Room 104 is a double bedroom that was converted to a conference room for the weeks of the four annual plenary meetings. This was an entirely legitimate use of resources. A tradition had been established for forty years that the British embassy provided liquid refreshment to Room 104. In addition the room's mini-bar was freely used. The bill was paid from a central hospitality fund. I never heard any justification for this but the practice had been long accepted as normal.

Inevitably it was abused with excessive drinking and worse. It was usually at the end of long days of work, plus a steady intake of alcohol. Tired and emotional delegates would top up their alcohol levels until the early hours. The mild disagreements of the day would be inflamed into wild angry confrontations. There were occasional reports of threats of violence although I never witnessed any. The woman delegates fairly objected to the menacing male atmosphere of 104. An agreed smoking ban was not respected. Eventually, the delegation agreed to abandon the room. An occasion of sin disappeared.

The improvement was instant. There are still delegates who have drink problems. They no longer behave boorishly. When they have over-indulged, peer pressure has persuaded them to avoid evening social events. The excesses of the past will never again be tolerated.

My work on illegal drugs for the COE has been arduous, bruising but ultimately rewarding. In 2003 I was a hate figure on Swedish websites. They painted me as a drug-pushing fiend. My report was objective and scientific. It compared the changes in illegal drug use in two prohibitionist countries, Sweden and the UK, and two pragmatic ones, Switzerland and the Netherlands. The pages of charts and figures that I published from unimpeachable original sources proved an increase of use and problems in the prohibitionist countries and stability or a decline where pragmatism ruled.

The opposition was chauvinistic, embittered but never rational. Allied with the Swedes were Slovaks and Poles. My report was disgracefully rejected by one vote in the Strasbourg hemicycle. It was a victory of prejudice over science. This was six years before Alan Johnson's equally prejudiced bullying of Professor Nutt on a shameful day in 2009 when the Commons lynched science.

I have despaired of the possibility of deep-seated reforms. Sweden will never become Holland. The UK will never become Switzerland. My second more ambitious drugs report has been successful at all stages.

It seeks compromise, not confrontation, with a European convention to change the emphasis of anti-drug policy from criminal justice measures to health remedies. It has had almost universal support from all British parties, the COE, the Council of Ministers and the Pompidou group. A new European convention could result. Its effect could be profoundly beneficial for millions of Europe's citizens whose lives are being wrecked by the scourge of drugs.

Added spice to Euro politics is provided by language delights. To his bemused fellow-members of the Council of Europe, on one occasion Labour MP Laurie Cunliffe declared, 'You're pussy-footing.' In French this was translated as '*jouer cache-cache*' although it's a different activity from hide and seek. To the Italian translator the idiom was new. Her creditable effort was 'kicking the cat'. Better acquainted with the lingo of international pornography, the Turkish interpreter disguised his idea of the precise meaning with a delicate 'taking part in an English vice'. Cunliffe's message on Euro finance was displaced by distracting thoughts of children's games, animal abuse and sexual foreplay. This is no way to conduct international conversations.

The oldest of European institutions, the Council of Europe has only two official languages. The pride of members from Francophone countries ensures the survival of French, but it's in full retreat. The irresistible worldwide rush to English accelerates yearly among the parliamentarians from forty-seven countries.

A new language is evolving in European forums. Translated idioms are just one obstacle to comprehension in the language of Euro-speak, *lingua anglica* or Eurolish. The great majority of European politicians struggle to master a simplified English that will allow them to be understood. Their efforts put British politicians to shame but it is a frequent mistake to overestimate the fluency of those who use second-language English.

There are glorious exceptions. Some of the best English in European institutions is spoken by the Dutch and the Danes. One Bulgarian MP, Elena Poptodorova, speaks with the faultless Southern Counties cut-glass accent learnt from wartime B movies. Only she and the Queen still speak this way. In the struggle to maintain the dominant role of their mother tongue, the French strive for the unattainable linguistic parallelism. But, even in the simplest of translations this is rarely achievable.

No two languages run neatly side-by-side on parallel tracks for long. As repositories of centuries of the shared experiences of nations, they are all unique. Rendering languages down into a common Eurolish is done by evaporating off their subtleties, humour and colour. What is left is a pallid blancmange of utility-speak, as drably universal as wartime rationed clothes.

There is a constant search for immediate communication. Simple expressions that can be used in a multitude of situations are gratefully adopted. In the Strasbourg hemicycle, votes are not lost or won, every decision is expressed as 'That is the case' or 'That is not the case'. The semi-fluent have the answers to all questions. Do you speak French? 'That is not the case.' Are you well? 'That is the case.' They are the longwinded positive and negative of Eurolish – as expressive and tedious as semaphore.

The pressures of instant translation are coarsening Eurolish. Exotic metaphors are stamped on and banished back to their original languages. A Danish member dramatically announced in mid-rant, 'We are now in the middle of the river.' Close questioning revealed that this was the Danish equivalent of being at the crossroads, not knowing which direction to take. Mildly provocative to the Welsh is the French cry of 'Revenons à nos moutons'. It's far from obvious that we are being urged to get back to the subject, not being told to return to our woollybacks. My colleague Mike Hancock froze the translators into stuttering silence with the English expression 'They knocked the stuffing out of them'.

Frequently, speakers in minority languages are translated two or three times. One speaker who unexpectedly insisted on addressing the Council in Macedonian was translated into Serbo-Croat, then German and finally into English. It is unlikely that the English version bore anything but the vaguest resemblance to the Macedonian original.

The degradation from English to Eurolish works in two ways. While life and colour fade from the feeder languages of Eurolish, the clichés and platitudes spread like viruses. Most European languages have adopted the verbal polyfiller of replacing 'now' with 'at this moment in time' or 'finally' with 'at the end of the day'. The entire continent of Euro-babble is now covered with level playing fields. The pap of predictable platitudes smothers original vivid phrases. The pollution of conformity spreads inexorably.

Even President Chirac has been infected. He is fond of saying that anything disagreeable is *'pas ma tasse de thé'*. Tea? Not his *verre de vin* would make better sense. The President should set an example and challenge the littering of his mother tongue.

A further inducement to debase the common tongue is the dislocation between a speaker and a live audience. Those listening in translation can unnerve the best orator. Empathy is impossible when the meaning hits the listener's brain five seconds after the words are said. The best example is the dislocation of meaning and body language that I described earlier in Bulgaria. They shake their heads from side to side indicating assent and nod them up and down when they disagree.

Professional politicians feed off the responses from their audiences. Delays, mistakes and misunderstandings of translation leave listeners baffled and the speaker distressed that his words are not answered with appreciation or understanding. Even worse is a delayed laugh when the penny has dropped at the moment the speaker has progressed from his joke to his serious point. The only remedies are to slow delivery, coarsen thoughts, simplify adjectives and abandon all but the obvious metaphors or idioms. No swift changes of mood are possible. Speeches must be divided into coherent compartments of gloom, humour, inspiration that will be as synchronous as possible with the flow of translation.

There is no hope that Eurolish will be a language that will be pleasant to the ear. In the less fascinating moments of Euro debate, I occasionally listen to my colleagues in translation. The dullest speaker can sound seductive in Italian, threatening in Turkish or abusive in German. The prospect is bleak. Eurolish is incurably regressive. Europeans will speak to Europeans in the turgid verbiage that dulls the brains and enfeebles inspiration. Stripped of invective and passion, no poetry will ever be written in Eurolish. On the other hand it's unlikely that anyone will ever declare war in it.

In 2003 I had a head-on clash with the French clerks. We were about to debate a report about the rights of minority languages. I told the Council of Europe clerks that I intended to make a speech in Welsh. The right-wing French government was reversing many of the gains achieved by Breton-medium schools achieved under the previous socialist government. My intention was to berate the French for their centralist neurotic defence of the French language against the midge bite of a threat from the Breton language. It was a point worth making because the Council of Europe Tower of Babel is well disposed towards minority languages.

The clerks were horrified and baffled. They said it would be impossible. The French clerk voiced traditional disdain for the minority languages that had the impertinence to exist in France. 'But if you speak in Welsh, someone else might want to speak in Alsatian, Provençal and Occitan,' he said, knowing that such an absurdity should never be permitted. 'Why not?' I asked.

Until two hours before the debate was due to start, Welsh was still outlawed. I dug my heels in. I would speak in Welsh and refuse to stop. The only way they could silence me would be to switch off my microphone. Perhaps not a convincing advertisement for a Council of Europe's report proudly proclaiming its record of the promotion of minority languages. Eventually they surrendered. I could use Welsh but I would have to provide a written translation and an interpreter.

A written translation? Yes. An interpreter? Difficult. There were no other Welsh-speakers available. Straining our marriage vows to breaking point I asked my non-Welsh-speaking wife to read a translation. She was wisely worried. There was trouble ahead. There was a couple of hours' delay in the order of debates during which Sam was ensconced in the interpreter's booth. It was a revelation. There was close camaraderie among the interpreters. They were respectful and correct when the microphones were live: contemptuous, cynical and mocking when they were not in sound contact with the hemicycle. One interpreter expressed her contempt for a Ukrainian. His speech was quietly delivered. As maliciously interpreted, he sounded like an aggressive ranting lunatic. The chairman's Austrian accent made him sound like a Schwarzenegger village yokel. He was irritated by a technician who repeatedly switched off his microphone. He protested that he might need to intervene in debates, so he needed a live mike all the time. This was interpreted from the silent booth in a childlike wail, 'I want my mike. Who has stolen my toy? Give it back to me or I will have a tantrum.'

Sam and I had hurriedly rehearsed the speech. There were a few key words and names understandable to her that should have guided her. The nightmare would have been that one of us would have finished too early or too late. It was extremely courageous of Sam. She has always been up for a challenge.

Inevitably, I went astray in my speech. Never have I learnt the knack of reading a speech from a script with any passion or conviction. Even though no one could understand a word that was coming from my lips, I did feel an uncanny empathy with the audience who were staring at me in amazement. Most were astonished at an impassioned rant delivered with strange war-cries in a language that the chairman called 'Velch'. I busked a bit in mid-speech and wandered off the script into unplanned territory. Entirely by luck and nothing to do with judgement, Sam finished her translation five words after I ended. The perfect result, exactly what professional interpreters do.

There was universal acclamation. The wise Hungarian Liberal Eörsi said this makes it easier for 'all of us to use our languages'. At a reception at the British embassy in the evening, it was the main talking point with agreeable support coming from the Portuguese and Romanian delegations. The British embassy staff were a bit sniffy.

It was a triumph for Sam. Her voice was heard in all the headphones in the Assembly. A fellow delegate and pal of Sam's, Geraldine Smith, was genuinely surprised. 'It was so professional. I thought it was one of the regular interpreters.' Good day for Breton, Welsh and all European minority languages. Sam and I purred quietly. What a team!

The COE has a little brother. The Western European Union (WEU) is a largely unknown organisation. Staffed by people of high quality and crammed with talkative MPs, its existence has been hanging by a thread for a decade. But it has given me some wonderful opportunities to influence top politicians. Its invisibility was sadly proved when the Leicester MP Jim Marshall died in 2004. His main political interest was his chairmanships of the Technological and Political committees of the WEU. He invested enormous energies in building an international reputation as a resourceful and talented politician. Bizarrely, there was no mention of his WEU work in any of his obituaries. Strenuous work abroad had not created a ripple of interest in his constituency or at Westminster.

The British contribution to the COE and the WEU peaked with the election of the splendid Birmingham MP Terry Davis as secretary general in 2004. In his five-year tenure he did a magnificent job. In his acceptance speech, he affirmed the highest ambitions of the council and especially its British members.

> I have a vision of Europe as part of a world where men and women are treated fairly and equally, a Europe where people live in peace on the basis of mutual respect without any discrimination based on gender, sexual orientation, ethnic origin or religious belief, a Europe with no borders, no visas, no passports – a Europe where people have the time and opportunity to enjoy not only their own culture but the cultures of other people. The Council of Europe is the best way to turn that vision into reality.

Within days of Terry standing down at the end of his term, the reforms he introduced were being dismantled by an institution that was deeply hostile to Anglo-Saxon ways. A linguistic fog and national self-interests confined the Europe-wide stages of the COE and the WEU.

But contemporary politicians now enjoy new platforms, without boundaries or limits, in the novel world of cyberspace.

30

The artful blogger

The World Wide Web is a godsend to some politicians and a headache to others. Old and young fogies resent change. The web disturbs their familiar settled routine. To the curious and adventurous the web has opened up fresh prairies of knowledge, fun and broad avenues of contact with constituents. We can become better MPs.

My ten-year odyssey in cyberspace has been an exhilarating adventure. My website and blog have been honoured with prizes, cursed by MPs, denounced as 'unfit for children', lavished with praise, excoriated with censure and banned by the House of Commons. It continues joyously with a daily addition to the permanent two million plus mountain of words and tens of thousands of pictures that chronicle a decade in the life of a backbencher.

The site has multiplied the value of my work and allowed me to harangue flagrantly and sumptuously in choice words and images. Will the web improve the political process? Would a 'nyebevan.co.uk' have provided an earlier NHS? Would a 'winstonchurchill.com' have helped us win the war? Why not? Certainly the political giants of the past would have revelled in the immense possibilities to proselytise and campaign. But even some of my closest respected friends have disagreed. The late, brilliant, Tony Banks felt threatened by new technology. He saw his talents in the spoken not the written word. He told me he was squatting on two domain names: 'tryanothermp.com' and 'whydontyoufuckoff.com'. Elevation to the Lords was an escape route for him from pestilence of importuning constituents who had the effrontery to contact him.

In some respects, the web has restored the anarchic freebooting independence of the pioneers of embryo socialism. One hundred and fifty years ago, in my constituency, the Chartists spread the word with locally printed pamphlets. John Frost had his produced by Partridge, the Newport printer, and distributed them door to door. Word of mouth did the rest, spreading the Chartist creed in songs and poems. The web now gives the same freedom to capture a near-infinite audience.

Politicians who have had their mouths bandaged by the whips or feel ignored or misrepresented by the media can become their own publishers. The scope and creative possibilities have few boundaries. Politicians can be exuberantly ON-line and creatively OFF-message: uncensored, unspun, uninhibited.

Some early MPs' forays into cyberspace were dreary. The first builders of steel bridges copied the techniques of the builders of wooden bridges. The first wedding videos aped the traditional style of still pictures. The first politicians' sites were stale copies of traditional propaganda and electioneering. There were no interviews and little use of sound and movement. CVs, press releases and political leaflets remain as deeply boring in cyberspace as when they are pushed through letterboxes.

Constituents will surf only those sites offering news, gossip or humour not available elsewhere. Surfers must be seduced and trapped by the enticing promise that the blog will reveal exciting new gossip, truths or confidential insights. Winston Churchill and Aneurin Bevan would have worked wonders with such a launch pad for their ideas in the 1930s. When Bevan was a member of the Monmouthshire County Council, he was never allowed to make a speech. That was the job of the senior county councillors.

Nyebevan.co.uk would have been a rich tapestry of wild humour, prophetic insights and blazing idealism. His web-fluency would not have been inhibited by the stutter that plagued his early speeches. His ideas would have soared beyond the Miners' Institutes to a world audience. He would have fed off the shoal of emails that would have tested and enriched his own beliefs. Churchill suffered years of brooding, enforced silences. His prophetic ideas, at times, had no ready outlets.

US politicians have blazed the trail with their money-raising rabble-provoking blogs. We are at the embryo stage of development. The launch of my site in 1999 was a baptism of unexpected adulation. Not because it was that good. It was not. But other MPs' sites were woeful. Tom Steinberg wrote in the *Parliamentary Monitor* that my site was 'a triumph of irreverent style, run by this delightfully unconverted Welsh Labour MP. Filled with opinion pieces, kept lovingly up to date and built around a simplest-is-best design, Mr Flynn shows the power that is there to be exploited by politicians who have the courage.'

In its first years the site won the *New Statesman* New Media Award for best politician's site. It was named the best site in Wales by the *Western Mail*. Anne Campbell, a former MP, wrote that it was 'a wonderful excuse for Paul's prolific writing. I laughed out loud at his Dear Raving Bigot letter.' The Assessment and Qualifications Alliance lifted a great chunk of gossip about backbenchers for an examination question paper. *Westminster Watch* declared the site to be the 'stickiest of all MPs' websites – the one to stay on all day'. The *Daily Mirror* printed a chunk of my doggerel about New Labour imposing Alun Michael on the Welsh Assembly. Allegedly penned by Rupert Blair, it concluded,

> You gloomy Taffies, now rejoice,
> I've given you your own small voice,
> An extra gift is this wise wish,
> Be joyful, humble and – more English.

The only sour note was a report that Margaret Moran MP wrote for the *House Magazine* on the *New Statesman* award ceremony. Margaret herself was nominated for an award. She remarkably managed to complete her article without mentioning the name of the winner.

My constituents purred with approval that their on-line off-message MP was voted the best at Westminster at anything. The *Express on Sunday* was inadvertently helpful with a headline 'Outrage over MP's hotline to drugs dealer'. It was exaggerated hot air written by someone who did not understand the Internet. One of the many links on the site was to Howard Marks, the former imprisoned drugs dealer and drug laws reformer. The *Express* wrote the story up to imply that I was pushing drugs. Two dim-witted MPs swallowed the *Express* line. There was a pompous word from Charles Clarke copied to the Prime Minister. Charles repeated the calumny that I was promoting the illegal drugs market. I told Charles that he had fallen for a piece of tabloid hype. There is also a link to the Labour Party on the site 'even though I do not support the party's disastrous drugs policy that results in 1,000 heroin deaths a year'.

Tory John Greenway helpfully said my site was 'unfit for children'. This was manna. I copied his words onto my home page. Ann Widdecombe had a 'Kiddies Corner' on her site. No self-respecting child would ever visit that. But a website that was 'unfit for children' was a guaranteed magnet for young surfers. The cunning plan of the home page was to journalistically intrigue, puzzle and seduce readers to delve deeper into the site where the serious campaigning messages lurked.

On 21 March 2007 I started a daily blog. I have not missed a day since. More than 1,000 posts have been written and 10,000 comments received. Improved technology eases the process of daily blogging from abroad and, with a dongle, I can post from the back seat of a moving car. Blogging was like learning to swim or ride a bike for the first time at an advanced age. A delicious thrill. I hesitated before starting. Blog pope Iain Dale, speaking ex cathedra, opined that most MPs think that their colleagues who blog are 'clinically insane'. Those MPs will be the average timid career-hungry boring MPs who are terrified of saying anything interesting. Recording original thoughts is dangerous. They can boomerang back later and bite.

The House of Commons ignored blogs until the new communication allowance included payments for running websites (the allowance has now, following the expenses fiasco, been removed). The full majesty of the Commons thought police excoriated my blog. They were unhappy with a comment about Peter Hain, when I compared him to Shapeshifter, a *Star Trek* character 'who liquefies at the end of each day and sleeps in a bucket to emerge in any chosen shape the following morning'. Nor did they like my restrained comment that Lembit Öpik is a 'clown and a turkey whose specialty is valuing mindless political populism over intelligence'. Tory Nigel Evans was described as 'a tabloid newspaper made flesh'. I described the cash donated to two of my Labour colleagues, Richard Caborn and Ian McCartney, from the nuclear industry as 'cash for comrades'.

There were complaints because I had said that in her first parliament Ann Widdecombe was 'everyone's loathed ogre. Sour, unattractive and humourless she spat her puritanical venom at foe and friend.' I was being excessively kind to Nicholas Soames in saying that 'a serious politician was struggling to emerge from his globular mountainous shape'. Removing all criticism of politicians would have filleted out the idiosyncratic spice and malice that attract blog readers. This might make sense in terms of Commons courtesy but under the oppressive rules of the Commons, blogs would become bland, anaemic and unreadable. Journalists enjoy almost unfettered freedom. Matthew Parris has described Tony Blair as 'a mad, delusional cheat', Margaret Thatcher as 'blinkered, brutal and imaginatively stunted', David Cameron 'a podgy puffball' and John Redwood as 'an emotionally illiterate Vulcan'.

This is the stuff of political banter. My contributions were, and continue to be, remarkably restrained, with the occasional mild reproof to recidivist MPs. My website is the window into a political world striving to record the daily shifts of the political drama. I have marked all the deaths of our soldiers in Iraq and Afghanistan including a tally of the total when each new death occurs. The exchange of views with my correspondents has been informative and stimulating. Some have changed my opinions.

I restrict the time I spend on it to less than an hour a day – usually late in the evening. Most blogs are about 800 words long, covering three subjects, and illustrated. The statistics tell their own story: 1,000 blogs, 10,000 comments and 270,000 hits. The response has been marvellous. Between 500 and 2,000 people read the daily offering. Constituents and journalists drop in to the site to find out what's going on. No longer do I bother to send out press releases. The media have been kind to me. But there are frustrations in trying to push complex serious arguments through the needle's eye of the news editor's judgement. Reducing a complex intelligent argument to a single sentence often distorts and misrepresents. I have long given up on explaining my views on drugs, war and royalty to the bovine monosyllabic local press.

We can talk to constituents and the wider world unedited, unspun and unabbreviated. Comments can also be dressed up with attractive pictures. Here is a platform to present campaigns that challenge orthodox opinion on the impossible Helmand mission, the over-prescription of medicinal drugs, the exploitation of the third world, the counter-productive illegal drugs policy.

Blogging has become addictive. My website has been in business for ten years. It fulfilled the communication function. The need to write creatively every day is a welcome discipline and jump-starts my synapses into their daily callisthenics. There have been strong reactions to some of the many obituaries I have written to honour my friends. Some have lived exemplary lives, unseen and under-appreciated. One was intended as a counterblast to the faux-tributes paid to her by politicians who had previously undermined her.

No more will we hear the beautifully expressive voice of Gwyneth Dunwoody, authoritative, acerbic, impassioned or persuasive. She employed all the skills of her past training as an actress to dominate the backbench and select committees.

She was waspish and wise at a meal I enjoyed with her and two other colleagues a month ago. There was no hint or sign of any illness. She was irritated and often contemptuous of the easy rise to cabinet of new women MPs. She thought they had it easy compared with her generation. One of the few repeatable comments is her claim that Pat Hewitt's career faltered because she spent too much time with her voice coach.

She was the last of a generation of women MPs of exceptional talent who succeeded mainly because they were tougher than their male counterparts. Gwyneth was generously endowed with strength, guile, humour, courage and integrity. Rest in Peace, Comrade.

I believe that a main platform of political debate in future will be on the blogosphere. The merging of the coalition parties in the Welsh Assembly was lubricated by Welsh blogs. Ways forward were suggested at a time when parties were not talking directly. Possible areas of agreement were floated on the blog of a Plaid Cymru MP, Adam Price. They were basis for the Labour–Plaid One Wales coalition that has been a startling success.

One intriguing new blog menace is 'swarming'. My defence of the smoking ban provoked an instance of it, when nearly 700 comments were recorded and the site had many thousands of hits. Two other swarms, from Christian fundamentalists and global warming deniers, also stung. A 'queen bee' may lead the swarms or they can arise spontaneously from supportive blogs. Either way they present a conundrum for blogging politicians. Ignore them or spend an inordinate amount of time answering them. Failure to produce replies to comments leads to accusations that the arguments are not being answered. I posted a 1,000-word riposte to those who oppose the smoking ban. It did little but provoke even more comments.

Luckily a small group of well-informed and impassioned correspondents valiantly battled against the smokers. The debate was generally very enlightening. It's significant that none of my constituents has ever raised this issue with me.

Swarmers have all the characteristics of members of cults: an exaggerated view of the importance of their issue, a reluctance to challenge their own prejudices, a mistaken sense of victimhood plus a fanatic's lack of proportion and common-sense. The anti-smoking-ban lobby amassed a mere 0.38 per cent of the vote in a parliamentary by-election. I am very happy to continue to offer a platform for intelligent debate. But I am now less hospitable when I hear the sound of buzzing.

31

Icons and knaves

Politicians are odd and fascinating. To encourage MP-watching as a national sport, I have listed some of them with their characteristics. Many I admire. Others I loathe. Several are described here for their unique peculiarities, others for exemplary talents or because they are typical of groups of like-minded wayward souls. My judgements are inspired by admiration and hero-worship, spiced with a little malice.

Carne Ross was a troubled senior diplomat in the Foreign Office. Talented and idealistic, his job was to know the secrets about our relations with Iraq. He was contemptuous of claims that there were WMDs or any serious military threat from Saddam Hussein. He knew that Saddam could be controlled by cutting the illegal sales of oil through our allies in Jordan and Sudan. This was an easy bloodless alternative to war. It was not considered because Bush was determined to go to war. We meekly followed behind. The price in blood and treasure was grievous.

Carne did not speak out at the time. He gave evidence anonymously to the Butler inquiry then resigned from his high-flying post. There was no ready alternative. Although he and the other whistleblowers could have leaked productively to MPs, none of them considered that. This is a worry for MPs.

He thought of resigning and making a fuss at the start of the war. He said it would be like standing in front of a runaway train. He complained that those who question policy in the FO were stigmatised as troublemakers.

Their careers would end in appointment to an embassy in Belarus rather than Washington. He frankly admitted that he had a period of depression when he resigned from the FO. He has now set up a non-profit-making diplomatic service concentrating on the plight of the people of Western Sahara. His view is that UK foreign policy is based on narrow, commercial self-interest. Because we need a few paltry contracts with Morocco we have ignored the persecution of the people of the Sahel.

Carne is a brilliant young man of high idealism. What a tragedy that there is no place for him in our Foreign Office. The Iraq War was the worst decision taken by the British government since the invasion of Suez. The integrity of our political system has been debased. Carne Ross should have a future role in restoring it to its highest standards.

Alan Simpson is the greenest of all MPs. He is one of my main parliamentary heroes because of his brilliant presentation of environmental issues. Eloquent, serious and extremely funny and entertaining, he has put his convictions into action. He has converted his house in the Lace Market, central Nottingham, into a new energy-efficient home. It has a microchip power unit, which he believes is the way homes need to be heated.

The *Independent*'s Colin Brown said of him: 'Alan Simpson is an MP who stuck to his principles. He gives politicians a good name.' For Alan Simpson, the turning point came with the birth of his daughter Elie. After carving out a successful career as a familiar and colourful figure on the Labour back benches, enough was enough. The MP arrived at a stark conclusion: if his daughter were to enjoy a secure future, more would have to be done to combat global warming. Disillusioned with an increasingly ineffective Parliament, he decided Westminster was no longer capable of listening to his demands for more radical action.

Tony Blair and Gordon Brown, the frequent recipients of Simpson's critical tongue, may weep few tears at his departure at the next election, but many believe Parliament will be a poorer place. And for those who fear politics is increasingly dominated by spin and is bereft of principle, Alan's decision may offer some reassurance.

The 59-year-old has become a fully paid-up member of Parliament's awkward squad, the band of irrepressible troublemakers on both sides of the House who refuse to be silenced by whips and are prepared to sacrifice careers for principles. Alan summed up his philosophy:

> I never went into Parliament to have a career. I went in to change the world. I'm leaving because I still want to change the world, and I don't think you can do that in this Parliament. My worry is that it has become a comfort zone in which MPs are paid more and more to stand for less and less.

He has been described as the rebel without applause.

Lembit Öpik has an impenetrable shellback and invites mockery. Even his famous personality did not help when he lost ignominiously in an internal Lib Dem election to an unknown baroness. 'Anyone but Lembit' was the winning vote. His abilities are manifest but wayward.

He is suffering the fate of all devoted parliamentary jokers and media tarts. It's entertaining to see him yelping and cavorting. But ultimately it's self-lacerating. He boldly flouted the law on his motorised pogo stick. But the joke was on Lembit. While he was parading outside a party conference on his Segway, he was accused of neglecting his duties in a debate inside.

It's on with the motley again for Lembit. He can take pride in his status as a valued Commons character. But he has sabotaged his own gravitas. He adds colour to the accepted grey persona of MPs. But his Montgomery constituents may punish him in the ballot box.

Ann Widdecombe has gone from a loathed ogre to a parliamentary treasure. In an unkind moment, I called her Doris Karloff, a jibe understood only by cinema fans of a certain age. The *Daily Mirror* repeated the nickname in a banner headline. Unfazed, she was reported to answer her phone with 'Karloff here'.

Now she has metamorphosed into Parliament's beloved warm agony aunt and good-natured fox-hugger. She is the benign earth mother spoiling the nation with great dollops of common sense. National television will be the gainer and Parliament will lose out when she stands down at the next election.

Ann Cryer has suffered cruel blows. She is the antithesis of the New Labour princesses who have flounced into Parliament on New Labour assisted places schemes and will flounce out when the going gets rough. Ann is grassroots Labour and one of Parliament's most fearless operators. From the dross of greed and grab on the expenses scandal she shines out as an honourable member. Even that did not protect her from the sneers of the gutter media. An act of great personal generosity was twisted to imply that she was implicated in the scandal. That was unjust.

Ann contradicts the image of the strident assertive MP. She is quietly spoken, modest and free from ambition. Her exemplary courage is rooted in the strength and certainty of her socialist convictions. She saw injustices among her Muslim women constituents and fearlessly challenged them. Her campaign on forced marriages resulted in a change in the law. She has highlighted the dangers of consanguineous marriages in defiance of the traditions of her constituents. She braved the anger of male opinion and emerged triumphant. Lesser politicians have remained silent or, in one case, accused her of 'racism'.

She suffered two tragic bereavements. Her first husband, MP and former MEP Bob Cryer, died at the wheel of his car when he was driving her to London. Her second husband John died after a long battle with cancer. After suffering the rigours of repeated surgery and treatments, he decided when to say 'No more'. They were both fine men of principle and integrity. Ann is rightly proud of her family. Her son John is the former MP for Hornchurch and continues a tradition of the Labour Party at its very best. The Cryer family have been the conscience of the Labour Party.

Stephen Pound is a parliamentary jewel. Ripples of laughter spread from his perch on the back benches. His flow of banter, insults and jokes is a continuous Greek chorus to the main speakers. His flow is unstoppable. Bruce George MP was startled to hear animated talk from the next cubicle to the one he was using in the Commons Members' toilet. Stephen was multi-tasking, one of the tasks being an interview for Radio Ulster.

His maiden speech was a hilarious caricature of the dreary formula of lavishing sugary praise on the constituency:

> A giant circus elephant collapsed on Castlebar Hill . . . and died. The great pachyderm, with its last few breaths, bravely staggered forward and is, to this day, to be found beneath the road, unfortunately just over the constituency border in Ealing, Acton & Shepherd's Bush. I suspect that his last thought was to leave Ealing North.

Occasionally the clown's mask slips and a serious and honest politician is revealed:

> I am asked why I – as a Christian, and a person who tries to lead my life in the imitation of Christ – would, as I intend to, support the bill [The Sexual Offences Amendment Bill 1999]. My son is not yet sixteen. I love my son, and I hope that I will always love my son. I do not know whether he will be gay, straight or bisexual – that is up to him; that is what he will be – but, if he comes out as a gay man at the age of sixteen or seventeen, I would like to show my love and respect for him by saying that I value and respect his sexuality just as much as I respect his sister's sexuality.

Throughout the Livingstone stitch-up he was embarrassingly loyal to lost causes, first to Glenda Jackson then to Frank Dobson. Why? He explained, 'I'm a cringing coward. I always vote the way they tell me to vote. I'm a balls-achingly, tooth-grindingly, butt-clenchingly loyal apparatchik.'

All MPs felt a stab of pain. The fit, non-smoking, cricketing, light-drinking 63-year-old David Taylor died without warning on Boxing Day 2009.

David Taylor was a supremely resourceful backbencher, a polymath

and a unique parliamentary craftsman. In the three final days of David's
parliamentary life before the Christmas recess he asked a remarkable ten
oral questions and initiated a parliamentary debate. As always, his words
were authoritative, penetrating and humorous.

His nimble, well-furnished mind deployed every weapon in the
backbenchers' armoury. Ministers braced themselves for the inevitable
David Taylor question. His formula for oral questions was a courteous
introduction that flattered the answering minister, then a deadly
adjectival triple fusillade, usually lubricated with humour and a final
unanswerable coda.

> I exculpate the minister, who is a very able man of great integrity, but
> what should be done about the lamentable failures of that ill-conceived,
> incoherent and incompetent organisation? Perhaps the guilty parties
> could be locked up for egregious negligence as a pilot group in one of
> the minister's fabled titan prisons – if there is one big enough.

The House of Commons Library kindly measured for me the extent to
which he mastered oral questions including the newly fangled topical
ones. He tops all tables with a massive eighty-four topical questions
and 121 other orals. Many were opportunistic, called because of his
permanent presence in the chamber. He scored highly in the value-for-
money league table of MPs who work the hardest for the lowest unit cost.

His stylish audacious use of language was a delight. He extended the
stale vocabulary of the Commons with adventurous English. Occasionally
he overindulged his alliteration, asking, 'Is it forever the fate of football
fans to be fleeced by flaky foreign financiers?'

His independent unique approach to parliamentary procedure has left
its legacy. A 'David Taylor vote' is the only way of registering a positive
abstention. When in doubt, David voted in both the No and the Aye
lobbies. It's hard to explain to constituents. But it's good sense until
Parliament comes up with a better idea.

He was never what Tony Wright called a When politician, concerned
about when he was going to get a job, a promotion or a prized favour.

David was a Why MP, asking: Why is that happening? Why can't it be improved? Why are we repeating errors?

Ambition or ministerial office never captured his interest. He never sought self-aggrandisement or empty publicity. His satisfaction came from worthwhile reforms. He spoke with sensitivity and understanding on the care of the elderly and the strains of family life. He inspired campaigns for improved residential care, for the smoking ban and the humane treatment of laboratory animals. Yvette Cooper praised his contribution to improved cancer services.

He was first elected in 1997 as a fully fledged expert in accountancy and computers. He flailed PFI as 'prohibitive in cost, flawed in concept and intolerable in consequence'. He excoriated the Rural Payments Agency for their 'failure to properly specify, design and control a major public sector computer development'. He passionately denounced the parliamentary system that allows the 'executive to take liberties with democracy, generating an atavistic herd instinct that strangles independent thought and objectivity'. He devised a practical strategy for correcting the harm of the 10p tax debacle.

But he was loyal to the core values of the Labour Party. He described himself as 'typical working class' and a 'mushy peas rather than a guacamole socialist'. His never-failing courtesy and lack of malice secured the affection of all colleagues. He served his constituency with maternal zeal. David's iconic success and character make him an admirable model for the new parliamentarians.

Ann Cryer told she was glad she kept a scrap of paper ripped out of the order book and passed to her by David a fortnight before his death. He scribbled on it, 'Happy Birthday. If I was you I would sue those dyslexic scoundrels on the *Guardian* who say you are 70 today, when you are obviously 60.'

He decided to leave Parliament and not contest his Leicester seat after a taxing campaign in 2005. So thin was his campaigning team he was forced to act as his own agent. He promised his family that he would not stand again. He announced his retirement in 2008 before the expenses scandal broke. David became one of the lynch mob's casualties. He allowed his daughter to rent a room in his flat for a rent of £250 a month. He declared the rent and deducted that sum from his total claims. He had bought the flat with his own capital, not with money that can be claimed through parliamentary allowances. He had done nothing wrong.

David was his own savage judge. He decided that the rent was low and paid the Fees Office £8,000 in recompense. He had failed in his own eyes to live up to his own high standards of integrity. I argued with him that he was guiltless. He was not convinced and he suffered a barrage of hate including death threats. He was deeply wounded.

Perhaps David Taylor may have been the first fatal victim of the crushing mindless abuse that followed the expenses scandal. The chortling critics did not differentiate between the guilty and the innocent. The life of a lovely man was ended prematurely. His colleagues will miss his friendship, his modesty, his infectious laugh and his kindness. Parliament is bereaved.

After Windsor MP Alan Glyn had adopted me as his pair in 1987 he trained me in the seamy by-ways of Parliament's social life. By then he was past his best. After a creditable, colourful career as a distinguished soldier and GP, his life had settled into a comfortable routine of idle self-indulgence.

Being an MP had become a tiresome habit as familiar and dreary as pulling on an old boot. Each day was a slow slide into an amiable alcoholic haze, enlivened by regular embassy receptions, visits abroad and the occasional re-recital of his speech on defence. He delivered it year after year with hardly a syllable being changed. He dreamt of elevation to the House of Lords with his Windsor parliamentary seat passing on to a member of his family. He was fobbed off with a knighthood in exchange for his resignation from Parliament. Like most politicians he was disappointed with his career. It was a familiar story. His ambitions were beyond what was practically attainable.

He was in his early seventies but he looked about 110. Late nights and a prodigious consumption of fine wines and food had weakened Alan Glyn's constitution. For the final twenty years of his life he teetered on the brink of survival. His friends thought they had a tragedy on their hands during a by-election campaign. A Tory team of senior MPs, including Alan, had booked into a hotel in the constituency ready to be on parade early next morning. Alan was put to bed before midnight with brain and body generously alcoholised.

Not unexpectedly he failed to appear for breakfast next morning. Phone calls to his room were not answered. Alarmed that the old buffer might have finally given up the ghost, his friends hammered on the door. Even that failed to rouse him. The hotel's master key was tried. The door unlocked but would not budge. Could the object that was blocking it be Alan's body? Had he finally succumbed to the ravages of age, alcohol and heart trouble? Reverentially the door was inched open. The obstruction was a fallen wardrobe. There was no sign of Alan. They searched the bathroom, under the bed, behind the curtains. How could he have left the room with the door blocked? Inexplicable. They heard snoring. It was coming from the fallen wardrobe. Alan was inside. He never provided a plausible account of the night's adventure. The favoured explanation is that he needed the bathroom in the middle of the night. In the confusion of an unfamiliar room, he mistook the wardrobe door for the bathroom door. No one was sufficiently indelicate to enquire what happened inside. But his struggles to get out toppled the wardrobe. Hours later Alan was still inside sleeping like a baby.

Understandably Alan's constituency party wanted to dump him. They tried in 1983 but he won the battle with a promise that it would be his last parliament. He had another excuse: 'Margaret might want me to stand down so that a cabinet member could take my place in the by-election.'

To nail him on retirement, his constituency party organised a valedictory dinner prior to the 1987 election. It was a grand occasion. The wine flowed. The tributes to the retiring MP were extravagant. What was there to lose? He was going. They lavished praise: 'Alan has been a brilliant MP, a dedicated physician, a gallant soldier who almost liberated Hungary single handed. Whoever will replace him, they could never be better than Doctor Alan.'

With difficulty Alan staggered to his feet. He was deeply moved. Tears flowed. 'My dear friends. I had no idea how much you appreciate my work for you. You are so kind. I cannot desert now. I will not run away. I will continue to be your MP.'

The emotion and alcohol worked. They all cheered. The slow realisation dawned. 'God! What have we done?'

They were saddled with him for another five years.

Although I had known him since I was a child, George Thomas never failed to shock, even after his death. He combined the roles of vice-president of the Methodist Conference and a secret cottaging homosexual.

George was very kind to my first wife Ann and me in 1962. He escorted us around the House of Commons on our honeymoon in London. It was slightly embarrassing that he greeted all the attendants and police as 'brother'. Thousands of other constituents benefited from his dedicated care of his 'flock'. Other suffered his wrath. He had a lifelong feud with fellow Cardiff MP James Callaghan. Many backbenchers loathed his waspish ridicule.

His family background was classic anthracite Old Labour. All four of his siblings left school at age thirteen. His two sisters went into service, his elder brother went down the pit and his younger brother worked in a shop. George's native wit gained him a place in the local valley's grammar school and he became a schoolteacher.

He rediscovered his valleys accent which he had lost as a London schoolteacher. His Welsh-accented 'Order, Order' became a trade mark for the first parliamentary radio broadcasts.

His persona as MP and Speaker was one of elevated righteousness. He preached the old-time religion with passion. He suffered, or perhaps enjoyed, the ever-present threat of exposure. Homosexuality was not only a sin but a crime throughout most of his parliamentary life. Leo Abse spilled the beans after Thomas's death. He once confided in Leo, when he was Speaker, that he was finished because he had contracted a venereal disease. Leo once loaned him £800 to pay off a blackmailer. For years he had been paying blackmailers. It's extraordinary that the secret of one of the best-known politicians in the land with a famous voice was never revealed.

In his final years he drifted from his working-class roots. He became a grovelling royal groupie and backed James Goldsmith's Referendum Party. His legendary meanness is recalled by an account of his visit to the Commons post office the day after he resigned as MP and Speaker. He was no longer entitled to the free postage service for the thank-you letters he was sending to admirers. Aghast at the price of a stamp he railed, '27p?! Don't you know I'm a pensioner?'

Brian Haw is Britain's most successful advocate for bringing home the simple message of guilt daily to those who voted to send British troops to Iraq. All MPs are humbled by him. Driving home to my warm flat at the end of day, I have passed him in Parliament Square hundreds of times, settling down for another night under the stars. Often I have a stab of guilt because I had not raised in Parliament that day the futility of Iraq and Helmand. He has been doing it for seven years.

Mark Wallinger is a refreshingly artless artist with a stunted ego. It may be conceptual bullshit or worse, but it's superb politics. He reproduced, in an exhibition, Brian Haw's 100 yards of protest. The artistic merit escaped me, but politically Haw's display constantly twitches the conscience of legislators. Uniquely, after winning the Turner Prize, Wallinger did not talk about himself and his genius but about Brian Haw and the big lie.

This was the best Turner Prize decision ever. Forget the pretentious art; let's have full-blooded politics!

Kim Howells is emblematic of those woeful junior ministers on eternal odysseys of futility, ever moving sideways from meaningless jobs as the lackeys of their seniors. Their lives are buried in the decision-free world of jersey warmers. They peak reading speeches by civil servants for late-night adjournment debates. They are doomed forever to be the substitute and never the cabinet member.

Kim was given an award for his work in 2006. Was it for his comment in July 2006 that calling for a cease-fire in Lebanon was a meaningless gesture? Only Israel, USA and the UK failed to demand a ceasefire. It would not have been meaningless for the children buried alive at Qana, the thousand killed and the million whose homes were destroyed in the subsequent invasion. Was it for his flippant dismissal on 7 February 2006 of a warning that his Afghan drug eradication programme would lead to the alienation of Afghans and the deaths of more British soldiers? He described the questioner as a 'muesli-eater'. Then, only twelve British soldiers had died. Was it for the serial failure of his anti-drugs policy and repeated assurances that drugs production in Afghanistan was dropping? It cost British taxpayers £250 million to engineer a 60 per cent increase in heroin production to the highest level ever. The price of the drugs on the streets of Britain is the lowest ever. Was it for his impassioned speech on Britain's 'shared values' with Saudi Arabia? Bribery, torture, anti-democracy, feudalism...?

Kim's lifetime trait is to move in a crab-like direction. He has moved seamlessly from a Blairite to a Brownite minister, doing what he does best – clinging to office. Has any significant reform ever resulted from his perpetual sideways motion? To his and our relief he has now fallen off the ministerial shelf, and is now the government's patsy on the Intelligence and Security Committee.

Tony Banks was the kindest, most humane, funniest person in politics. Never once did he fail to be a welcome companion and a principled courageous advocate of his passionate beliefs. He stood down from Parliament in order to spend less time with his constituents. His plan was to concentrate, as Lord Stratford, on the issues of animal welfare, sport and international solidarity. Frank, open and unafraid, for twenty years he was the brilliant star in the parliamentary firmament.

He appeared to be in robust health. A youthful sixty-two, lean and fit, he was never seriously ill. He loved to indulge his passion for quality champagne but was never drunk. At the wedding of my stepdaughter in May, he posed for a photograph by hoisting his beloved wife Sally off her feet to demonstrate how wives should be carried over thresholds.

Newport will recall the two visits Tony made to speak at Chartist events. Few realised that this most accomplished public speaker suffered agonies of nerves before appearing in public. So steamed up was he at the Chartist Dinner in November 2004, he turned on me and said, 'You're my friend. Why did you put me through this misery?' Then he spoke brilliantly with a thoughtful and extremely funny speech. Afterwards he purred with pleasure. He looked back on the evening with great satisfaction. He also visited Newport in 2001, when Chelsea was playing at home – a sacrifice beyond any call of duty. The evening finished happily after the event with Tony sipping champagne while watching Chelsea win on the television.

He wrote a generous introduction to *Commons Knowledge*, referring to me as his 'companion on the back benches'. There were many happy hours that I spent listening to his commentary of verbal barbs and witty jibes enlivening the tedium of parliamentary business. His strongest anger was directed at the greedy, the selfish and those who abuse animals. He was one of the least mercenary and the most generous of MPs. When accused by a journalist of being on a gravy train, he offered to show him the fruits of more than twenty years in the Commons – two overdrawn bank accounts and savings of less than £18,000.

The unveiling of the bronze statue of Margaret Thatcher in the Members' Lobby of the Commons in 2007 churned up fond memories of Tony. In 1991 he delighted the Tory government by suggesting that a statue of recently deposed Prime Minister Thatcher should be erected in the Members' Lobby. It was an oral question and the answering minister thanked Tony for this magnanimous gesture. He pointed out that parliamentary tradition required that no statue had ever been erected to a living person. Tony said this was unfair and frustrating. All those people in eastern Europe who had overthrown their Communist rulers had been able to vent their anger by pulling down the statues of Lenin, Marx and Stalin. Tony explained, 'We have got rid of the old bag, but we have no statues to pull down. So let's put one up so that we can then vent our feelings.'

Many years later a more diplomatic Tony was elected the chair of the Works of Art Committee. He fulfilled the task with flair and distinction. This time his Thatcher wheeze had added subtlety. He sincerely held the view that Thatcher's achievement as the first woman prime minister deserved commemoration. He collected money for a splendid marble statue, which Mrs. Thatcher unveiled with great pleasure and pride. Soon after it was beheaded by a vandal. The marble statue was intended eventually for a minor empty plinth in the Members' Lobby. The understanding was that it would be placed there alongside existing marble statues of the same dimensions. This would leave the remaining major vacant plinth for a new bronze statue of the expected recipient Tony Blair. The other bronze statues are of the giants of twentieth-century politics, Lloyd George, Churchill and Attlee. Mrs Thatcher's bronze statue now occupies that prime position. Few would disagree that she is the worthy fourth giant of the Commons in the twentieth century. Tony Banks did not foresee the crumbling reputation of Tony Blair following the Iraq inquiry.

Only once did I refused to sign one of Tony's Early Day Motions. It was written in fury. It emerged that, during the Second World War, MI5 had proposed using pigeons as flying bombs. Tony denounced human beings as obscene, perverted, cruel, uncivilised and lethal. He added that he also looked forward to the day when the inevitable asteroid slams into the Earth and wipes them out, thus giving nature the opportunity to start again. Calling for the end of humankind was a step too far, and would not be understood by my constituents. Tony continued with his fearless attacks. During a Tory sex scandal, he suggested installing Durex machines in Westminster so that the Tories would have fewer illegitimate children.

Tony's funeral was an emotion-churning hour of tears and laughter. The news that day was led by accounts of a lost whale that was stranded in the Thames. Tony's widow Sally made the touching point that the whale was probably Tony reincarnated. First it had cavorted outside the Commons at Westminster, and then it struggled to swim further up the river until it reached Chelsea where it died.

David Mellor said his task of paying tribute to Banksy was similar to that of a third-rate composer who asked if the special musical tribute he had written for the funeral of Rossini was good. He was told, 'Musically, it would have been better if you had died and Rossini had composed a piece to commemorate you.' Mellor suggested that in the interests of an entertaining tribute it would have been better if he had died and Tony was paying the tribute.

Mellor told a story very much against himself. It had been suggested he made love wearing a Chelsea shirt; he was relieved to hear Tony on the radio dismissing the calumny as absolutely unbelievable. No one, said Tony, has ever scored five times wearing a Chelsea shirt.

Many welcomed being insulted by Tony. After Ann Widdecombe went blonde she was delighted to be dubbed Marilyn. Tony served as a faithful party servant. He was the replacement London whip, or the agency whip as he called himself. The party called him up on special occasions. He could not continue as a serious whip because the job demanded absolute mindless loyalty. From the front bench he insulted Terry Dicks MP for sneering against 'arty-farty' ballet dancers. Tony said that Terry had proved that in certain parts of the country, the Tories can put up a pig's bladder on a stick as a candidate and get elected.

Brian Davies, the founder of the International Fund for Animal Welfare, was a close friend of Tony and Sally's. He was with him when he died. He told the funeral crowd of Banksyites that his last morning had been a good morning. They were enjoying a nice meal after having a glass of wine. It was apparent immediately that Tony had suffered a massive stroke. Brian carried him to a bed and rang the emergency services. As Tony lay on the bed one of the beloved Davies family dogs climbed alongside Tony and snuggled up to him. Tony stroked her with his hand. That was his last conscious act. His compassion for animals was not confined to the cuddly ones. A story was told of his frantic efforts to move a sea-slug to safety where it would not be damaged by the boat he was in. That was after the sea-slug had bitten him.

Iain Dale produced a volume, *The Wit and Wisdom of Tony Banks*, as a tribute to a parliamentary character. A biography is long overdue.

Dr Russell Rhys is a treasured constituent. He is a prosperous former communist cultural entrepreneur and arts patron. He has created a unique mini-paradise in Caerleon named the Ffwrwm. A fiercely individualist provocateur and socialist, he is loved and loathed in equal measure. His indiscretions are outrageous. His natural charm is tempered with a light touch of arrogance and the occasional reckless insult.

He has stunned audiences into shocked silence with his uninhibited directness and flouting of language taboos. As a passionate Welshman, he is a spellbinding storyteller of the ancient tales of the Mabinogion and Arthurian legends. Now eighty-five, he has long retired as a medical doctor. But his work is fondly remembered. He was never beguiled by new fashions in drugs and surgery. He once told me, 'I don't know how many patients I have saved. But I know precisely the number that I have killed.'

The Ffwrwm is a haven of tranquility in the heart of Caerleon. Arts, antiques, crafts and fine food nestle together among the statuesque sculptures of the ancient garden. Russell has pursued a private passion to create the most eclectic collection of sculptures anywhere in Wales.

It is entered through an historic arch fronting Caerleon's main street, and consists of an art gallery, craft workshops and a restaurant, all set in the glories of an eighteenth-century walled garden. The restaurant is well known for its home cooking, specialising in Welsh recipes. The walled garden contains unusual shrubs and trees, including a very rare tulip tree, and many attractions in relation to King Arthur.

But there is another colourful side to Russell's character. Possibly a lack of sensitivity led him into a comment that brought a live Welsh-language television programme to a juddering halt. I was sitting next to him on a discussion on the age of consent for sexual activity. Russell's offer to comment was welcomed by the chairman: 'Let's hear from the medical man.' Russell said, 'The age is of consent is of great importance in Wales, especially in rural Wales' – the audience was mystified – 'where it's vital to know the precise age of the sheep.' There was a dumbfounded silence. The chairman sounded like someone having a heart attack. He scrabbled through his papers to find a new subject. The audience was white-faced, silent, horrified. Russell had insulted the Welsh nation in a live broadcast in Welsh. A puzzled Russell whispered to me, 'Well, that went down like a lead balloon.'

In the early 1980s there was a formal public inquiry into an application to build rows of condominiums on the ridge of Christchurch Hill above Caerleon. Russell was prominent in the group opposing the plans. Explanation of the meaning of the word 'condominium' was provided to the Welsh Office inspector conducting the inquiry. Another innovation were the Jacuzzis in each building. 'What is a Jacuzzi?' the inspector asked. Russell offered his expert professional view in a further effort to damn the proposal. 'I suppose the best way to define a Jacuzzi in layman's language', said Russell, 'is that it's a wanking pit.' The inspector was not amused.

In spite of Russell's indelicate intervention the local group were successful in resisting what would have been a visual atrocity. Caerleon is grateful to Russell as the originator of not only the Ffwrwm but also an annual arts festival. At the heart of it is a sculpture symposium, which produces a crop of fine wooden statues to add interest and distinction to the Caerleon streetscape. It was Russell's persuasive, contagious enthusiasm that inspired others to create an exciting festival that is a splendid yearly romp.

He has one remaining great ambition. He dreams of a statue of a goddess located in the river Usk in Caerleon. The world's second highest rise and fall of tide would inundate the lady on the incoming tide and reveal her beauty on the falling tide. The waters would dress and undress her. A start has been made and the lady's head exists. Some obstacles have been overcome but problems remain. It's a great visionary concept. An alternative I have urged on him is to have a massive Excalibur sword that would be revealed and hidden by the massive tides. This would strengthen Russell's advocacy of Caerleon as the authentic Camelot. He is not impressed with the idea.

Russell relishes his full life of politics and the arts. He has deployed his alchemy to turn his wild Celtic dreams into tangible beauty. Lucky man.

John Hutton is the archetypical Blairite minister. He is a blank page that bears the imprint of the last lobbyist who sat on him. He is personality-free and the despair of serious parliamentarians.

He trained himself to be a Blair clone. He dressed like Blair and abided by the commandments of Blairism. He even started to imitate the way that Blair speaks, starting every other sentence with 'Look!' In all his many jobs he has parroted the usually bad ideas that lobbyists have crammed into his head. Five years after New Labour dismissed new nuclear as an 'unattractive option' the party was led astray. Hutton fell head over heels in love with new nuclear and said, 'Nuclear is the UK's new North Sea oil.' He resigned as Secretary of State for Defence. It was reported that he wanted to send 2,000 more troops to Afghanistan even though they would do little but be fresh targets for IEDs. This was a populist but deadly policy. He appeared to have caved in to pressure from the military.

In August 2009 it was reported that John was to be appointed to nuclear power company EDF's stakeholder advisory panel. This would have been a disturbing example of the 'revolving door' that the Public Administration Committee had condemned. In 2008 EDF had been awarded a contract worth £12 billion by government. PASC emphasised the grave danger that contracts could be awarded for the wrong reasons. The hopes of future employment for a retired minister might influence decisions on contracts. PASC stressed this peril. My conviction is that former ministers should be banned for life from working in companies that have received contracts from them in their ministerial incarnations. The angry blog that I did on Hutton's possible job with EDF was reprinted in the *Guardian* Diary. Subsequently it was announced that John Hutton had declined the position with EDF, for the time being.

A glimpse of the mind-set of New Labour ministers was illustrated in a PASC cross-examination. John Hutton had promulgated unattainable choice in schools and hospital with religious fervour.

PAUL FLYNN: You said you asked the public whether they wanted choice. Can you remember how many of them said they wanted no choice?

JOHN HUTTON: I think a tiny number.

FLYNN: Then it's a fairly stupid question. Asking the public whether they want choice is like asking whether they favour mother love and thornless roses.

HUTTON: Yes, I think it confirms that choice is a popular idea.

FLYNN: Do you not think there is a danger that it would keep the problem with targets (which you seem to have said were more a measure of failure than success) by offering them choice which is not deliverable in many instances?

HUTTON: We should offer choice where we know we can deliver it.

The *Independent* invited John to pontificate on Afghanistan in October 2009. He parroted uncritically the military line. 'Our long-term strategy is also clear: it is to give the emerging Afghan democracy the means to do this job for itself.' Democracy? With election-rigging Karzai, his crooked family and criminal law enforcers?

'The purpose of the Nato mission . . . is to ensure that Afghanistan does not become a safe haven for international terrorism that would endanger our national security.' Fantasy. Already the Taliban had control of 80 per cent of the territory of Afghanistan. They have not invited al Qaeda in to set up a safe haven. They already have one in Pakistan and potentially in Somalia and Yemen.

'We need enough troops now to hold and secure the ground, so that the Afghan government and the UN mission can deliver economic and social reconstruction.' To take one turbine to the Kajaki dam needed 4,000 Nato troops. A year later it was still not working. Ambitious reconstruction is impossible with the Taliban in control. There were 9,000 British soldiers, 2,000 of them front-line, in only one of Afghanistan's thirty-four provinces. Russia failed to make the country secure with 120,000 troops.

Does this self-deluding nonsense pass for sense in the Ministry of Defence? After eight years of our presence Afghanistan is a hopeless shambles. Karzai is corrupt, denying basic human rights and dependent on lawless warlords and the depraved thieves of the Afghan police.

No New Labour minister made an effective stand against the war in the way that Robin Cook and (belatedly) Clare Short made against the Iraq War. Kim Howells found his conscience and voice only after leaving office. Labour governments since 1997 have a commendable record of achievements in stealth socialism in spite of ministers like John Hutton. The country and the Labour Party would have been better served by ministers with backbones.

B ritain's first and last drugs czar, Keith Hellawell, represents the growing army of the anti-drugs establishment who profit from the continuing failure of drugs prohibition. By chance I bumped into him in Parliament Square on the night that he was appointed in 1997. I told him he was a fall guy appointed to take the rap when prohibition fails again. He disagreed. The only abiding achievement of his four-year stint was that he had the most expensive haircut in government. Not only did he make no progress whatsoever on his targets to reduce drug harm, he has left his office with drug use, drug crime and drug deaths at record levels.

Giving evidence before the Home Affairs Select Committee, he bemoaned the fact that, when he became drugs czar, the proportion of spending on rehabilitation was 'only 13 per cent'. When asked what it is now under his administration, he said that he did not know. The rest of his performances were equally woeful. Perversely, he made his name initially as a reformer. In May 1994 the *Guardian* quoted him: 'The present policies are not working. We seize more drugs, we arrest more people but when you look at the availability of drugs, the use of drugs, the crime committed because of and through people who use drugs, the violence associated with drugs, it's on the increase. It can't be working.'

Very sensible. Even courageous for a chief constable. The title 'czar' was a new gimmicky wrapper for the tired failed policies of drug prohibition. Keith Hellawell was content to do the government's bidding in exchange for a salary bigger than the Prime Minister's. Once he called for the death penalty for armed criminals. Profoundly unconvincing as ever, he had no answer to those interviewers who asked him for any example of the death penalty reducing crime. His spell as drugs czar ended ignominiously. He had lost the respect of government ministers and the drugs treatment world.

His self-imposed targets exposed and mocked the futility of prohibition.

In that period, the government made alcohol *more* widely available even though alcohol is involved in 80 per cent of crimes of violence and abuse. Those who use cannabis as a medicine are jailed despite the consensus on its benefits. Soft on a hard drug and hard on a soft drug.

David Blunkett kindly pointed out that Hellawell changed his mind three times on cannabis. In fact, it was five times. Once, shortly after an unimpressive, unscientific report from New Zealand had suggested that cannabis was a gateway drug, he vehemently denounced cannabis use. A few months later he visited a school where the pupils told him that they did not regard cannabis as a significant drug of abuse. The drugs czar changed tack and said that heroin and cocaine were the serious threats. We suffered four wasted years of avoidable crime and deaths because of the timidity of politicians expressed through their fall guy. As an emeritus czar he makes himself available as a keynote speaker – typical fees for a keynote speech range between £5,000 and £12,000, his agent's website confirmed.

Nothing much changed after Hellawell's contract ended. The government continued to dance to the lowest common denominator of popular prejudice and more money was mindlessly thrown at drugs. There is hope from a European Convention, Portugal's de-penalisation success and the revolt of South America states against the USA and UN prohibition hegemony. The drugs czar episode was a low point in New Labour shallow gimmickry.

Gordon Prentice is Parliament's Sleazebuster General. His campaigns against absent Lords and revolving doors for former ministers and lobbyists are succeeding. He is in that select group of politicians whose ambitions are eclipsed by principles. Although I know him very well, I have failed to convince him that his talents should be offered to rescue the Labour government from its third-term torpor. His charisma, ability and political horse sense are needed to challenge the party's exhausted old guard. He resisted all attempts from me and others to nominate him for top roles. His focus is on individual campaigns.

Gordon relentlessly pursued Jonathan Aitken. In his autobiography,

Jonathan recalls the deadly effect of Gordon's persistent parliamentary questions on whether Jonathan's perjury had influenced decisions. The issue could not be quietly forgotten as many establishment figures hoped. Doggedness paid off and justice was done.

Gordon often apologised to fellow members of the Public Administration Committee for complaining for the umpteenth time about the Lords Laidlaw and Ashcroft. Their absentee status and their lavish (possibly illegal) contributions to the Conservative Party were his constant themes. In the Commons he asked, 'Lord Laidlaw is a self-confessed tax exile and he gave more than £100,000 to the Conservative Party last year. Is it not inappropriate for any political party to accept donations from someone who is a self-confessed tax exile?' The campaign was a great success. Collaboration with Lord Campbell-Savours and the biggest ever rebellion by Labour lords forced the reform that Gordon sought.

Gordon led the campaign against replacing Trident in 2007. The government's line was: 'Renewing the current Trident system is fully consistent with the Non-Proliferation Treaty and with all our international legal obligations.' Gordon hit back:

> I simply do not believe that. When I asked ministers three weeks ago to supply me with the Attorney General's advice, I was told that it was confidential. I am not prepared to take these matters on trust, not after Iraq, not after weapons of mass destruction and not after the forty-five minutes assertion. If the Prime Minister came here and told us that we had to invade Iran, do you think the military would go along with that without having sight of the Attorney General's opinion?

Speaker Martin interrupted Gordon here with a piddling procedural point. This was not the first time that Speaker Martin had tried to silence Gordon. It was rash of him to bait the one MP whom Simon Hoggart had described as Parliament's most practised troublemaker. The process of nemesis was started by Gordon in a brave call for a new Commons

Speaker to be elected early. He then publicly told Michael Martin to go in the debate that forced his resignation.

Sketch writers delight in Gordon's stroppiness and independence. Quentin Letts spotted his great talent. He had been 'consistent value for money, pulling apart a succession of crooks, conmen and blue-sky thinking pseuds'.

'It was pretty brutal,' Letts continued, 'with the wonderfully arch tone of disbelief, Mr Prentice kept repeating words Lord Warner had used. He also interjected with the occasional, languid "yerrrrrs", laced with doubt. Both witnesses lost their tempers.'

Gordon battles on as Britain's most admirably independent-minded MP. I hope his constituents and the country notice.

Chris Mullin is a parliamentary wonder and oddity. He arrived with an interesting hinterland as a successful writer and former editor of *Tribune*. His diaries reveal his principled trampolining from backbencher to minister, back to backbencher, promotion to minister and back to backbencher. The most telling revelation in his diaries is that he was never asked to make a decision in his first job of a junior minister. He was used as a department's dogsbody to attend tedious functions that senior ministers wished to avoid.

He emerged saint-like from the expenses scandal. I was delighted to support his proposal fourteen years ago to link MPs' salaries with the level of the basic pension. When he first withdrew from ministerial office he told Tony Blair that he wanted the greater influence that backbenchers enjoy. Blair admired his talents and wanted him in the tent.

Chris is a former aviation minister. He asked his civil servants again and again how many passes to the Commons the aviation industry had. His civil servants refused to tell him. When he persisted with his question, a civil servant asked, 'Why do you want to know?' The incestuous relationship between the lobbying industry and civil servants was deep. They were ambitious spenders and gluttons for growth. Nothing has changed.

He chaired the Home Affairs Committee with intelligence and courage.

His report on drugs was the most progressive work of the committee in twenty years. His diary revealed the tedious depth of futility of life at the bottom of government as the minister for folding deckchairs. His diaries are self-deprecating, frank and hilarious. They added greatly to his reputation for straight talking. He is probably the most respected and trusted voice on the Labour benches.

Peter Freeman was born generations too early. He was mocked as the friend of the lobster and denounced as eccentric for views that are now progressive. He was the MP for Newport from 1945 until his agonising death in 1956. His life was tumultuous, extraordinary and ultimately tragic.

He raced like a shooting star across the parliamentary firmament, trailing a dazzling aurora. His trajectory was sometimes capricious but always defined by originality, conviction and idealism. Peter was a backbenchers' backbencher untouched by the tyranny of the party whips, electoral pressure or the media. Assertive, intelligent, principled, rich and unambitious for office, he was the living nightmare for party disciplinarians. Many contemporary backbenchers have been castrated, mesmerised and lobotomised by ambition. The legacies of their careers will not be celestial. Their trails will not be those of stars but of slugs.

Newport was a hospitable habitat for Peter the vegetarian, after the sneering, doltish abuse heaped on him by the local aristocracy, 'the county set', in his previous rural parliamentary seat of Brecon. Newport Labour Party has a great history of progressive causes. It was a delicious pleasure to remind Tony Blair of the city's radical independence. On the day after he appointed the new Archbishop of Canterbury, there was a meeting of the Parliamentary Labour Party. Tony was taken aback when I told him that the new archbishop had always been a reliable supporter of all Labour Party policies, adding, 'As interpreted by Newport West Labour Party.' In his distinguished eleven-year stint in the city Rowan Williams echoed and built on the courage and originality of the Chartists and Peter Freeman.

An old school friend of mine, Mike Bloxsome, wrote the only

biography of Freeman. In *The Green Casanova* he reveals Freeman's visionary passions. He tried to ban fox hunting with dogs three-quarters of a century before the Commons were convinced. The animal rights movement has not yet caught up with the strength and purity of his convictions. He urged a laughing House to ban the practice of boiling lobsters alive in Parliament's kitchens. He refused to take morphine for his dreadful cancer because it had been tested on animals, and thereby suffered a cruel death.

To the dim witted, Peter's conduct and views seemed random and contradictory: the successful entrepreneur who planned to reshape the worker-employer relationship; the impassioned internationalist who longed for a Welsh parliament; the prophetic social reformer who was an adherent of a faith (theosophy) that has almost vanished; the world class sportsman: a rampant womaniser who was moved to a tender, self-sacrificial, lifelong devotion. In 1945 he looked up an old girlfriend in Vienna. She had raced out of a bombed building and fallen down a lift shaft. She was in a wheelchair for life. He married her. Newportonians remember her quaint Viennese accent.

All were facets of a coherent unique political personality. Posterity should now grant Peter Freeman's memory the respect, gratitude and admiration denied to him during his lifetime. *The Green Casanova* presents the world environmental movement with a new hero.

W alt (Sonny) Waters was one of the dozens of admirable councillors that I have worked with in nearly forty years as a councillor and MP. As a group they are undervalued. I owe them a debt as idealists, mentors and exemplars.

Walter Waters had a wonderful life. He was a distinguished sportsman in baseball, hockey, rugby and his beloved boxing. He became an international boxing referee and he trained many young boxers. He was named Newport Sports Personality of the Year in 1981.

His full eighty-three years were lived in the service of others. He was one of a family of ten children. He worked on the railways for thirty-six years, with only five days on the sick. He was drafted in the war as a Bevin Boy and worked in the south Wales coal mines. That was not enough national service, because he was then called up to military service when the war ended. He met his beautiful wife Betty in a Butlin's holiday camp. The marriage was blissfully happy, blessed with children and grandchildren.

He possessed a sunny personality, guile- and malice-free. He was always smiling and had something optimistic to say. He was humorous and mischievous. One story was told of the comeuppance he gave to two relatives who were predatory on children's Christmas chocolates. He carefully cut open some Maltesers and replaced the contents with goose fat. The chocolate thieves had a lesson they never forgot. He insisted that his grandchildren learned poems by heart. One interesting verse read at his funeral inspires high ambition against the odds:

> According to statistics, which can be proved by means of a wind tunnel, the bumblebee cannot fly. This is because its size, weight and shape in relation to its total wingspan, makes flying impossible. But with great determination, the bumblebee does fly and makes a little honey every day.

The incident that increased my admiration for him occurred at a Labour Party meeting. I had railed against boxing as a brutal sport that unnecessarily inflicted brain damage. Walter spoke after me. I expected a strong defence. He was entitled to be angry with me because I had attacked the sport that had enjoyed his lifetime devotion. He announced that he had read the BMA reports and he was giving up his beloved work. He became a great advocate of head protection for young boxers. This change of mind led him into conflict with friends and family. It was a principled decision based on the scientific evidence and he stuck to it. In spite of his Catholic upbringing, he opted for a humanist funeral rich in music, poetry and anecdotes. Warm, touching tributes were paid by relatives and friends. A talented musical quartet of young Waters played.

At the age of sixty Walter began his twelve years of service as a Gwent county councillor. Others had more prominent careers on the council, few are remembered with the same affection that he enjoyed. In spite of having limited educational opportunities himself, he was elected chair of governors of both Durham Road and St Julian's schools.

His daughter Karen told me:

> I saw in Dad a man willing to reflect upon social changes around him. In the 1950s when we were children he was very much a man's man and left the baby stuff – nappies, baths and pushing prams etc. to my mum. It was considered women's work. However, when the grandchildren came along he said to me that when he saw his sons and sons-in-law looking after the children, it made him realise how much men had lost out by not having that sort of contact with their children as babies. I was proud of my dad for recognising that ... Mind you, he never offered to change any of the grandchildren's nappies!

He served his constituents and the Labour Party with dedication and distinction. Without grandstanding or self-aggrandisement, he faithfully carried out the micro-surgery of hundreds of small decisions that served his St Julian's constituents. There is pride and happiness in a life well lived.

John Bercow is a bonus of champagne quality. His enthusiasm and leadership will liberate Parliament's creaking exasperating procedures. I promoted his campaign for the speakership with a flurry of blogs and radio interviews. At the time when journalists asked 'John who?', I put him as my sure favourite on my blog. Matthew Parris said he often speaks as though he is 'chiselling his words out of granite'. The ponderous tone is there. It is a fair price to pay for his precision and gravity.

When a Member of Parliament has died, past Speakers have abided by the Commons 'tradition' of coldly announcing the death and then immediately moving on to next business. Speaker Bercow won the affection of the House by trampling on tradition with a brief and lovingly crafted tribute to David Taylor: 'David was a highly assiduous, principled and independent-minded Member who respected the House and was respected by it. Truly, he was a House of Commons man.'

John's backbench contributions were marvels of construction and feats of memory. Every one of his words sweats with potency. As Speaker he staggered an audience of thirty-five assorted MPs by welcoming them by name and constituency. He could also have reeled off from memory the dates when they were first elected. Previous Speakers have struggled to remember the names of all members. They resorted to the device of calling 'The Hon. Member' and pointing.

The continuing hostility of his Tory colleagues limits the pace of Bercow's reforms. Parliamentary questions are tiresome, self-indulgent and flatulent. He has risked unpopularity by cutting short the rambling and repetitive questions of the great and the glorious. His campaign for simple, pithy questions has succeeded. Ministers and backbenchers are learning new tricks.

I am his collaborator with a crusade for tweet-length questions. It's a fascinating new self-imposed discipline to make the essential points as briefly as possible. Dropping non-essential verbiage concentrates the essential meaning. Tweet questions are better questions. One day Parliament's bible, Erskine May, will insist on Twitter rules. A major Commons reform is in early stages of gestation. Here are a few I have tried:

> PAUL FLYNN (Newport West): When can we debate our reliance on the corrupt, depraved, drug-addicted, murdering thieves of the Afghan police?

> PAUL FLYNN (Newport West): 221 British dead, yet this House has never voted on the Afghan War. Isn't time we did?
> PAUL FLYNN (Newport West): Why are expensive new nuclear developments advancing at the speed of a striking cobra while good value, clean marine developments are moving at the pace of an arthritic sloth?

Traditionalists will fret but sharper questions and answers in simple, direct language will engage the public with Parliament. Of the four Speakers that I have served with, John Bercow is the only one with the character and talent to become a great Speaker.

D oug Cumpstone had a great life. He was not just a father-in-law to me. He was a daily practical and emotional life support service for twenty-five years and it was a privilege and a joy for us to share our lives with him.

He was born on the eleventh day of the eleventh month in 1927, and was named after Douglas Haig. The train-driver from Fochriw married Newport war widow Elsie and they enjoyed forty years of happiness, blessed with the birth of Lynne Samantha. Doug was silently proud of the life he had made for himself. Until his final eighty-third year, he enjoyed exceptional health and strength. I was astonished one day to see him 14 feet up a tree in my garden sawing off a branch. He was then eighty years old.

The Cumpstones are a tough tribe. Uncle Idris was shot throught the heart in 1917. Of course he died eventually – at the age of ninety-six. The bullet is a treasured memento. Doug's driving proved he was no paragon of virtue. To improve others' knowledge of the Highway Code, he drove with one hand on the wheel and the other closed in a fist, ready to shake at other drivers. Sam developed a technique of sliding down in the passenger seat to become invisible to the pedestrians that he sent scurrying out of his way.

Doug was an instinctive socialist and trade unionist, proud of his record as Mr Aslef in Newport. He had a commanding presence, tall and handsome. He was a man of culture, who derived pleasure from the beauty of poetry, knowledge of history and a love of music. He was touched when he heard that his fourth great-grandchild, born in August 2009, was named Elsie after his wife, who died in 1992. 'If this one is as good as my Elsie,' he said, 'she'll have nothing to worry about.'

32

Innocent until proved Labour

The MPs' expenses row has undermined the respect that we have enjoyed in recent times. The trust the public has intermittently given us over the past century may never be restored. The expenses scandal of 2009 has caused a mood in the House similar to a clinic for depressives. Some sensitive souls were distraught with worry and embarrassment. Others shunned their constituencies to avoid face-to-face abuse. There were disturbing accounts of MPs' spouses being verbally abused in public and children being bullied.

As a veteran campaigner for freedom of information and income transparency, I played a minor role in the revelations. I was shocked when I heard the allegation that Home Secretary Jacqui Smith was claiming as her main home an area in her sister's London house. There were also damaging accidental claims for porn videos. I was asked my view in a live radio interview. I said, 'Her reputation is in serious trouble and her authority is badly damaged and I think she should herself look at her position. I don't see much point in her continuing in high office now.'

She did eventually resign. Sooner would have been better than later. When I made the comments I had no idea that hundreds of MPs had flipped their homes to make similar indefensible claims. On my select committee I had been vocal in denouncing MPs' double incomes. My comments were filmed for two national TV programmes. While I stick by my comments, I regret they were broadcast alongside exaggerated abuse that unfairly and disproportionately attacked Labour MPs. It was not my intention to be linked to the cumulative and irrational build-up of anti-MP hysteria. Some deserved condemnation. Many did not.

The modern expenses system was a generous reaction to the mean treatment that MPs suffered in the 1960s and 1970s. Then they had to pay for their own stamps. The only lodgings they could afford were seedy London hotels. When I arrived in 1987, I was told the facts about my wages and allowances. I was encouraged to claim in full. It was even suggested that waste would be avoided if I sent in a claim every month for a twelfth of the annual total of my London home allowance. No receipts were required. After all, we were Honourable Members who could be trusted not to make unnecessary claims.

I read the *Daily Telegraph*'s detailed publication of MPs' expenses with a nauseous mix of schadenfreude and fear. Reading the fine details of MPs' expenses was bordering on the prurient. A few of the claims may be proved to have criminal intent. Other MPs were unjustly pilloried. At a meeting of the Parliamentary Labour Party I protested that Norwich MP Ian Gibson had been hounded out of the Commons by an ignorant Star Chamber court. His only sin was that the *Daily Telegraph* devoted too many square inches of publicity to him.

The *Telegraph* kept to their political agenda. Every MP is assumed to be innocent until proved to be Labour. One giant lacuna in their revelations was the absence of any assessment of David Cameron and his deputy George Osborne's mortgage claims.

Balance came from a surprising source when the *Mail on Sunday* reported that Cameron paid off a loan on his London home shortly after taking out a £350,000 taxpayer-funded mortgage on his constituency house. He nominated it as his second home. The cost is significant because it allowed him to claim around the maximum of £20,000 in interest only over the past five years. George Osborne was accused of taking out a mortgage of over 100 per cent to maximise his claim. David Cameron claims that using all his £20,000 for interest payments is perfectly correct. No, it was not. The allowance is designed to allow MPs a London dwelling to provide access to Parliament. The costs are meant to be spread over mortgage interest, council tax, utilities and living expenses. They are not intended to be used to buy millionaires' pads in MPs' constituencies. Parliament outlawed this abuse by limiting the amount that can be spent on interest. In both Cameron's and Osborne's alleged situations the potential misuse was far more serious that anything that Ian Gibson had done.

Proof of the *Telegraph*'s duplicity and distorted news values was in a report that MP Frank Cook had claimed for a £5 church offertory donation. They devoted four times the space to Frank Cook's claim than they gave to the news that two soldiers had been killed in Afghanistan. If the story is true, Frank's attempt to recoup a church offertory donation of £5 is either maniacally mean or certifiably stupid. This is not credible sleaze. It was a stupid accounts mistake.

There was a perceptible rising wrath from non-millionaire Tory MPs. Outer London ones had already lost £37,000 of their income before the Kelly committee acted. They fear that Cameron is using the scandal as an excuse to clear out traditionalists who stand in the way of his modernising project, while largely protecting members of his inner circle. Peter Viggers, Anthony Steen and Douglas Hogg have all been slipped the black spot by Cameron as bed-blockers. When will he act against Michael Gove, Francis Maude, Chris Grayling and Alan Duncan?

In evidence to the Kelly Committee I raised the misuse of the second homes allowance. Some MPs own several, in one case over twenty, houses. Why should the taxpayer pay for housing in those cases?

However, my main plea was for Kelly to rule that an MP's job is a full-time one. This principle should underpin all measures to reform the system of remuneration. It is known that some MPs earn up to £250,000 a year from moonlighting. Those who take additional paid employment, which could be considered a second job, should declare the hours spent and the income received. Voters can decide if they are able to carry out the core job of an MP. Parliamentary salaries should be adjusted to reflect the additional income derived from second jobs. Former ministers and former senior civil servants should be barred from taking jobs in those areas in which they served.

There is a gathering storm on MPs' pensions. Our pensions continue to improve while other occupational pensions are declining in value. MPs should not have a pension system that is more favourable than those outside of Parliament. There was no nightmare on expenses in Newport. I had not flipped my home and I had paid my full capital gains tax. In order to head off any criticism I held a well-advertised public meeting as soon as the full details were published. I wondered beforehand whether this was the stupidest or the wisest move I had ever made. Other MPs were lying low, avoiding all publicity. But there was no criticism and the meeting was warm and supportive.

I hold my hands up in guilt because I did not protest earlier against an indefensible system that invited abuse. There was press hysteria and many blameless MPs were attacked. But the fault is ours. We have only ourselves to blame.

33

New Socialism

The socialist Sunday schools of my childhood had inspiring commandments. Their direct values still hold good. Love learning, which is the food of the mind. Honour the good, be courteous to all, bow down to none. Be a friend to the weak, and love justice. Do not be revengeful, but stand up for your rights and resist oppression. Do not think that those who love their own country must hate other nations and wish war. Look forward to the day when all will be free citizens of one world.

These are splendid simple concepts that remain the foundation of my socialism. In spite of the disappointment and lost opportunities, the Labour government since 1997 achieved major advances.

It has been mainly stealth socialism, which Tony Blair was loath to recognise in case the *Daily Mail* noticed and excoriated him. The minimum wage provided a decent income for millions and ended the worst excesses of stingy employers. The most difficult feat for government is to reduce the gap between rich and poor. The rich are very good at getting richer by doing the things that made them rich in the first place. But a million pensioners and 800,000 children have been pulled out of poverty by direct government intervention. Fragile peace has been brought to Northern Ireland through the micro-surgery of patient diplomacy.

Families have been helped with trust funds, tax credits and increased child benefits. The pension credit, winter fuel allowance and free TV licences for over-75s have substantially improved pensioner income. Sure Start and New Deal have been successful initiatives. We have increased aid to the developing world and made progress on animal welfare with the hunting bill and a ban on fur farming. Devolution and Lords reform are advances that will not be reversed. None of these would have been introduced by a Tory government.

But Labour's inheritance is pockmarked with failing concepts and fashionable lost causes. The recent past was an age of extravagance, self-indulgence and the profligate plundering of the planet. As a party we wallowed in the easy victories and the comforts of power. The future will be an age of austerity, thrift and reverence for our fragile human habitat. This is a splendid time to top up the knowledge banks and create a New Socialism.

We are on the brink of the Obama revolution. Political certainties are collapsing and the world economy is convulsed. There is encouragement from the Welsh experience. Welsh Labour is receptive to fresh ideas, having spurned many of the superficial canards of New Labour. The Westminster Labour Ministry of Truth is irritated when a sister Labour body has the temerity to stray from the revealed, but shifting, nostrums of New Labour.

The Labour movement has been hurt by bewildering self-destructive polices from Westminster. On the gravest error – the Iraq War – the Labour Party in Wales had its objections silenced by bureaucratic procedure.

This is the authentic exasperated anger at the wayward drift of New Labour from our core values. Our subservience to American's neo-cons was our foulest hour. Many opportunities have been neglected and much of the value of Labour's electoral victories was dissipated in fruitless meandering into political dead ends. Happily, Labour in Wales has embarked on its voyage across the clear red water.

There has been loyalty to the benefits of universal services. Services that are reserved for poor people very quickly become poor services. Universal services are cheap to administer and have no stigma of dependence. Free school breakfasts are provided in Wales for all pupils, not just for those branded as needy. This is efficient practical politics. 'Old Labour', 'Classic Labour', 'Real Labour' is not the rusted wreck of the past failures. It must be the 21st-century smart socialism that is pragmatic and rooted in the realities of the unavoidable global crises.

The post-2010 general election Labour Party will seek a renaissance. We cannot wash the memory of recent failures out of our heads with a cocktail of rhetoric and make-believe. New Socialism can be nurtured into fresh life from the detritus of New Labour. We will refresh our idealism and nourish it with our abiding values.

Epilogue

Future bright

Having passed seventy, retirement is a consideration. Tony Banks urged me to follow his example and leave Parliament in 2005. Sadly he had only one year liberated from constituency chores. Tony's clincher argument was to insist that I should think of all the things I could do when I retire.

Tony was a wise and good friend. We had much in common. I did my thinking. What is the idyllic life at seventy-plus? It should be full, packed with thinking, fun, stimulating company, the buzz of fresh ideas, pulse-racing new technologies plus a daily fix of the heart-stopping drama of politics.

Occasionally it would be fulfilling to make a minute ripple in British and Euro politics. Getting the odd bon mot or joke across to an audience of millions via the media provides a warm glow. An adequate salary would be a comfort that distanced me from the distractions of the low incomes that I have had for most of my life. Trips now and again to politically exciting places would be wonderful stimuli. The company of like-minded consenting political aficionados to fill the spaces between the meetings would be bliss.

Added zing would come from having the worry cells creatively throbbing. I'd need the daily fix of the worthy, wild and mad demands of my constituents. Occasionally, some of them would be helped and show appreciation. Satisfaction would come from working with my dedicated staff, the family of the Labour Party and even a rare flicker of understanding from the media that my intentions are worthy. The Tory press would daily stoke up my reservoirs of outrage and indignation to keep me angry and hungry for retribution and reform.

Retirement would mean painful withdrawal symptoms. No chance to tell the Prime Minister face to face how he is failing. No smug select committee witnesses to be humbled. No unsung heroes to be celebrated. My beloved constituency under-promoted by a novice.

Unlike Tony Banks I came to Parliament in middle life and I have been in the job for a mere twenty-two years. I'm just settling in. Like most megalomaniacs I suffer the delusion that I am a little bit indispensable. I recall an MP's wife saying, 'Who could represent this place better than my husband?' I hear the same question in my head. The answer, of course, is 'Thousands of people'. But we cling to our fantasies.

One incident did give me a moment of uncertainty. I cursed myself. Stupid! Imbecile! Past it? How could I have done it? A mind-jarring error left me reeling. Worse because it was totally unexpected after a promising day. Everything had been going well. After a full morning in Parliament, I was due to fly to Norway. I walked up to Victoria staion and caught the Gatwick Express. Searching for the flight on the displays at Gatwick, I recalled that it was going from 'Terminal 1'. The flight was not listed. Slowly truth dawned. There is no Terminal 1 at Gatwick. I checked the ticket – the plane was leaving in precisely two hours' time from Heathrow. I rushed to the bus stop, calculating on the way how long a bus would take down the M25, past the roadworks near the junction with the M4, at peak time of 5.30 p.m. The only chance of catching the plane was to use a taxi. The driver estimated fifty minutes for the journey if he was not held up. It was just possible. With difficulty I tried to control my anxiety but I failed to give my full attention to the lovely wintry sunset that I was passing through on the M25. There were no hold-ups, only speed restrictions. I arrived with half an hour to spare. Chance to cool down my burning ulcers and chat to the ever-calm lord Tom Burlison, my companion on the trip. Such was the depth of my embarrassment, I could not tell him he was talking to an incompetent idiot.

'Am I losing it?' is a question that seventy-year-olds ask themselves. No, I console myself; I have always been like this. When I was a teenager my mother often said I was like an 'absent-minded professor'. An absent mind is tolerable, a crumbling one is not. It must have been too many things on my mind. As my last two flights were from Gatwick, this one must be as well. There was a stark welcome from Oslo which was agreeably Nordic: temperatures below freezing, piles of stained snow in the streets and pristine snow on the fields.

The waiter at my hotel gave me simple instructions on the location of the Norwegian Parliament. 'Take the next corner and turn right, and the Storting is in front of you.' I found a less than imposing yellow brick building with no sign. Could it possibly be? There was a far more imposing building on a hill nearby. I asked a passer-by. Sympathetically she pointed to the massive building across the road. It's hardly a Taj Mahal or a Big Ben and my question was understandable, I reassured myself. I knew the pitying look in her eyes that said, 'This berk would not know his Heathrow from his Gatwick.'

Five years later and I am now on a roll. Life has never been more productive. The Euro Drugs Convention needs two years' more work. Voices against the follies of future Iraq, Helmand and Iran adventures are needed.

In December 2009, *The Wales Yearbook* awarded me the 'Welsh MP of the Year' prize. The citation was written in the generous terms that are usually confined to obituaries:

> The panel of judges were particularly impressed by Paul Flynn's record as an extraordinary and effective backbencher and his willingness to challenge difficult issues irrespective of convention or the whips.
>
> The award is less 'for the year' but recognising Paul Flynn's service to Newport and a wider constituency throughout Britain, over many years.
>
> Denis Balsom, Editor, *The Wales Yearbook*.

Parliament's most under-represented group is the over-75s. Whose shame of wartime poverty spurs them on? My enthusiasm for speaking, questioning, writing and blogging multiplies yearly.

As a late developer, I sense the best is yet to be.

Index